S
MAT

SCHOOL MATHEMATICS

is issued in the following styles

PART I (two years' work); *with* and *without Answers*. *Also* in two sections, A and B (each covering one year's work); *without Answers only*.

PART II (3rd and 4th years); *with* and *without Answers*. *Also* in two sections, A and B (each covering one year's work); *without Answers only*.

PART III (for 5th year); *with* and *without Answers*.

By the same author

REVISION COURSE IN SCHOOL MATHEMATICS

Provides a complete revision of the syllabus in mathematics for G.C.E. Ordinary Level.

By H. E. PARR and J. R. SHELLEY

MODERN MATHEMATICS

For use with *School Mathematics*, enabling topics of 'modern' mathematics to be introduced into each year's work.

BELL & HYMAN LIMITED
37–39 QUEEN ELIZABETH STREET, LONDON SE1 2QB

SCHOOL MATHEMATICS

A UNIFIED COURSE

By

H. E. PARR, M.A.

*Formerly Chief Mathematics Master and Second Master, Whitgift School
Late Scholar of Jesus College, Cambridge*

PART I

BELL & HYMAN
LONDON

Published by
BELL & HYMAN LIMITED
Denmark House
37–39 Queen Elizabeth Street
London SE1 2QB

First published in 1949 by
G. Bell & Sons Ltd
Reprinted fifteen times
New decimalised and metricated edition
published in 1970
Reprinted 1970, 1972, 1975, 1978, 1980, 1983, 1984

PART ONE WITH ANSWERS ISBN 0 7135 1581 3
PART ONE, WITHOUT ANSWERS ISBN 0 7135 1582 1
PART ONE, SECTION A ISBN 0 7135 1583 X
PART ONE, SECTION B. ISBN 0 7135 1584 8

Printed and bound in Great Britain by
Cox & Wyman Ltd, Reading

PREFACE TO NEW EDITION

THE decimalization of the currency in 1971 would, in any case, necessitate a new edition of this book. In view of the probability that industry, and indeed the whole economy of the country, will be very largely metric by 1975, there would seem to be obvious advantages in making the changes caused by decimalization and metrication together. In this new edition, money sums have been decimalized in accordance with the recommendations of the Decimal Currency Board, and all the units of weights and measures have been made metric. A complete change to the metric system in everyday commercial life will doubtless take some years. In the meantime, the replacement of British Imperial units by metric ones will serve the purpose of familiarizing the pupil with the system he will increasingly encounter when he goes out into the world, tend to make him more metric-minded, and also save valuable teaching time which can be employed to better advantage in topics of modern mathematics.

In the case of sections of the book, chiefly mensuration, where the use of Imperial units makes the work fundamentally different, additional exercises in these units have been provided for the benefit of teachers who think that, during the change-over period, some practice in Imperial units is necessary.

The opportunity was taken to rearrange some of the subject matter, and also to introduce a few topics which have gained a place in the traditional course since this book was first published. Number systems have been included in Part I, and Part II contains sections on linear and quadratic inequalities and three-dimensional co-ordinates. A section on arithmetical and geometrical progressions has been added to Part III.

H. E. P.

PREFACE TO FIRST EDITION

THE mathematics syllabus which was recommended for secondary schools by the Jeffery Report in 1944 has now been adopted, with only minor modifications, by all the examining bodies, and has met with the approval of an increasing number of schools. Whatever may be the future of the external examination system after 1950, the majority of secondary schools will base their work in mathematics upon this syllabus, even though the time which is devoted to the subject should prove inadequate for its completion.

This book is designed to cover the ground of that syllabus from the age of eleven plus to the standard of the present school certificate. Part I deals with the first two years' work, and Parts II and III complete the course. The book pre-supposes a knowledge of the ordinary processes of arithmetic, weights and measures, money sums, and long multiplication and division of whole numbers; revision exercises on these topics will be found on pp. 158–167. Mathematics is treated as a unified subject, in the spirit of the Jeffery Report; and while certain topics would generally be described as chiefly geometrical, others as chiefly algebraic, and so on, it is hoped that no part of the subject is pursued to the temporary exclusion of the other parts.

Most teachers are of the opinion that it is unwise to keep a class on the same sort of topic for more than a week or so. In conformity with this view it will be found that subjects are broken into by other topics and subsequently resumed after an interval. Although it is intended that on the whole the order of the book shall be followed, it will often be possible for a teacher to pursue a particular topic further by omitting a few intermediate sections for the time being and coming back to them later.

The position of formal geometry has undoubtedly weakened a good deal during the last few years. It is hoped that most teachers will find that the amount of formal geometry in this book is sufficient for their requirements, and that those who consider there is too much will not find any difficulty in selecting which parts to omit. Algebraic and (in Parts II and III) trigonometrical methods have been employed wherever these make the work easier or more instructive.

The author has followed closely the recommendations of the Mathematical Association's various reports on the teaching of Arithmetic, Algebra and Geometry, and wishes to make his acknowledgements of the excellent hints and material contained in those reports. He wishes also to thank Mr. A. H. G. Palmer, M.A., for his valuable suggestions and assistance.

H. E. P.

CONTENTS

NOTE. This Part is issued complete, with and without answers. It is also issued in two separate sections, Section A and Section B, without answers. The following is the Table of Contents of the whole book.

SECTION A

TABLES

LENGTH

10 millimetres (mm)= 1 centimetre (cm)
100 centimetres   = 1 metre (m)
1000 metres   = 1 kilometre (km)

CAPACITY

1000 millilitres (ml)= 1 litre (l)= 1000 cm^3

WEIGHT

1000 milligrammes (mg)= 1 gramme (g)
1000 grammes   = 1 kilogramme (kg)
1000 kilogrammes   = 1 tonne (t)

MONEY

British
100 new pence (p)= 1 pound (£)

American
100 cents= 1 dollar ($)

French
100 centimes (c)= 1 franc (fr)

TIME

60 seconds (s) = 1 minute (min)
60 minutes   = 1 hour (h)
24 hours   = 1 day
7 days   = 1 week
365 days   = 1 ordinary year
366 days   = 1 leap year
100 years   = 1 century

ANGLE

60 seconds (60″)= 1 minute (1′)
60 minutes   = 1 degree (1°)
90 degrees   = 1 right angle

SECTION A

1. FACTORS AND MULTIPLES

IF one number goes exactly into another number, the first number is called a **factor** of the second, and the second number is called a **multiple** of the first.

Thus $63 = 7 \times 9$, ∴ 7 is a factor of 63, and so is 9.

Again $63 = 3 \times 21$, ∴ 3 and 21 are also factors of 63.

Also 63 is a multiple of any of the numbers 3, 7, 9 or 21, since each of these numbers goes exactly into 63.

Every number, obviously, has itself and 1 as factors. If a number has no other factors besides these, it is called a **prime number.** Thus 2, 3, 5, 7, 11, 13, 17, 19, 23 are all prime numbers. A factor which is a prime number is called a **prime factor.**

Thus, 7 is a prime factor of 42, and so are 2 and 3.

But 21, although a factor of 42, is not a prime factor.

EXERCISE 1 (Oral)

1 What numbers are factors of 24? Answer the same question for 72, 56, 132.

2 Which of the following numbers are factors of 12: 2, 3, 4, 5, 6, 12, 18, 24, 36? Which are multiples of 12?

3 Give a list of all multiples of 7 between 10 and 50.

4 Give the *prime* factors of 24, 72, 56, 132.

5 State the two prime numbers next bigger than 23.

6 What is the least number which has each of the numbers 2, 3, 5 and 7 as factors?

Indices Instead of writing 5×5, we shall usually write 5^2, which is read as '5 to the power 2'.

Similarly
$$5 \times 5 \times 5 = 5^3,$$
$$5 \times 5 \times 5 \times 5 = 5^4,$$

and so on. Be careful not to confuse 5^3 with 5×3.

5^3 is called a **power** of 5, and the little 3, which tells you the number of 5's which are multiplied together, is called an **index**. (The plural is 'indices'.) Thus the number 2^3 (which means $2 \times 2 \times 2$, or 8) is a power of 2, and the index is 3.

Instead of reading 5^2 as '5 to the power 2', we often say '5 squared', because (5×5) is the number of square units in the area of a square whose side is 5 units. Similarly, 5^3 is often read as '5 cubed', because $(5 \times 5 \times 5)$ is the number of cubic units in the volume of a cube whose edge is 5 units.

EXERCISE 2

Multiply out the following, and learn the results:

1 2^2, 3^2, 4^2, 5^2, and so on up to 18^2, 19^2, 20^2
2 3^3, 3^4, 5^3, 5^4

Example 1 *Express* $2 \times 3 \times 2 \times 3 \times 5 \times 2 \times 5 \times 3 \times 2$ *in index form.*

The number is $2 \times 2 \times 2 \times 2 \times 3 \times 3 \times 3 \times 5 \times 5$
$$= 2^4 \times 3^3 \times 5^2.$$

Example 2 *Express* 4312 *in prime factors, using index notation.*

```
 2 | 4312
 2 | 2156
 2 | 1078
 7 |  539
 7 |   77
11 |   11
   |    1
```

Hence $4312 = 2^3 \times 7^2 \times 11$.

Example 3 *Multiply* 3^2 *by* 3^4.

$$3^2 \times 3^4 = (3 \times 3) \times (3 \times 3 \times 3 \times 3)$$
$$= 3 \times 3 \times 3 \times 3 \times 3 \times 3$$
$$= 3^6.$$

Notice that the answer is *not* 3^8, which you would get if you multiplied the indices 2 and 4.

The **square root** of a number is that number whose square is equal to the given number.

For example, $9 = 3^2$, so 3 is the square root of 9.

The symbol for the square root of 9 is $\sqrt{9}$.

Example 4 *Express 15 876 in prime factors, and hence find its square root.*

$$\begin{array}{r|r} 2 & 15876 \\ \hline 2 & 7938 \\ \hline 3 & 3969 \\ \hline 3 & 1323 \\ \hline 3 & 441 \\ \hline 3 & 147 \\ \hline 7 & 49 \\ \hline 7 & 7 \\ \hline & 1 \end{array}$$

Hence $15\,876 = 2^2 \times 3^4 \times 7^2$.

Notice that each prime factor occurs an *even* number of times.

In the square root each prime factor must occur half the number of times it occurs in 15 876.

$\therefore$ the square root of $15\,876 = 2 \times 3^2 \times 7$
$$= 126.$$

When finding the prime factors of a number, start with 2. When 2 will divide into the number no longer, try 3; then try 5, 7, 11, 13 ... in order. You will probably know already that 2 is a factor only if the last digit is even or 0; 3 is a factor only if the sum of the digits of the number adds up to a multiple of 3; and 5 is a factor only if the last digit of the number is 0 or 5.

EXERCISE 3

Put the following numbers into prime factors, using index form:

1 $2 \times 7 \times 7 \times 2 \times 2 \times 11 \times 13 \times 13$

2 $5 \times 3 \times 5 \times 3 \times 5$

3 $2^2 \times 2^3$

4 $3^2 \times 11^2 \times 3^5 \times 11$

5 $7 \times 7 \times 7 \times 5^2 \times 7 \times 5^3$

6 $10 \times 5 \times 2^2$

7 $6^2 \times 8$

Write the following in a simpler form, using indices:

8 $a \times a \times a \times b \times b$

9 $a \times b \times c \times a \times c$

10 $x^3 \times x^4$

11 $a \times a \times a^2$

12 The square of $2^2 \times 3$

13 The square root of $3^4 \times 11^2$

14 The square of $a \times b^2$

15 The square root of $x^4 \times y^2$

Express in prime factors:

16 12	**17** 96	**18** 441	**19** 256	**20** 540
21 4851	**22** 686	**23** 3465	**24** 684	**25** 360
26 75	**27** 169	**28** 1728	**29** 840	**30** 6552
31 289	**32** 3610	**33** 6534	**34** 35 280	**35** 8750

Simplify:

36 $2^5 \div 2^3$ **37** $3^6 \div 3^3$ **38** $b^2 \div b$ **39** $a^3 \div a$

40 The square of x^2 **41** The square of x^3

42 $(2^3)^4$ **43** $(b^3)^4$

44 $(b^4)^3$ **45** $(5 \times 7)^2 \div (5 \times 7^2)$

Find the prime factors of the following numbers, and then write down their square roots, leaving the answers in index form:

46 4356	**47** 1936	**48** 625	**49** 4900
50 39 204	**51** 7056	**52** 16 900	**53** 19 600

H.C.F. and L.C.M.

The **Highest Common Factor** (usually written H.C.F.) of two or more numbers is the greatest number which is a factor of each of them.

Thus 12 is the H.C.F. of 24, 36 and 60.

The **Lowest Common Multiple** (L.C.M.) of two or more numbers is the least number which is a multiple of each of them.

Thus 30 is the L.C.M. of 5, 6 and 15.

EXERCISE 4 (Oral)

State what are the H.C.F.'s of:

1 4, 6	**2** 8, 12	**3** 24, 36
4 10, 15, 30	**5** 26, 39	**6** 18, 30, 12, 42

State what are the L.C.M.'s of:

7 6, 8	**8** 6, 8, 12	**9** 16, 20
10 10, 25, 4	**11** 9, 12, 18	**12** 9, 14, 21

Notice that the H.C.F. of several numbers is generally a small number, but the L.C.M. is generally big. If the L.C.M. is large, it should be left in prime factors.

Example 5 *Find the H.C.F. and the L.C.M. of* 84, 1386 *and* 210.

$$
\begin{array}{c|c}
2 & 84 \\ \hline
2 & 42 \\ \hline
3 & 21 \\ \hline
7 & 7 \\ \hline
 & 1
\end{array}
\qquad
\begin{array}{c|c}
2 & 1386 \\ \hline
3 & 693 \\ \hline
3 & 231 \\ \hline
7 & 77 \\ \hline
11 & 11 \\ \hline
 & 1
\end{array}
\qquad
\begin{array}{c|c}
2 & 210 \\ \hline
3 & 105 \\ \hline
5 & 35 \\ \hline
7 & 7 \\ \hline
 & 1
\end{array}
$$

Hence
$$84 = 2^2 \times 3 \times 7,$$
$$1386 = 2 \times 3^2 \times 7 \times 11,$$
$$210 = 2 \times 3 \times 5 \times 7;$$

∴ the H.C.F. $= 2 \times 3 \times 7 = 42.$
The L.C.M. $= 2^2 \times 3^2 \times 5 \times 7 \times 11.$

Example 6 *Find the L.C.M. of* 56, 70 *and* 98.
$$56 = 2^3 \times 7,$$
$$70 = 2 \times 5 \times 7,$$
$$98 = 2 \times 7^2;$$

∴ the L.C.M. $= 2^3 \times 5 \times 7^2.$

EXERCISE 5 (Oral)

State the H.C.F. and the L.C.M. of:

1 $2 \times 3,\ 2^2 \times 3 \times 5$ **2** $3 \times 7,\ 2^2 \times 7$

3 $2 \times 11^2,\ 3 \times 11$ **4** $2^2 \times 7,\ 2^3 \times 5^2 \times 7,\ 2^2 \times 7 \times 13$

5 $3^4,\ 3^2 \times 5^2$ **6** $a^2,\ a^3,\ a^4$ **7** $x,\ x^3$

8 $2^4 \times 3^2 \times 5^3,\ 2^5 \times 3^3 \times 5^2 \times 7,\ 2^2 \times 3^3 \times 5 \times 7$

EXERCISE 6

Find the H.C.F. and the L.C.M. in Nos. 1–9, leaving the L.C.M. in prime factors:

1 72, 162   **2** 126, 198   **3** 210, 336, 294

4 455, 286   **5** 616, 2156   **6** 132, 506

7 45, 72, 240   **8** 69, 92, 161   **9** 42, 735, 882

10 Find the L.C.M. of $2^3 \times 7^2 \times 13$ and $2^2 \times 7 \times 13^2$. How many times does the L.C.M. contain the first number, and how many times does it contain the second?

11 Find the H.C.F. of $2^3 \times 5^2 \times 11$, $2^2 \times 5 \times 11^2$ and $2^2 \times 11 \times 17$. How many times is the H.C.F. contained in each of the numbers?

12 If a bag of sugar weighs 360 grammes, how many bags must be taken to weigh an exact number of kilogrammes?

13 Find the least number which is divisible by all the numbers 1, 2, 3, 4, 5, ... up to 12.

14 What is the least number by which $3^3 \times 7$ must be multiplied in order that the result may have an exact square root?

15 What is the least number by which 24 must be multiplied to make the result an exact square?

16 Three bells toll at intervals of 3, 4 and 6 minutes respectively. If they all toll together at a certain moment, how many minutes will pass before they do so again?

17 Find the least number of boys in a school, if it is possible to divide the school into classes of 25 or 30 or 35 and have no boys over in each case.

18 Find the least sum of money into which 30p, 36p and 54p all divide exactly.

19 A courtyard 360 cm long and 210 cm wide is to be paved with square tiles. Find the length of the edge of the largest tiles that can be used without cutting any.

20 Trees are planted on both sides of a road, at 60 m apart on one side and 75 m apart on the other side of the road. At one end of the road two trees are directly opposite one another. After what distance, measured from that end, would you again find a pair of trees directly opposite one another?

21 Find the smallest number which leaves a remainder 2 when divided by either 8 or 12 or 14.

22 If a land mile = 5280 ft and a sea mile = 6080 ft, find in sea miles the least distance which is an exact number of land miles and also of sea miles.

2. NUMBER SYSTEMS

The symbols 1, 2, 3, 4, . . . 9 are called **arabic numerals,** because they were introduced into Europe in the fourteenth century by Arabian merchants trading with Italian ports. The Arabs borrowed them from the Hindus, who also invented the symbol 0 for zero. The essential feature of the arabic system of numerals is that the value of a symbol depends on its position in the number, a device called the **Principle of Place Value.** Thus,

$$4325 = (4 \times 10^3) + (3 \times 10^2) + (2 \times 10) + (5 \times 1).$$

This method of representing numbers is called the **denary system,** because it is based on powers of 10, and 10 is said to be the **base** of the system. The symbols used are the nine digits and zero, ten in all.

Any number can be taken as the base. For example, if 2 is the base, the only symbols required are 0 and 1, and

$$1101 = (1 \times 2^3) + (1 \times 2^2) + (0 \times 2) + (1 \times 1)$$
$$= \quad 8 \quad + \quad 4 \quad + \quad 0 \quad + \quad 1 \quad = 13.$$

If 8 is the base, the symbols required are 0, 1, 2, . . . 7, and

$$245 = (2 \times 8^2) + (4 \times 8) + (5 \times 1)$$
$$= \quad 128 \quad + \quad 32 \quad + \quad 5 \quad = 165.$$

Whatever base is used, the number of symbols needed always equals the base.

In order to show what system is being used, we put a small denary number, called a **suffix,** at the foot of the number. Thus, 32_{10} (read as 'three-two to the base ten') means thirty-two; 32_4 (read as 'three-two to the base four') means $(3 \times 4) + (2 \times 1)$, or fourteen.

The system of numerals using 2 as the base is particularly important because it is the one employed by computers. It is called the **binary system.**

Converting from denary to any other base

To express 5213_{10} with a base 8, we divide repeatedly by 8, and the remainders in reverse order give the required number:

$$
\begin{array}{l}
8 \mid 5213 \\
8 \mid 651 \text{ rem. } 5 \\
8 \mid 81 \text{ rem. } 3 \\
8 \mid 10 \text{ rem. } 1 \\
8 \mid 1 \text{ rem. } 2 \\
 0 \text{ rem. } 1
\end{array}
\qquad \therefore \; 5213_{10} = 12135_8.
$$

Example 1   *Express 21_{10} with a base 2.*
Repeated division by 2 gives:

$$
\begin{array}{l}
2 \mid 21 \\
2 \mid 10 \text{ rem. } 1 \\
2 \mid 5 \text{ rem. } 0 \\
2 \mid 2 \text{ rem. } 1 \\
2 \mid 1 \text{ rem. } 0 \\
 0 \text{ rem. } 1
\end{array}
\qquad \therefore \; 21_{10} = 10101_2.
$$

Converting to denary from any other base

One method is to write out the number in full:

$$432_5 = (4 \times 5^2) + (3 \times 5) + (2 \times 1) = 100 + 15 + 2 = 117_{10}.$$
$$10101_2 = (1 \times 2^4) + (0 \times 2^3) + (1 \times 2^2) + (0 \times 2) + (1 \times 1)$$
$$= 16 + 4 + 1 = 21_{10}.$$
$$526_8 = (5 \times 8^2) + (2 \times 8) + (6 \times 1) = 320 + 16 + 6 = 342_{10}.$$

A quicker method can often be done mentally. Thus, for 526_8, we say: 5×8 is 40, plus 2 makes 42; 42×8 is 336, plus 6 makes 342. $\therefore \; 526_8 = 342_{10}.$

NUMBER SYSTEMS

Calculations with base other than 10

When performing the ordinary operations of arithmetic in any scale other than ten, we must remember that the digits no longer denote successive powers of ten, but of the base which is being used. This means that the carrying figures are found by dividing by the base, not by ten.

Example 2 *Add* 232_5 *to* 344_5.

We say $2+4 = six = (1 \times 5)+1$. Put down 1 and carry 1; $3+4+1 = eight = (1 \times 5)+3$; put down 3 and carry 1; $2+3+1 = six = (1 \times 5)+1$; put down 1 and carry 1 into the fourth place from the right.

```
  232
+ 344
 1131
```

Ans. 1131_5

Example 3 *Subtract* 43_8 *from* 72_8.

We cannot subtract 3 from 2, so we borrow one from the eights column and call it eight in the units column, making $2+8$, or ten; 3 from 10 leaves 7. In the eights column we can either add 1 to 4 and subtract 5 from 7, or take 1 from the 7, leaving 6, and then subtract 4 from 6. In either case it leaves 2.

```
  72
- 43
  27
```

Ans. 27_8

Example 4 *Multiply* 6734_8 *by* 27_8.

When multiplying by the 2, we say $2 \times 4 = eight = (1 \times 8)+0$; put 0 and carry 1; $(2 \times 3)+1 = seven$, so we put 7; $2 \times 7 = fourteen = (1 \times 8)+6$, so we put 6 and carry 1; $(2 \times 6)+1 = thirteen = (1 \times 8)+5$, so we put 5 and carry 1. When multiplying by the 7, we say $7 \times 4 = twenty-eight = (3 \times 8)+4$; put 4 and carry 3; $(7 \times 3)+3 = twenty-four = (3 \times 8)+0$; put 0 and carry 3; $(7 \times 7)+3 = fifty-two = (6 \times 8)+4$; put 4 and carry 6; $(7 \times 6)+6 = forty-eight = (6 \times 8)+0$; put 0 and carry 6.

The addition is then done as in Example 2.

```
   6734
     27
  15670
  60404
 237304
```

Ans. 237304_8

Example 5   *Divide* 110111_2 *by* 101_2.

$$101 \;)\; 110111 \;(\; 1011$$
$$\underline{101}$$
$$111$$
$$\underline{101}$$
$$101$$
$$\underline{101} \qquad \textit{Ans. } 1011_2$$
$$\underline{\cdots}$$

EXERCISE 7

1 Convert to denary numbers: 43_8, 2314_8, 7_8, 27_8, 127_8.

2 Find the denary equivalents of 421_5, 202_3, 1011_2, 3231_5, 1111_2, 2211_3.

3 Express with the base 8: 47_{10}, 252_{10}, 725_{10}, 866_{10}, 9_{10}, 39_{10}, 129_{10}.

4 Write 28_{10} with base (i) 8, (ii) 5, (iii) 3, (iv) 2.

5 Write 5432_{10} with base (i) 8, (ii) 5, (iii) 3, (iv) 6.

In Nos. 6–29, carry out the calculations and give the answers in the system indicated.

6 $21_8 + 27_8 + 66_8$

7 $234_5 + 324_5$

8 $2102_3 + 2202_3$

9 $2071_8 + 754_8$

10 $11011_2 + 1011_2$

11 $56_8 + 27_8 + 65_8$

12 $777_8 + 717_8$

13 $10101_2 + 1001_2 + 111_2$

14 $72_8 + 41_8 + 267_8$

15 $403_5 - 121_5$

16 $201_3 - 122_3$

17 $11011_2 - 1101_2$

18 $152_8 \times 43_8$

19 $124_5 \times 32_5$

20 $222_3 \times 111_3$

21 $333_4 \times 333_4$

22 $11111_2 \times 1001_2$

23 $11001_2 \times 111_2$

24 $3256_8 \div 46_8$

25 $3140_8 \div 42_8$

26 $3212_5 \div 14_5$

27 $20010_3 \div 12_3$

28 $10010_2 \div 110_2$

29 $111001100_2 \div 10111_2$

3. FRACTIONS (I)

Common fractions Fig. 1 shows a line AB divided into eight equal parts. Each part, such as AX, is called one-eighth of AB. This is written

$$AX = \tfrac{1}{8} \text{ of AB.}$$

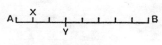

Fig. 1

If AY contains three of these equal parts, it is called three-eighths of AB. This is written

$$AY = \tfrac{3}{8} \text{ of AB.}$$

A number such as $\tfrac{3}{8}$ is called a **fraction.** The number 8 is called the **denominator** of the fraction; it tells us into how many equal parts AB is divided. The number 3 is called the **numerator** of the fraction; it tells us the number of eighths which are taken.

You have already met examples of fractions. One penny is $\tfrac{1}{100}$ of £1, therefore 37p is $\tfrac{37}{100}$ of £1. One centimetre is $\tfrac{1}{100}$ of 1 metre, 29 cm is $\tfrac{29}{100}$ of 1 m; 40 m is $\tfrac{40}{1000}$ of a kilometre.

EXERCISE 8

1 Write as fractions: seven-eighths, eleven-twelfths, three-tenths, nineteen-hundredths.

2 Write in words: $\tfrac{3}{14}$, $\tfrac{5}{7}$, $\tfrac{8}{27}$, $\tfrac{28}{1000}$.

3 How many pence are there in $\tfrac{1}{10}$ of £1, $\tfrac{1}{5}$ of £1, $\tfrac{1}{4}$ of £1, $\tfrac{7}{10}$ of £1?

4 Express as fractions of a metre: 7 cm, 57 cm, 60 cm, 3 mm.

Conversion of fractions

In Fig. 2, the line AB is divided into four equal parts by the marks above the line, and into eight equal parts by the marks below the line, so that the larger divisions are quarters and the smaller ones eighths.

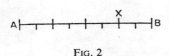

Fɪɢ. 2

Now AX is $\frac{3}{4}$ of AB, and it is also $\frac{6}{8}$ of AB.
Hence we see that

$$\frac{3}{4} = \frac{6}{8}.$$

If the line AB were divided into sixteenths, there would be twelve of these parts in AX, and so AX would be $\frac{12}{16}$ of AB.

If AB were divided into twenty equal parts, each quarter of the line would contain 5 of these parts, and so AX would contain 3×5, or 15, parts. AX would therefore be $\frac{15}{20}$ of AB.

We have thus found a set of fractions

$$\frac{3}{4}, \frac{6}{8}, \frac{12}{16}, \frac{15}{20}$$

which are all equal. You will notice that each of the last three fractions can be obtained from $\frac{3}{4}$ by multiplying the numerator and the denominator of the fraction $\frac{3}{4}$ by some number.

For example, if the numerator and denominator of $\frac{3}{4}$ are both multiplied by 2, we get $\frac{6}{8}$; if by 4, we get $\frac{12}{16}$; if by 5, we get $\frac{15}{20}$.

We can also say that $\frac{15}{20}$ becomes $\frac{3}{4}$ if we divide numerator and denominator by 5; $\frac{6}{8}$ becomes $\frac{3}{4}$ if we divide both numerator and denominator by 2, and so on.

More examples of fractions treated in this way:

$\frac{5}{15} = \frac{1}{3}$ (dividing numerator and denominator by 5),

$\frac{30}{42} = \frac{5}{7}$ (,,   ,,   ,,   by 6),

$\frac{2}{3} = \frac{8}{12}$ (multiplying numerator and denominator by 4),

$\frac{4}{5} = \frac{80}{100}$ (,,   ,,   ,,   by 20).

The conclusion we reach is that **the value of a fraction is unaltered if we divide the numerator and denominator by the same number, or if we multiply the numerator and denominator by the same number.**

Sometimes we can carry out the process of dividing numerator and denominator by the same number several times. This is called 'reducing a fraction to its **lowest terms**'. A fraction will not be reduced to its lowest terms unless we divide its numerator and denominator by their H.C.F., but the work is best done in stages.

Example 1   *Reduce $\frac{144}{180}$ to its lowest terms.*

$\frac{144}{180} = \frac{36}{45}$ (dividing numerator and denominator by 4)

$\qquad = \frac{4}{5}$ (,,   ,,   ,,   by 9).

After a little practice the work may be set out thus:

$$\begin{array}{c} 4 \\ \cancel{36} \\ \cancel{144} \\ \hline \cancel{180} \\ \cancel{45} \\ 5 \end{array}$$

but the numbers must be crossed out neatly so as not to obscure the working.

Example 2   *Express $\frac{7}{16}$ with a denominator 48.*

The new denominator (48) is 3 times the original one (16).

$\therefore$ the new numerator must be 3×7, or 21.

$$\therefore \frac{7}{16} = \frac{21}{48}.$$

Example 3 *Arrange in order of size, beginning with the smallest, the fractions $\frac{3}{4}$, $\frac{5}{8}$, $\frac{7}{12}$, $\frac{7}{9}$.*

$4 = 2^2$
$8 = 2^3$ $\therefore$ L.C.M. of denominators $= 2^3 \times 3^2$
$12 = 2^2 \times 3$ $= 72$.
$9 = 3^2$

(In an easy example such as this, you could find the L.C.M. mentally.)

Expressed with denominator 72, the fractions are

$$\frac{54}{72}, \quad \frac{45}{72}, \quad \frac{42}{72}, \quad \frac{56}{72}.$$

$\therefore$ the order is $\frac{7}{12}$, $\frac{5}{8}$, $\frac{3}{4}$, $\frac{7}{9}$.

EXERCISE 9

Reduce the fractions in Nos. 1–15 to their lowest terms:

1 $\frac{9}{12}$ **2** $\frac{14}{18}$ **3** $\frac{60}{75}$ **4** $\frac{45}{72}$ **5** $\frac{12}{12}$
6 $\frac{44}{165}$ **7** $\frac{200}{360}$ **8** $\frac{144}{189}$ **9** $\frac{800}{1600}$ **10** $\frac{210}{385}$
11 $\frac{546}{910}$ **12** $\frac{315}{405}$ **13** $\frac{384}{448}$ **14** $\frac{154}{176}$ **15** $\frac{39}{52}$

16 Express with denominator 12 the fractions $\frac{5}{6}$, $\frac{3}{4}$, $\frac{2}{3}$, $\frac{1}{2}$.
17   ,,   ,,   36   ,, $\frac{5}{9}$, $\frac{7}{18}$, $\frac{11}{12}$, $\frac{2}{3}$, $\frac{1}{2}$.
18   ,,   ,,   100   ,, $\frac{4}{5}$, $\frac{3}{50}$, $\frac{7}{10}$, $\frac{8}{25}$.

19 If $\frac{7}{12}$ has the same value as the fraction $\frac{x}{60}$, say what number you think x stands for.

20 Simplify $\dfrac{3 \times a}{4 \times a}$, $\dfrac{b \times c}{c \times d}$, $\dfrac{t}{t^2}$, $\dfrac{3 \times a \times b}{6 \times a \times b}$.

Arrange in order of size, beginning with the smallest, the groups of fractions in Nos. 21–26:

21 $\frac{1}{2}$, $\frac{5}{6}$, $\frac{2}{3}$, $\frac{7}{12}$ **22** $\frac{3}{10}$, $\frac{1}{4}$, $\frac{3}{14}$, $\frac{2}{7}$ **23** $\frac{4}{15}$, $\frac{7}{30}$, $\frac{5}{21}$, $\frac{3}{14}$
24 $\frac{5}{6}$, $\frac{7}{8}$, $\frac{8}{9}$, $\frac{3}{4}$ **25** $\frac{2}{15}$, $\frac{3}{25}$, $\frac{7}{50}$, $\frac{13}{100}$ **26** $\frac{3}{55}$, $\frac{5}{99}$, $\frac{2}{45}$, $\frac{1}{22}$

27 Express with denominator $24x$ the fractions $\dfrac{5}{6x}$, $\dfrac{7}{12x}$, $\dfrac{3}{8}$.

28 Express with denominator $6x^2$ the fractions $\dfrac{2}{3}$, $\dfrac{1}{2x}$, $\dfrac{5}{x^2}$.

Simplify the following fractions; if there is no simpler form, say so:

29 $\dfrac{x \times a}{y \times a}$ **30** $\dfrac{a \times b \times c}{b \times c \times d}$ **31** $\dfrac{b^2}{b^3}$ **32** $\dfrac{a^2}{b^2}$ **33** $\dfrac{4x^2}{2x}$

34 $\dfrac{2^3}{3^3}$ **35** $\dfrac{3x}{3y}$ **36** $\dfrac{3a^2}{6 \times a \times b}$ **37** $\dfrac{26x}{39x^2}$

Kinds of fractions   Fig. 3 illustrates the fact that $\frac{3}{8}$ is the same as $3 \div 8$. The line AB is 3 units long, AC is 1 unit. Each

Fig. 3

unit is divided into eighths, and AX contains 3 of these divisions.

$$\therefore \text{AX} = \tfrac{3}{8} \text{ of a unit.}$$

But AB contains 24 of these same divisions, so AX is $\frac{1}{8}$ of AB.

$$\therefore \text{AX} = \tfrac{1}{8} \text{ of } 3 = 3 \div 8.$$
$$\therefore \tfrac{3}{8} = 3 \div 8.$$

Hence $\dfrac{\text{numerator}}{\text{denominator}} = \text{numerator} \div \text{denominator.}$

A fraction such as $\frac{3}{8}$, in which the numerator is less than the denominator, is called a **proper fraction**.

A fraction such as $\frac{11}{8}$, in which the numerator is greater than the denominator, is called an **improper fraction**.

The **integers**, or whole numbers, 1, 2, 3, 4, 5, ... may be replaced by the fractions $\frac{1}{1}$, $\frac{2}{1}$, $\frac{3}{1}$, $\frac{4}{1}$, $\frac{5}{1}$, ... where convenient; for $\frac{3}{1} = 3 \div 1 = 3$, and so on.

Notice that $\frac{11}{8} = \frac{8}{8} + \frac{3}{8} = 1 + \frac{3}{8}$, and this is written simply $1\frac{3}{8}$.

Similarly, $\frac{23}{8} = \frac{16}{8} + \frac{7}{8} = 2 + \frac{7}{8} = 2\frac{7}{8}$.

A number such as $2\frac{7}{8}$ is called a **mixed number**, as it consists of a whole number 2 and a proper fraction $\frac{7}{8}$.

Example 4 *Write $\frac{25}{7}$ as a mixed number.*

$$\frac{25}{7} = \frac{21}{7} + \frac{4}{7} = 3\frac{4}{7}.$$

(The mental work is to say '7 into 25 goes 3 times and 4 over'; ∴ the whole number is 3 and the fractional part is $\frac{4}{7}$.)

Example 5 *Write $\frac{241}{72}$ as a mixed number.*
First divide 241 by 72.

$$72)241(3$$
$$\underline{216}$$
$$\underline{\underline{25}}$$

The answer is $3\frac{25}{72}$.

Example 6 *Express* (i) $3\frac{6}{7}$, (ii) $5\frac{6}{13}$ *as improper fractions.*

(i) $3\frac{6}{7} = 3 + \frac{6}{7} = \frac{21}{7} + \frac{6}{7} = \frac{27}{7}.$

The mental work is to say $(3 \times 7) + 6 = 27$, and then to put 27 over 7 to make the fraction.

(ii) $5\frac{6}{13} = \frac{(5 \times 13) + 6}{13} = \frac{65 + 6}{13} = \frac{71}{13}.$

EXERCISE 10 (Oral)

Express as mixed numbers (or as integers):

1 $\frac{10}{3}$ **2** $\frac{21}{8}$ **3** $\frac{20}{5}$ **4** $\frac{13}{4}$ **5** $\frac{17}{6}$
6 $\frac{90}{12}$ **7** $\frac{15}{5}$ **8** $\frac{52}{9}$ **9** $\frac{27}{2}$ **10** $\frac{79}{12}$

Express as improper fractions:

11 $5\frac{2}{3}$ **12** $1\frac{5}{16}$ **13** $9\frac{2}{11}$ **14** $3\frac{3}{5}$ **15** $2\frac{5}{8}$
16 $4\frac{4}{7}$ **17** $6\frac{3}{4}$ **18** $10\frac{1}{10}$ **19** $5\frac{3}{11}$ **20** $4\frac{1}{4}$

Find the values of:

21 $\frac{9 \text{ cm}}{6}$ **22** $\frac{£6}{5}$ **23** $\frac{48p}{6}$ **24** $\frac{72p}{4}$ **25** $\frac{4 \text{ m}}{10}$
26 $\frac{96p}{12}$ **27** $\frac{£3}{20}$ **28** $\frac{6 \text{ kg}}{40}$ **29** $\frac{7 \text{ cm}}{35}$ **30** $\frac{3 \text{ h}}{60}$

EXERCISE 11

Express as mixed numbers:

1 $\frac{78}{16}$ **2** $\frac{127}{22}$ **3** $\frac{147}{18}$ **4** $\frac{135}{15}$ **5** $\frac{158}{100}$

6 $\frac{1256}{85}$ **7** $\frac{793}{64}$ **8** $\frac{653}{16}$ **9** $\frac{1732}{121}$ **10** $\frac{331}{13}$

Express as improper fractions:

11 $12\frac{4}{13}$ **12** $16\frac{14}{15}$ **13** $27\frac{5}{12}$ **14** $46\frac{3}{17}$ **15** $18\frac{10}{11}$

16 $15\frac{1}{8}$ **17** $8\frac{3}{17}$ **18** $28\frac{3}{100}$ **19** $21\frac{4}{11}$ **20** $12\frac{7}{24}$

Addition of fractions To add two or more fractions together, we must express them all with the same denominator. This *common denominator* should be the L.C.M. of the denominators of the fractions which are to be added. When this has been done, the numerators are added, and the resulting fraction reduced to its lowest terms. If the result is an improper fraction, it must be changed into a mixed number.

Example 7 *Simplify* $\frac{2}{3} + \frac{1}{4} + \frac{1}{12} + \frac{3}{8}$.

$$\frac{2}{3} + \frac{1}{4} + \frac{1}{12} + \frac{3}{8} = \frac{16}{24} + \frac{6}{24} + \frac{2}{24} + \frac{9}{24}$$

(24 is the L.C.M. of 3, 4, 12 and 8)

$$= \frac{16+6+2+9}{24}$$
$$= \frac{33}{24}$$
$$= \frac{11}{8} = 1\frac{3}{8}.$$

EXERCISE 12

Complete the following:

1 $\frac{2}{3} = \frac{}{12}$ **2** $\frac{3}{7} = \frac{}{84}$ **3** $\frac{5}{18} = \frac{}{54}$ **4** $\frac{4}{5} = \frac{}{75}$

5 $\frac{7}{9} = \frac{}{81}$ **6** $\frac{2}{11} = \frac{}{33}$ **7** $\frac{5}{6} = \frac{}{48}$ **8** $\frac{1}{5} = \frac{}{30}$

Simplify:

9 $\frac{1}{12}+\frac{1}{12}$ **10** $\frac{3}{10}+\frac{2}{5}$ **11** $\frac{7}{16}+\frac{5}{16}$ **12** $\dfrac{5}{x}+\dfrac{4}{x}$

13 $\frac{1}{4}+\frac{3}{4}$ **14** $\frac{5}{8}+\frac{7}{8}$ **15** $\frac{10}{21}+\frac{4}{21}$ **16** $\frac{1}{2}+\frac{3}{4}$

17 $\frac{1}{3}+\frac{1}{5}$ **18** $\frac{1}{3}+\frac{1}{4}+\frac{1}{6}$ **19** $\frac{2}{5}+\frac{1}{10}$ **20** $\dfrac{b}{3}+\dfrac{2b}{7}$

21 $\dfrac{2}{3x}+\dfrac{2}{x}$ **22** $\frac{1}{2}+\frac{1}{3}+\frac{1}{4}$ **23** $\dfrac{3}{4a}+\dfrac{1}{5a}$ **24** $\dfrac{1}{2a}+\dfrac{2}{a}$

25 $\frac{3}{5}+\frac{1}{10}+\frac{2}{25}$ **26** $\frac{1}{4}+\frac{5}{12}+\frac{3}{8}$ **27** $\frac{7}{10}+\frac{11}{12}+\frac{4}{9}+\frac{2}{3}$

28 $\frac{4}{11}+\frac{5}{6}+\frac{7}{9}+\frac{10}{33}$ **29** $\frac{2}{3}+\frac{3}{4}+\frac{4}{5}+\frac{7}{12}$ **30** $\frac{5}{8}+\frac{13}{20}+\frac{1}{10}+\frac{1}{3}$

When adding mixed numbers, any improper fraction should be put as a mixed number. Then the whole numbers are added together, and the fractions are written with a common denominator and added as in the last exercise.

Example 8 *Simplify* $2\frac{1}{2}+1\frac{3}{8}+3\frac{1}{5}$.

$$2\frac{1}{2}+1\frac{3}{8}+3\frac{1}{5}=2\frac{1}{2}+1\frac{5}{8}+3\frac{1}{5}$$
$$=6+\frac{20}{40}+\frac{25}{40}+\frac{8}{40}$$
$$=6+\frac{53}{40}$$
$$=6+1\frac{13}{40}=7\frac{13}{40}.$$

EXERCISE 13

Simplify:

1 $2\frac{1}{2}+3\frac{3}{8}$ **2** $\frac{10}{7}+2\frac{2}{21}+3\frac{1}{3}$ **3** $1\frac{5}{18}+2\frac{2}{9}$ **4** $1\frac{3}{14}+2\frac{2}{7}$

5 $\frac{9}{4}+\frac{9}{12}+\frac{9}{16}$ **6** $2\frac{5}{8}+\frac{5}{8}+3\frac{1}{5}$ **7** $3\frac{1}{3}+\frac{1}{6}+1\frac{2}{7}+4\frac{3}{28}$

8 $1\frac{1}{6}+2\frac{5}{8}+\frac{1}{12}$ **9** $3\frac{1}{7}+\frac{2}{9}+1\frac{4}{63}$ **10** $1\frac{7}{18}+2\frac{1}{3}+4\frac{5}{9}$

11 $\frac{5}{4}+\frac{4}{9}+\frac{5}{6}$ **12** $1\frac{7}{10}+2\frac{4}{5}+1\frac{3}{4}$ **13** $\frac{17}{6}+\frac{8}{15}+\frac{47}{20}$

14 $\frac{2}{7}+3\frac{1}{4}+1\frac{1}{14}+3\frac{1}{28}$ **15** $4\frac{2}{5}+3\frac{5}{7}+1\frac{3}{35}$ **16** $2\frac{1}{2}+1\frac{8}{13}+1\frac{7}{26}$

17 $2\frac{1}{3}+1\frac{3}{4}+\frac{4}{5}+1\frac{5}{6}$ **18** $1\frac{4}{9}+1\frac{1}{3}+4\frac{7}{12}$ **19** $1\frac{11}{16}+\frac{3}{4}+\frac{1}{8}+1\frac{17}{24}$

20 $1+2\frac{1}{3}+3\frac{1}{2}+4\frac{1}{3}+5\frac{1}{4}$

Subtraction of fractions To subtract one mixed number from another, deal first with the whole numbers, and write the fractions with a common denominator.

Example 9 *Simplify* $3\frac{7}{12} - 1\frac{1}{3}$.

$$3\frac{7}{12} - 1\frac{1}{3} = 2 + \frac{7}{12} - \frac{4}{12}$$
$$= 2 + \frac{7-4}{12}$$
$$= 2 + \frac{\cancel{3}^{1}}{\cancel{12}_{4}} = 2\frac{1}{4}.$$

In the next example the fractional part of the second mixed number is greater than the fractional part of the first, and we have to take 1 from the whole number 6 and change it to $\frac{24}{24}$.

Example 10 *Simplify* $8\frac{7}{12} - 2\frac{5}{8}$.

$$8\frac{7}{12} - 2\frac{5}{8} = 6 + \frac{14}{24} - \frac{15}{24}$$
$$= 6 + \frac{14-15}{24}$$
$$= 5 + \frac{24+14-15}{24}$$
$$= 5 + \frac{23}{24} = 5\frac{23}{24}.$$

EXERCISE 14

Simplify:

1 $\frac{5}{8} - \frac{3}{8}$ **2** $\frac{7}{12} - \frac{5}{12}$ **3** $1 - \frac{1}{4}$ **4** $\frac{5}{x} - \frac{2}{x}$

5 $2 - \frac{2}{7}$ **6** $3 - \frac{3}{4}$ **7** $5 - \frac{7}{10}$ **8** $1\frac{3}{4} - \frac{1}{2}$

9 $\frac{5}{6} - \frac{1}{3}$ **10** $\frac{5}{8} - \frac{1}{4}$ **11** $\frac{9}{10} - \frac{2}{5}$ **12** $\frac{9}{2a} - \frac{2}{a}$

13 $2\frac{5}{8} - 1\frac{1}{4}$ **14** $3\frac{11}{14} - 1\frac{2}{7}$ **15** $3\frac{3}{4} - 2\frac{1}{8}$ **16** $6\frac{5}{12} - 3\frac{3}{4}$

17 $4\frac{1}{5} - 1\frac{3}{5}$ **18** $5\frac{3}{10} - 1\frac{9}{10}$ **19** $5\frac{1}{6} - 2\frac{4}{9}$ **20** $\frac{35}{16} - \frac{19}{12}$

21 $2\frac{7}{45} - 1\frac{9}{25}$ **22** $5\frac{19}{24} - 1\frac{3}{4}$ **23** $7\frac{2}{3} - 4\frac{7}{9}$ **24** $4\frac{1}{4} - \frac{53}{52}$

Multiplication of fractions What you already know about the meaning of a fraction shows that multiplying a fraction by a whole number presents no difficulty. A sensible meaning for $5 \times \frac{3}{10}$ is to say that it equals $\frac{15}{10}$, or $\frac{3}{2}$.

Now consider $\frac{3}{10} \times \frac{5}{6}$.

We assume this to mean the same as $\frac{5}{6}$ of $\frac{3}{10}$, or $\frac{3}{10}$ of $\frac{5}{6}$, either of which would mean $\frac{5 \times 3}{6 \times 10}$.

We thus have the following rule for multiplying fractions:

Multiply the numerators together to give the numerator of the answer; multiply the denominators together to give the denominator of the answer.

More shortly, $\qquad \dfrac{a}{b} \times \dfrac{c}{d} = \dfrac{a \times c}{b \times d}$.

It is obvious that we could divide the numerator and the denominator of the fraction $\frac{5 \times 3}{6 \times 10}$ by 3 and by 5. This is more often done *before* the multiplication, as in these examples:

Example 11 *Multiply $\frac{3}{10}$ by $\frac{5}{6}$.*

$$\frac{3}{10} \times \frac{5}{6} = \frac{\overset{1}{\cancel{3}}}{\underset{2}{\cancel{10}}} \times \frac{\overset{1}{\cancel{5}}}{\underset{2}{\cancel{6}}} = \frac{1 \times 1}{2 \times 2} = \frac{1}{4}.$$

Example 12 *Simplify $\frac{10}{27} \times \frac{9}{35}$.*

$$\frac{\overset{2}{\cancel{10}}}{\underset{3}{27}} \times \frac{\overset{1}{\cancel{9}}}{\underset{7}{\cancel{35}}} = \frac{2 \times 1}{3 \times 7} = \frac{2}{21}.$$

If either of the quantities is a mixed number, change it to an improper fraction first, except in an easy case like $4\frac{1}{3} \times 2$, which is obviously $8\frac{2}{3}$.

Example 13 *Multiply $3\frac{8}{9}$ by $3\frac{3}{5}$.*

$$3\frac{8}{9} \times 3\frac{3}{5} = \frac{\overset{7}{\cancel{35}}}{\underset{1}{\cancel{9}}} \times \frac{\overset{2}{\cancel{18}}}{\underset{1}{\cancel{5}}} = \frac{7 \times 2}{1 \times 1} = 14.$$

Notice that $3\frac{1}{2} \times 4\frac{1}{4}$ is *not* $(3 \times 4) + (\frac{1}{2} \times \frac{1}{4})$.

Example 14 *Simplify* $2\frac{1}{2} \times 1\frac{1}{5} \times 3\frac{1}{8} \times 6\frac{2}{5}$.

$$2\frac{1}{2} \times 1\frac{1}{5} \times 3\frac{1}{8} \times 6\frac{2}{5} = \frac{\overset{1}{\cancel{5}}}{\underset{1}{\cancel{2}}} \times \frac{\overset{3}{\cancel{6}}}{\underset{1}{\cancel{5}}} \times \frac{\overset{5}{\cancel{25}}}{\underset{1}{\cancel{8}}} \times \frac{\overset{4}{\cancel{32}}}{\underset{1}{\cancel{5}}} = \frac{1 \times 3 \times 5 \times 4}{1 \times 1 \times 1 \times 1} = 60.$$

EXERCISE 15 (Oral)

Simplify:

1 $\frac{1}{2} \times \frac{1}{2}$	**2** $\frac{1}{2} \times 2$	**3** $\frac{1}{3}$ of $\frac{3}{5}$	**4** $\frac{2}{7} \times 2$
5 $5 \times \frac{3}{7}$	**6** $\frac{2}{3}$ of $\frac{3}{8}$	**7** $\frac{1}{4}$ of $\frac{8}{9}$	**8** $\frac{2}{3} \times \frac{3}{4}$
9 $\frac{5}{12} \times \frac{3}{10}$	**10** $1\frac{1}{4} \times 3$	**11** $1\frac{1}{5} \times 5$	**12** $\frac{1}{7} \times \frac{14}{15}$
13 $1\frac{1}{2} \times \frac{1}{3}$	**14** $2\frac{1}{2} \times 3\frac{1}{2}$	**15** $1\frac{1}{2} \times 1\frac{1}{2}$	**16** $8 \times \frac{7}{16}$
17 $\frac{5}{24}$ of $\frac{12}{25}$	**18** $\frac{5}{7} \times 21$	**19** $\frac{2}{11} \times 3\frac{3}{4}$	**20** $\frac{3x}{5} \times \frac{5}{6x}$

EXERCISE 16

Simplify:

1 $2\frac{1}{7} \times 1\frac{1}{3}$	**2** $\frac{5}{27} \times \frac{18}{35}$	**3** $1\frac{5}{9} \times \frac{3}{7}$
4 $1\frac{2}{7} \times 9\frac{1}{3}$	**5** $2\frac{5}{8} \times 4\frac{4}{7}$	**6** $3\frac{3}{5} \times 3\frac{1}{3}$
7 $\frac{2}{3} \times \frac{3}{4} \times \frac{4}{5}$	**8** $2\frac{1}{3} \times 4\frac{2}{7}$	**9** $3\frac{6}{13} \times 1\frac{11}{15}$
10 $\frac{1}{3} \times 2\frac{2}{5} \times 8\frac{3}{4}$	**11** $22\frac{3}{4} \times \frac{3}{28}$	**12** $1\frac{1}{6} \times 1\frac{1}{5} \times \frac{10}{7}$
13 $2\frac{8}{9} \times \frac{3}{13}$	**14** $\frac{2}{25} \times 4\frac{3}{8}$	**15** $2\frac{22}{25} \times 3\frac{3}{4}$
16 $3\frac{7}{9} \times \frac{3}{17} \times 4\frac{1}{2}$	**17** $1 \times 2\frac{1}{2} \times 3\frac{1}{3} \times 4\frac{1}{2}$	**18** $1\frac{1}{54} \times 2\frac{4}{7} \times \frac{3}{5}$
19 $8\frac{1}{6} \times 3\frac{1}{7} \times \frac{2}{11}$	**20** $2\frac{7}{10} \times \frac{5}{36} \times \frac{8}{9}$	**21** $3\frac{3}{14} \times 2\frac{5}{8} \times 2\frac{8}{9}$

Division of fractions Obviously $\frac{3}{4} \div 5$ is the same as $\frac{1}{5}$ of $\frac{3}{4}$, which we have seen is $\frac{1 \times 3}{5 \times 4}$ or $\frac{3}{20}$.

Notice that 5 is $\frac{5}{1}$, and to *divide* by $\frac{5}{1}$ we *multiply* by $\frac{1}{5}$.

Next consider $\frac{3}{4} \div \frac{5}{7}$, or $\dfrac{\frac{3}{4}}{\frac{5}{7}}$.

This is $\dfrac{\frac{3}{4} \times 7 \times 4}{\frac{5}{7} \times 7 \times 4}$ or $\frac{21}{20}$.

But this is just the same answer as we should get if we multiplied $\frac{3}{4}$ by $\frac{7}{5}$.

Hence to *divide* by $\frac{5}{7}$, we have to *multiply* by $\frac{7}{5}$.

The rule for division of two fractions is thus:

Turn the divisor the other way up and multiply.

Example 15   *Simplify* $1\frac{5}{7} \div 6$.

$$1\tfrac{5}{7} \div 6 = \frac{\overset{2}{\cancel{12}}}{7} \div \frac{6}{1}$$

$$= \frac{12}{7} \times \frac{1}{\underset{1}{\cancel{6}}} = \frac{2 \times 1}{7 \times 1} = \frac{2}{7}.$$

Example 16   *Simplify* $3\frac{1}{4} \div \frac{1}{6}$.

$$3\tfrac{1}{4} \div \tfrac{1}{6} = \frac{13}{4} \div \frac{1}{6}$$

$$= \frac{13}{\underset{2}{\cancel{4}}} \times \frac{\overset{3}{\cancel{6}}}{1} = \frac{13 \times 3}{2 \times 1} = \frac{39}{2} = 19\tfrac{1}{2}.$$

Example 17   *Simplify* $3\frac{3}{5} \div 2\frac{7}{10}$.

$$3\tfrac{3}{5} \div 2\tfrac{7}{10} = \frac{18}{5} \div \frac{27}{10}$$

$$= \frac{\overset{2}{\cancel{18}}}{\underset{1}{\cancel{5}}} \times \frac{\overset{2}{\cancel{10}}}{\underset{3}{\cancel{27}}} = \frac{2 \times 2}{1 \times 3} = \frac{4}{3} = 1\tfrac{1}{3}.$$

The **reciprocal** of a number is 1 divided by that number. Thus the reciprocal of 3 is $\frac{1}{3}$; that of $\frac{1}{3}$ is 3; that of $\frac{2}{3}$ is $1 \div \frac{2}{3}$ or $1 \times \frac{3}{2}$, which is $\frac{3}{2}$.

We now see that **dividing by a fraction is the same as multiplying by the reciprocal.**

EXERCISE 17 (Oral)

Simplify:

1 $\frac{1}{2} \div 2$	**2** $\frac{1}{2} \div 3$	**3** $\frac{3}{4} \div 3$	**4** $\frac{3}{4} \div 4$	**5** $\frac{2}{3} \div 2$
6 $\frac{2}{3} \div 3$	**7** $1\frac{3}{4} \div 7$	**8** $1\frac{3}{4} \div 4$	**9** $\frac{8}{25} \div 4$	**10** $\frac{8}{25} \div 8$
11 $1 \div \frac{1}{2}$	**12** $2 \div \frac{1}{3}$	**13** $3 \div \frac{1}{4}$	**14** $\frac{1}{4} \div 3$	**15** $\frac{1}{2} \div \frac{1}{3}$
16 $1 \div \frac{2}{3}$	**17** $\frac{3}{4} \div \frac{3}{4}$	**18** $\frac{2}{3} \div \frac{3}{4}$	**19** $\frac{3}{8} \div \frac{3}{4}$	**20** $\frac{2}{3} \div \frac{1}{6}$

21 Give the reciprocals of (i) 6, (ii) $\frac{3}{4}$, (iii) $\frac{1}{10}$, (iv) $1\frac{1}{2}$, (v) $2\frac{3}{4}$, (vi) 100.

EXERCISE 18

Simplify:

1 $3\frac{1}{2} \div 1\frac{3}{4}$	**2** $1\frac{1}{9} \div 1\frac{2}{3}$	**3** $5\frac{5}{12} \div 3\frac{1}{3}$	**4** $1 \div 5\frac{3}{4}$
5 $1\frac{7}{8} \div 1\frac{7}{8}$	**6** $6\frac{3}{7} \div \frac{9}{14}$	**7** $2\frac{2}{11} \div \frac{8}{22}$	**8** $2\frac{2}{15} \div 1\frac{19}{45}$
9 $\frac{3\frac{1}{3}}{\frac{5}{9}}$	**10** $\frac{\frac{3}{4}}{2\frac{1}{7}}$	**11** $10 \div \frac{1}{100}$	**12** $3\frac{1}{2} \div 14$
13 $\frac{5}{3\frac{1}{3}}$	**14** $7\frac{4}{5} \div 1\frac{3}{10}$	**15** $\frac{3}{5} \div \frac{5}{3}$	**16** $1\frac{1}{55} \div 5\frac{8}{11}$
17 $3\frac{3}{8} \div 2\frac{13}{16}$	**18** $\frac{21}{32} \div 15\frac{3}{4}$	**19** $4\frac{2}{3} \div \frac{7}{18}$	**20** $\frac{3\frac{3}{4}}{8\frac{3}{4}}$

Problems involving fractions

Example 18 *If $\frac{3}{5}$ of a school are boys, and there are 96 girls in the school, how many children are there altogether?*

Since $\frac{3}{5}$ of the school are boys, $\frac{2}{5}$ of the school are girls.

$$\therefore \frac{2}{5} \text{ of the school} = 96.$$
$$\therefore \frac{1}{5} \quad \text{,,} \quad = \frac{96}{2}.$$
$$\therefore \frac{5}{5} \quad \text{,,} \quad = \frac{96 \times 5}{2}$$
$$= 48 \times 5 = 240.$$

$\therefore$ the total number of children $= 240$.

Example 19 *A pile of paper is $10\frac{1}{2}$ cm high, and each sheet is $\frac{7}{100}$ cm thick. Find the number of sheets in the pile.*

The number of sheets $= 10\frac{1}{2} \div \frac{7}{100}$

$$= \frac{\overset{3}{\cancel{21}}}{2} \times \frac{\overset{50}{\cancel{100}}}{7} = 150.$$

EXERCISE 19

1 A can contains 12 litres of water. How much must be poured out to leave $5\frac{3}{4}$ litres?

2 A man left $\frac{1}{2}$ of his money to his wife, $\frac{1}{5}$ to each of his two sons, and the rest to his daughter. What fraction did the daughter receive?

3 How many jugs each holding $1\frac{1}{2}$ litres can be filled from a cask holding 30 litres?

4 A boy bought 28 apples and found that $\frac{2}{7}$ of them were bad. How many apples were fit to eat?

5 A boy's stride is $\frac{7}{9}$ of a metre. Find how many strides he takes in walking a distance of 966 m.

6 After spending $\frac{5}{6}$ of his money, a boy finds that he has 24p left. How much had he at first?

7 A man walks at $5\frac{2}{5}$ km per hour. How far does he walk in 1 hr 20 min?

8 After using $\frac{5}{8}$ of his fuel stock, a householder had $10\frac{1}{2}$ tonnes left. How many tonnes had he at first?

9 The distance all round a rectangular field is 437 m, and the width of the field is $92\frac{1}{4}$ m. Calculate the length.

10 When a man has travelled $7\frac{1}{2}$ km he has gone $\frac{5}{9}$ of his journey. Find the total journey.

11 Find the number of hours it takes a train to travel $262\frac{1}{2}$ km at $62\frac{1}{2}$ km per hour.

12 The product of two numbers is 20 and one of the numbers is $6\frac{1}{4}$. Find the other number.

13 How many $\frac{3}{4}$-kg packets of sugar can be made up from 54 kg?

14 By what must $2\frac{5}{8}$ be multiplied to make $1\frac{3}{4}$?

15 How many pieces of string $2\frac{1}{2}$ cm long can be cut from a length of 84 cm, and how much remains?

16 Which of the expressions $\dfrac{3}{4\frac{1}{2}}$ and $\dfrac{4}{5\frac{1}{3}}$ is the greater, and by how much?

4. DECIMALS (I)

The powers of 10 have been defined to be 10^1, 10^2, 10^3, 10^4, ...; i.e. 10, 100, 1000, 10 000, ...

A fraction such as $\frac{3}{10}$, $\frac{47}{100}$, $\frac{21}{1000}$, whose denominator is a power of 10, is called a **decimal.**

When we have a number such as 2365, the 2 stands for 2 thousands, the 3 for 3 hundreds, the 6 for 6 tens, and the 5 for 5 units. We shall now extend this idea by putting a **decimal point** after the units figure, and figures *after* the decimal point to denote tenths, hundredths, thousandths ... in that order.

Thus 2·631 means

2 units + 6 tenths + 3 hundredths + 1 thousandth.
4·703 means 4 units + 7 tenths + 3 thousandths.

We can draw up a table, putting a thick line where the decimal point occurs.

	Hundreds 100	Tens 10	Units 1	Tenths $\frac{1}{10}$	Hundredths $\frac{1}{100}$	Thousandths $\frac{1}{1000}$
47·603 =		4	7	6		3
2·048 =			2		4	8
146·382 =	1	4	6	3	8	2

Of course 3·50, which is read as '3 point 5 nought' and not '3 point 50', is the same number as 3·5.

Example 1 *Express as decimals:* (i) $\frac{3}{1000}$, (ii) $\frac{56}{100}$, (iii) $24\frac{374}{1000}$.

(i) $\frac{3}{1000} = 0·003.$
(ii) $\frac{56}{100} = \frac{50}{100} + \frac{6}{100} = \frac{5}{10} + \frac{6}{100} = 0·56.$
(iii) $24\frac{374}{1000} = 24 + \frac{300}{1000} + \frac{70}{1000} + \frac{4}{1000}$
$= 24 + \frac{3}{10} + \frac{7}{100} + \frac{4}{1000} = 24·374.$

We usually write 0·56 instead of ·56, as the latter might be mistaken for 56.

Example 2   *Express* $4 \cdot 85$ *as a mixed number.*

$$4\cdot 85 = 4 + \tfrac{8}{10} + \tfrac{5}{100} = 4 + \tfrac{80}{100} + \tfrac{5}{100}$$

$$= 4 + \frac{\overset{17}{\cancel{85}}}{\underset{20}{\cancel{100}}}$$

$$= 4\tfrac{17}{20}.$$

EXERCISE 20

1 Make a table like the one on page 25, and write the following numbers: $\tfrac{4}{10}$, $39 \cdot 36$, $\tfrac{51}{100}$, $124 \cdot 06$, $256 \cdot 904$.

2 Write as decimals: $\tfrac{14}{1000}$, $22\tfrac{22}{100}$, $5\tfrac{104}{1000}$, $3\tfrac{8}{100}$, $14\tfrac{27}{1000}$.

3 Express as mixed numbers: $2 \cdot 786$, $8 \cdot 51$, $11 \cdot 05$, $10 \cdot 003$, $6 \cdot 843$.

4 Write as decimals: $\tfrac{124}{10}$, $\tfrac{304}{1000}$, twenty-four hundredths, $\tfrac{605}{10}$, $\tfrac{217}{100}$, $\tfrac{12345}{1000}$, $\tfrac{4816}{100}$, $\tfrac{20}{1000}$, $\tfrac{483}{100}$.

5 Express as fractions in their lowest terms: $0 \cdot 05$, $0 \cdot 17$, $0 \cdot 80$, $0 \cdot 08$, $0 \cdot 863$, $0 \cdot 75$, $0 \cdot 002$, $0 \cdot 125$, $0 \cdot 15$.

6 Write the fractions $\tfrac{1}{2}$, $\tfrac{1}{5}$, $\tfrac{3}{5}$, $\tfrac{4}{5}$ with denominator 10, and hence express these as decimals.

7 Write the fractions $\tfrac{1}{20}$, $\tfrac{1}{25}$, $\tfrac{3}{20}$, $\tfrac{3}{25}$, with denominator 100, and hence express these as decimals.

8 Express as decimals: $\tfrac{1}{4}$, $\tfrac{3}{4}$, $\tfrac{1}{8}$, $\tfrac{3}{8}$, $\tfrac{7}{8}$.

9 Given that 1 m = 100 cm, express the following lengths in metres: 4 m 50 cm, 5 m 85 cm, 6 m 9 cm.

10 Given that 1 dollar = 100 cents, express the following amounts in dollars and cents: $61 \cdot 38$ dollars, $7 \cdot 02$ dollars.

Learn by heart:

$\tfrac{1}{2} = 0 \cdot 5$, $\tfrac{1}{4} = 0 \cdot 25$, $\tfrac{3}{4} = 0 \cdot 75$,

$\tfrac{1}{8} = 0 \cdot 125$, $\tfrac{3}{8} = 0 \cdot 375$, $\tfrac{5}{8} = 0 \cdot 625$, $\tfrac{7}{8} = 0 \cdot 875$.

Addition and subtraction Decimals are added and subtracted by the same method as is used for whole numbers.

Keep the decimal points underneath one another.

Example 3   *Add together* 31·263, 0·58, 8·051, 43·7.

$$\begin{array}{r} 31·263 \\ 0·58 \\ 8·051 \\ 43·7 \\ \hline 83·594 \end{array}$$

Example 4   *Subtract* 14·683 *from* 23·25.

$$\begin{array}{r} 23·25 \\ 14·683 \\ \hline 8·567 \end{array}$$

Since there are no thousandths in the top number, we split up the 5 hundredths into 4 hundredths + 10 thousandths; 3 from 10 leaves 7, so we write down 7, and so on.

EXERCISE 21

Do the following additions:

1 1·8 + 2·2   2 2·7 + 0·3   3 1·08 + 4·12
4 0·072 + 0·028   5 1·74 + 2·43   6 3·901 + 4·709
7 6·74 + 5·4 + 0·87   8 14·27 + 6·128 + 5·647
9 0·783 + 3·61 + 2·417   10 16·41 + 2·3 + 10·87
11 14·18 + 0·72 + 11·06 + 5·82   12 3·2 + 0·41 + 1·603 + 2·07

Do the following subtractions:

13 0·86 − 0·34   14 1·7 − 0·9   15 4 − 2·73
16 6·412 − 3·14   17 8·67 − 6·13   18 21·2 − 9·48

In Nos. 19–26, the terms with plus signs should be added together, then those with minus signs, and the second total subtracted from the first.

Find the values of:

19 2·69 − 0·99 + 3·72   20 6·823 + 2·197 + 4·8 − 1·647
21 7·21 − 1·56 + 3·84 − 0·6   22 8 − 0·27 − 0·74 − 1·366
23 18·4 − 21·8 + 17·21   24 4·003 − 2·036 − 0·08 + 0·74
25 87·3 − 62·5 + 1·94 + 2·835 26 4·2 − 5·73 + 10·32 − 2·88

Multiplication and division by powers of 10

Multiplication   If we want to multiply 37·248 by 10, we say

8 thousandths × 10 = 8 hundredths,
4 hundredths × 10 = 4 tenths,
2 tenths   × 10 = 2 units, and so on.

The answer is obviously 372·48.

Similarly,   37·248 × 100 = 3724·8,
and   37·248 × 1000 = 37248.

Hence we have the rule:

To multiply a decimal by 10, 100, 1000, . . ., move the decimal point 1, 2, 3, . . . places to the right.

Division   If we want to divide 7·84 by 10, we say

4 hundredths ÷ 10 = 4 thousandths,
8 tenths   ÷ 10 = 8 hundredths,
7 units   ÷ 10 = 7 tenths,
∴ 7·84 ÷ 10   = 0·784.

Similarly,   7·84 ÷ 100 = 0·0784,
                    7·84 ÷ 1000 = 0·00784.

Hence we have the rule:

To divide a decimal by 10, 100, 1000, . . ., move the decimal point 1, 2, 3, . . . places to the left.

Notice that, both in multiplication and in division by a power of 10, the number of places through which the decimal point has to be moved, to the right or to the left, is the index of the power of 10 by which we want to multiply or divide.

EXERCISE 22 (Oral)

Simplify:

1 2·63 × 10	**2** 4·06 × 1000	**3** 21·9 × 100
4 0·056 × 10	**5** 0·0081 × 1000	**6** 6·732 ÷ 10
7 41 ÷ 100	**8** 4·230 ÷ 10	**9** 86·3 ÷ 1000

10 2·83 ÷ 100   **11** 6·32 × 1000   **12** 61·02 ÷ 10
13 0·643 × 10   **14** 420 ÷ 1000   **15** 356·47 ÷ 100
16 0·0008 × 100   **17** 0·01234 × 10 000   **18** 28·46 ÷ 10
19 1·7 × 100   **20** 4·26 ÷ 1000   **21** 540 ÷ 1000

Multiplication of a decimal by an integer

Example 5   *Multiply 4·72 by 6.*

$$\begin{array}{r} 4·72 \\ 6 \\ \hline 28·32 \end{array}$$

The multiplier 6 is put under the right-hand digit, 2, of the
number which we want to multiply. The decimal point in
the answer comes under the decimal point in 4·72.

Example 6   *Multiply 2·48 by 12.*

$$\begin{array}{r} 2·48 \\ 12 \\ \hline 29·76 \end{array}$$

The 2 in the multiplier 12 is put under the right-hand digit,
8, of 2·48.

The above method of short multiplication should be used
when multiplying by 11 or 12. To multiply by 20, multiply
by 2 and then move the decimal point one place to the right;
to multiply by 200, multiply by 2 and then move the decimal
point two places to the right.

EXERCISE 23

Find the values of:

1 0·3 × 4   **2** 0·5 × 8   **3** 4·2 × 7   **4** 0·005 × 6
5 1·07 × 6   **6** 0·06 × 12   **7** 0·8 × 20   **8** 0·9 × 11
9 0·03 × 70   **10** 0·002 × 4000   **11** 0·08 × 300
12 1·34 × 20   **13** 7·42 × 8   **14** 76·5 × 7
15 2·378 × 5   **16** 0·0756 × 8   **17** 4·39 × 20

18 0.8205×6 **19** 82.3×500 **20** 2.7182×5
21 0.6817×3 **22** 3.142×6 **23** 0.0125×8
24 7.135×6 **25** 3.76×12 **26** 2.46×1100
27 3.3×120 **28** 4.179×80 **29** 8.406×30

Multiplication of a decimal by any number

Suppose we want to multiply 34·521 by 26·31.

$$34.521 = \tfrac{34521}{1000}, \quad 26.31 = \tfrac{2631}{100}.$$
$$\therefore \ 34.521 \times 26.31 = \tfrac{34521}{1000} \times \tfrac{2631}{100}$$
$$= \tfrac{34521 \times 2631}{100000}.$$

We have to multiply 34521 by 2631 by ordinary multiplication, and then count five figures from the right and insert the decimal point.   The rule is thus:

Multiply the two numbers together as if they were whole numbers; **add together the numbers of decimal places in the two numbers, mark off this many decimal places in the product, and insert the decimal point.**

Example 7   *Multiply* 37·186 *by* 14·3.

$$
\begin{array}{r}
37186 \\
143 \\
\hline
37186 \\
148744 \\
111558 \\
\hline
5317598 \\
\end{array}
$$

Ans. 531·7598

Example 8   *Find the value of* $0.02 \times 0.03 \times 0.04$.

$2 \times 3 \times 4 = 24$, and there are $(2+2+2)$, or 6, decimal places in the answer.

$\therefore$ the answer is 0·000024.

Choose as the multiplier the number with the fewer figures, e.g. multiply 37·186 by 14·3 rather than 14·3 by 37·186.

If the product ends with 0, do not cross off this 0 before counting up the decimal places.

EXERCISE 24 (Oral)

Find the values of:

1 0.2×0.4	**2** 4×0.3	**3** 0.8×0.05
4 0.1×0.1	**5** $(0.03)^2$	**6** 0.03×0.5
7 1.7×0.3	**8** 0.2×0.2	**9** 1.1×0.1
10 $(0.5)^2$	**11** 0.2×0.07	**12** 0.07×0.04
13 0.8×0.9	**14** 1.13×0.03	**15** $(0.02)^3$
16 0.6×0.06	**17** 1.3×0.5	**18** 0.004×0.6
19 1.3×0.8	**20** 0.30×0.11	**21** 0.2×320
22 0.005×0.8	**23** 0.26×0.5	**24** $(0.1)^3$

EXERCISE 25

Find the values of:

1 4.12×2.1	**2** 2.47×13.2	**3** 48.35×1.04
4 0.123×0.56	**5** 29.8×1.24	**6** 0.00102×0.45
7 2.342×15.8	**8** 160×5.72	**9** 6.35×21.46
10 2.35×28	**11** 1.6×4.862	**12** 3625×0.058
13 0.052×7.6	**14** 14.63×1.23	**15** 6.12×0.034
16 5300×0.412	**17** 15.86×13.2	**18** 63.5×14.03
19 1.603×0.485	**20** 1.4×0.2716	**21** 0.0387×5.8
22 316.7×0.54	**23** 8.6×3.221	**24** 4200×0.093

Division There are many different methods of dividing one decimal by another, and only two of these methods are explained here. You should find which method you prefer, and keep to it until you know it thoroughly. Whatever method is used, it is always advisable to make a rough estimate of the answer. When, at a later stage, you can rely on this rough approximation to fix the position of the decimal point, you can ignore the decimal point during the working and insert it in your answer so as to make this agree with the rough check. In the meantime, learn one method properly.

Short division of decimals

Example 9   *Divide* (i) 86·45 *by* 7, (ii) 0·037 *by* 4.

$$\text{(i)} \quad 7 \mid \underline{86\cdot45} \qquad\qquad \text{(ii)} \quad 4 \mid \underline{0\cdot03700}$$
$$\qquad\quad 12\cdot35 \qquad\qquad\qquad\qquad 0\cdot00925$$

EXERCISE 26 (Oral)

Simplify (as decimals):

1 $8\cdot6 \div 2$	**2** $0\cdot57 \div 3$	**3** $9\cdot68 \div 8$
4 $0\cdot0126 \div 7$	**5** $61\cdot75 \div 5$	**6** $0\cdot786 \div 6$
7 $234\cdot3 \div 11$	**8** $41\cdot2 \div 8$	**9** $0\cdot099 \div 11$
10 $4 \div 5$	**11** $0\cdot05 \div 2$	**12** $0\cdot1 \div 4$
13 $1 \div 8$	**14** $23 \div 4$	**15** $0\cdot6 \div 12$
16 $64\cdot2 \div 3$	**17** $39\cdot27 \div 7$	**18** $2 \div 8$
19 $0\cdot132 \div 11$	**20** $16\cdot8 \div 12$	**21** $123\cdot4 \div 4$
22 $0\cdot0316 \div 5$	**23** $6\cdot741 \div 9$	**24** $1\cdot884 \div 12$

Long division of decimals

Method I.   Make the divisor a whole number.

Example 10   *Divide* 9·42718 *by* 0·476.

Rough check: $\dfrac{9}{0\cdot5} = \dfrac{90}{5} = 18.$

$\dfrac{9\cdot42718}{0\cdot476} = \dfrac{9427\cdot18}{476}$ (multiplying above and below by 1000).

```
              19·805
    476 | 9427·18
          476
          4667
          4284
          3831
          3808
          2380
          2380
```

Ans. 19·805

Method II.   Standard Form.

A number in **standard form** is one which has one figure (not 0)
to the left of the decimal point. By the standard form
method the decimal point is moved the same number of places
(to the right or left) in both numbers, so as to make the
divisor in standard form.

Example 11   *Divide* 9·42718 *by* 0·476.

Rough check: $\dfrac{9}{0·5} = \dfrac{90}{5} = 18$.

$\dfrac{9·42718}{0·476} = \dfrac{94·2718}{4·76}$ (multiplying above and below by
                                    10).

$$
\begin{array}{r}
19·805 \\
4·76\,\overline{)\,94·2718} \\
47·6 \\
\hline
46·67 \\
42·84 \\
\hline
3·831 \\
3·808 \\
\hline
0·02380 \\
0·02380 \\
\hline
\end{array}
$$

Ans. 19·805

EXERCISE 27

Find the values of:

1 132·6 ÷ 2·6	**2** 51 ÷ 6·8	**3** 78·02 ÷ 0·83
4 93·61 ÷ 0·023	**5** 628·56 ÷ 7·2	**6** 1·9812 ÷ 0·039
7 3415·3 ÷ 0·17	**8** 89·49 ÷ 19	**9** 16·512 ÷ 0·43
10 68·544 ÷ 1·7	**11** 0·93726 ÷ 0·123	**12** 686·93 ÷ 0·073
13 19·494 ÷ 5·4	**14** 53720 ÷ 1·7	**15** 4·8438 ÷ 0·069
16 30·2034 ÷ 21·3	**17** 1536·08 ÷ 280	**18** 0·96417 ÷ 0·027
19 113·706 ÷ 1·8	**20** 6·7268 ÷ 0·067	**21** 2·6144 ÷ 4·3
22 296·1 ÷ 35	**23** 7·999 ÷ 0·038	**24** 1128·423 ÷ 14·1
25 10·1854 ÷ 12·7	**26** 14·282 ÷ 0·74	**27** 3·9618 ÷ 0·031
28 11811·8 ÷ 28·6	**29** 0·4266 ÷ 0·15	**30** 0·54846 ÷ 0·0033

5. THE METRIC SYSTEM

The metric system was introduced in France during the French Revolution, but the system now to be described is a simplified version of the original metric system. It is the Système International (usually contracted to S.I.), the system of weights and measures which is now being adopted throughout the world.

The same prefixes constantly occur in the metric system, so you should learn by heart:

$$\textbf{kilo} = \textbf{1000}, \quad \textbf{centi} = \tfrac{1}{100}, \quad \textbf{milli} = \tfrac{1}{1000}.$$

Lengths The unit of length is the **metre.** This is divided into 100 equal parts, each called a **centimetre,** and the centimetre is divided into 10 equal parts, each called a **millimetre.** The **kilometre** is 1000 metres. The complete table of lengths is:

$$1 \text{ millimetre (mm)} = \tfrac{1}{1000} \text{ metre (m)}$$
$$1 \text{ centimetre (cm)} = \tfrac{1}{100} \text{ m}$$
$$1 \text{ kilometre (km)} = 1000 \text{ m}$$

Hence
$$10 \text{ mm} = 1 \text{ cm}$$
$$100 \text{ cm} = 1 \text{ m}$$
$$1000 \text{ m} = 1 \text{ km}$$

Weights The unit is the **gramme,** which is the weight of 1 cubic centimetre of water at 4° C. The complete table is:

$$1 \text{ milligramme (mg)} = \tfrac{1}{1000} \text{ gramme (g)}$$
$$1 \text{ kilogramme (kg)} = 1000 \text{ g}$$
$$1 \text{ tonne (t)} = 1000 \text{ kg}$$

In the metric system quantities are converted from one unit to another by simply moving the decimal point. For example,

$$4 \cdot 76 \text{ m} = 476 \text{ cm}, \quad 3 \cdot 7 \text{ kg} = 3700 \text{ g}.$$

Lengths and weights are expressed usually in one unit. Thus,
$$3 \text{ m } 6 \text{ cm } 4 \text{ mm} = 3 \cdot 064 \text{ m or } 306 \cdot 4 \text{ cm}.$$

EXERCISE 28

Express the following in the units stated:

1 4 m 32 cm (i) in m, (ii) in cm, (iii) in mm
2 2 km 40 m (i) in km, (ii) in m
3 57 m in km   **4** 8 g 90 mg in g
5 35 mg in g   **6** 3 km 3 m in km
7 5 kg 275 g (i) in kg, (ii) in g
8 75 cm (i) in m, (ii) in mm
9 1 m 26 cm 8 mm (i) in m, (ii) in cm
10 340 cm in m   **11** 2500 g in kg
12 640 000 cm in km   **13** 0·12 kg in mg
14 0·034 km in cm   **15** 2·63 tonnes in kg
16 750 mg in g   **17** 3 m 2 cm 4 mm in m
18 4762 kg in tonnes   **19** 2 tonnes in g
20 Mercury is about 13·6 times as heavy as water. Find the approximate weight of 1 litre of mercury. (A litre is 1000 cubic centimetres.)

In Nos. 21–23, find the sum of the given quantities in metres:

21 4 m 72 cm,   8 m 9 cm,   74 cm,   1 m 20 cm
22 30 cm 5 mm,   7 cm 8 mm,   62 cm,   1 m 35 cm
23 1 km 260 m,   2 km 45 m,   4 km 40 m

Express the following as compound quantities in terms of km and m:

24 6·876 km   **25** 14·06 km   **26** 4769 m
27 40·6 km   **28** 32 100 m   **29** 51 070 m

Express the following as compound quantities in terms of metres, centimetres and millimetres:

30 18·03 m   **31** 4006 mm   **32** 0·09371 km
33 10·603 m   **34** 265·7 cm   **35** 0·00504 km
36 3587 cm   **37** 2·064 m   **38** 2185 mm

The British system of money The pound is divided into 100 pence, i.e.

$$£1 = 100p.$$

An exact number of pounds, e.g. 59 pounds, can be written either as £59 or £59·00.

A sum of money less than £1 can be expressed in pence, or as a decimal of a pound with a zero preceding the decimal point. If the sum of money includes a half-penny, this is expressed as a vulgar fraction $\frac{1}{2}$. Thus,

$$83p = £0·83$$
$$8p = £0·08$$
$$3\tfrac{1}{2}p = £0·03\tfrac{1}{2}$$

A sum of money containing pounds and pence is expressed by writing the number of pence (preceded by zero if less than 10) after the decimal point. There is no need to write the sign for pence. Thus,

$$£29\ 37p \text{ is } £29·37$$
$$£29\ 6p \text{ is } £29·06 \ (not \ £29·6)$$
$$£29\ 80p \text{ is } £29·80 \ (not \ £29·8)$$
$$£29\ 26\tfrac{1}{2}p \text{ is } £29·26\tfrac{1}{2}.$$

Notice that there must always be two figures following the decimal point, and that there must always be one or more figures (a zero in some cases) between the symbol £ and the decimal point.

Other systems of money

In France, 100 centimes (c) = 1 franc (fr).
In America, 100 cents (c) = 1 dollar ($).

EXERCISE 29

1 Write the following amounts in £: 83p, 6$\frac{1}{2}$p, 3760p, 110p, $\frac{1}{2}$p, 428p.

2 Write the following amounts in pence: £5, £2350, £0·38, £28·40, £61, £1·27$\frac{1}{2}$.

3 Express in francs (i) 4 fr 65 c, (ii) 6172 c.

4 Express in dollars (i) 26 dollars 5 cents, (ii) 710 cents.

The British system of weights and measures, which is now gradually being superseded, has a long history going back to the times of the Saxons. They regarded standards of land measurement as much more important than standards of weight or capacity, for land was real estate, and could not lose its value like other forms of wealth. There were at that time in Europe several different feet used in surveying, but the Saxons clung to their own 'northern foot', which was about 13·2 in, or 335 mm. A farmer's holding of the ancient 'open field' system of ploughlands consisted of rectangular strips, side by side. 15 ft made 1 *land rod*, 40 land rods made a furrow length or *furlong*. A strip of land 40 rods long and one rod wide was called a *rood*, and 4 roods side by side made an *acre*. The land rod and the furlong remain unchanged to the present day.

The Normans made no alteration in the Saxon system of weights and measures, as William I was anxious to appear to the English, not as a conqueror, but as the lawful successor to the throne. In 1266 Henry III defined for the first time a 12-oz pound for coinage and a 15-oz pound for commerce:

'The English penny which is called a sterlyng, round and uncut, ought to weigh 32 grains of wheat taken from the middle of the ear. And the ounce ought to weigh 20 pennies. And 12 ounces make the London pound.'

Edward I in 1305 defined the system of measurement of lengths which has lasted until now, and he set up a new standard with which other measures could be compared:

'3 grains of barley dry and round make an inch. 12 inches make a foot. 3 feet make an ulna. $5\frac{1}{2}$ ulne make a rod. 40 rods in length and 4 in breadth make an acre.'

This ulna (Latin for *elbow*, and then shortened to *ell*) was later called a yard, and although Edward's original iron measure has long since disappeared, several standard yards which have survived from Elizabethan times show that his yard would not have differed from the standard British yard of 650 years later by more than 0·04 inches, or about a millimetre. The foot was smaller than the northern foot, but there were to be 16½ of them to the rod instead of the former 15.

In 1340 Edward III established a distinct system of weighing bulky goods, quite separate from that used for weighing coins. It was intended chiefly for weighing wool, raw wool being the principal export of England to Flanders and Germany at that time. The 12-oz and 15-oz pounds of Henry III continued, however, to be used.

Henry VII put the whole system on a clearly defined basis in 1497. He confirmed the use of the units of length instituted by Edward I. He also ordered the troy pound of 12 oz to be used for silver, gold and bread, and the merchants' pound of 16 oz for all other commodities. These standards were confirmed in 1588 by Queen Elizabeth I, who also in a later statute of her reign first mentioned the mile, containing 8 furlongs of 40 rods, each rod being 16½ ft, making 5280 ft in all. The standards of Elizabeth lasted unchanged until 1824, when a new standard yard and a standard pound were made and placed in the House of Commons, and called for the first time 'imperial standards'. These were lost in the fire which destroyed the Houses of Parliament in 1834, and new ones had to be made. In 1878 the troy pound was abolished in order to avoid the ambiguity of having two different pounds. The troy ounce was retained for weighing precious metals and stones, but for all other articles sold by weight the 16-oz pound was to be used.

It will be understood from this brief historical account that British units of length and weight have played a large part in our national life, as is shown by their frequent occurrence in proverbial sayings, nursery rhymes and songs. But in the modern world there are many advantages to be gained by a change to the metric system, and the benefits to industry, commerce and science will be far-reaching. There are considerable variations in practice within and between the different metric-using countries, but a metric system commanding international acceptance has now been agreed and has received widespread support. This international system (S.I.) is the one which the United Kingdom is adopting.

The metric units The metre was originally intended to be a ten-millionth part of a quarter of the earth's circumference. It was represented by a platinum rod, replaced in 1889 by an international prototype metre, a line standard of platinum-iridium. This was superseded in 1960 by a definition of the metre in terms of the wavelength of the orange radiation emitted under specified conditions by the krypton atom.

The kilogramme was originally defined as the mass of 1000 cubic centimetres of water under certain conditions, but this definition was eventually superseded by an international prototype in the form of a solid cylinder of platinum-iridium alloy, kept in Paris.

Relation between metric units and British Imperial units

By the Weights and Measures Act of 1963 the British yard was redefined as 0·9144 metres exactly, and the British pound weight was defined as an exact decimal fraction of a kilogramme. Although it is hoped that the change to S.I. in Britain will be completed by 1975, some British units will continue to be used for a long time to come. It will not often be necessary to convert from one system to the other, but the following list will give some idea of the relative size of units in the two systems.

1 inch   = 2·54 cm (exactly)   1 litre = 1¾ pints (approx.)
1 yard   = 0·9144 m (exactly)   1 kg   = 2·2 lb (approx.)
1 metre = 39·37 in (approx.)
8 km   = 5 miles (approx.)

6. THE CUBE AND THE CUBOID

Fig. 4 is a picture of a **cube,** a solid with which you will already be familiar. All the six faces are squares. Fig. 5 is the same cube, but the edges which cannot be seen are marked as dotted lines.

Figs. 6 and 7 are pictures of a **cuboid,** another name for which is a **rectangular block.** A brick and a closed match-box are examples of cuboids.

FIG. 4   FIG. 5

To make models of the cube and the cuboid which will be useful to you in your mathematical work, you will need some thin cardboard, a ruler, a set square, a pencil and a knife.

Copy Fig. 8 on the cardboard. It consists of six squares, each with a side 4 cm, and you must use a set square to make the corners true. Then put narrow flaps on seven of the sides, as shown in Fig. 9.

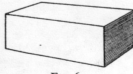   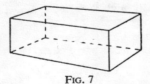

FIG. 6   FIG. 7

Cut the figure out carefully, and run the knife edge lightly along the dotted lines, not pressing hard enough to cut right through. Smear a little gum on the flaps, and fold the cardboard into the form of a cube, tucking the flaps neatly inside.

Fig. 8 is called the **net** of a cube.

Fig. 10 shows the net of a cuboid. Copy this on your piece of thin cardboard, making narrow flaps as you did for the cube. The rest of the work is as before. You will obtain a cuboid, or rectangular block, 4 cm by 3 cm by 1·5 cm.

Each of the six faces of the cube is a **square**; each face of

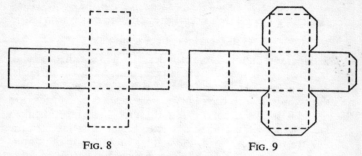

FIG. 8   FIG. 9

the cuboid is called a **rectangle,** because all its angles are **right angles.** The square is a particular kind of rectangle in which all the sides are equal.

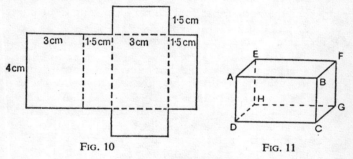

FIG. 10   FIG. 11

How to draw a cuboid

To make a sketch of a cuboid, first draw a rectangle ABCD to represent the front face (see Fig. 11); then draw short lines AE, BF, CG, DH from each of the four corners, all these lines being of the same length and in the same direction. Lastly, join EFGH. Dotted lines should be used for edges which are not visible. A similar method is used for a cube, except that we start with a square for ABCD instead of a rectangle.

This does not give a model drawing of the cube or the cuboid, for in a correct model drawing the angles of ABCD would not be true right angles, and also the edges AE, BF, CG, DH would converge as they receded from the eye. However, Fig. 11 gives a more useful drawing for our purposes.

Solid, surface, line, point

The cube and cuboid are examples of what is called a **solid**, that is, any part of space. These two solids have flat surfaces, but you will already have heard of solids such as the sphere and the cylinder which have curved surfaces. The surfaces are the boundaries of the solid. A flat, smooth surface is called a **plane.** Other examples of a plane, besides the faces of the cuboid, are the blackboard, the ceiling, and the top of a table.

Any two faces of the solids you have constructed meet in an edge. The edge is an example of a **straight line,** which is the meeting-place of two planes. Both the solids described above have twelve edges. Those of the cube are all equal in length, but the cuboid has four edges 4 cm long, four edges 3 cm long and four edges 1·5 cm long.

Both these solids have eight corners, where three edges meet. The corner is an example of a **point.**

To understand clearly what lines and points really are, it is important to remember that the lines ruled in your exercise book are in reality very thin rectangles; and that when we mark a point on the paper we are really drawing a very small circle. It is better to mark a point by means of two short lines crossing at the point, rather than by a dot.

A point, it should be realized, has a *position*, but no size.

A line has *length*, but no width.

A plane has a *length and a breadth*, but no thickness.

A solid has a *length and a breadth and a thickness*.

EXERCISE 30

1 Make a freehand sketch of a cube.

2 Make a freehand sketch of a cuboid 5 cm by 4 cm by 2 cm. Sketch also the net of this cuboid.

3 Fig. 12 represents three edges of a cube which meet at a corner.   Complete the drawing of the cube.

4 Fig. 13 represents three edges of a cube.   Complete the drawing.

5 Draw a cube, and mark the centres of all the six faces.   (The centre of a square can best be obtained

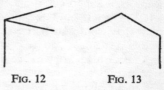

FIG. 12   FIG. 13

by joining opposite corners and seeing where these lines cut.)

6 Draw the net of a cuboid 4 cm by 2·5 cm by 1 cm.

7. AREA OF A RECTANGLE

Area   We measure a line by seeing how many centimetres (or some other convenient unit) it contains.   In a similar way we measure the **area** of a plane surface by seeing how many square centimetres it contains.   Fig. 14 shows a **square centimetre,** divided up into 100 square millimetres.

Area of rectangle   Now suppose a rectangle is 5 cm long and 3 cm wide.   We could divide up the area inside the rectangle (see Fig. 15) into three rows of five (or five rows of

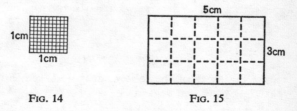

FIG. 14   FIG. 15

three), i.e. fifteen little squares, and each square is 1 square centimetre.   So the area is 15 square centimetres.

The same method could be used for any other rectangle,

provided its length and its breadth were an exact number of centimetres, and the rule is evidently: *multiply the length by the width to find the area.*

If the length and breadth of the rectangle were given in metres, it would be better to divide up the area into square metres instead of square centimetres. A square metre is the area inside a square whose side is 1 m. Similarly, if the length is in millimetres, we measure the area in square millimetres. The rule is the same whatever units are used:

$$\textbf{Length}\begin{pmatrix} m \\ in\ cm \\ mm \end{pmatrix} \times \textbf{Breadth}\begin{pmatrix} m \\ in\ cm \\ mm \end{pmatrix} = \textbf{Area}\begin{pmatrix} m^2 \\ in\ cm^2 \\ mm^2 \end{pmatrix}$$

We shall see later how we can put statements like this more shortly if we use letters. Suppose that the length of the rectangle is l units (whatever units are used), and the breadth b units, and let us suppose that the area is A square units. Then we can say that

$$A = l \times b.$$

Such a statement as this is called a **formula.**

By this rule the area of a square of side 5 cm is (5×5), or 25 square centimetres, and this is written as 25 cm². You will recall that we wrote (5×5) as 5^2, which was read '5 squared'.

Since a square centimetre is the area of a square whose side is 1 cm, or 10 mm, it contains 10×10 square millimetres, which we write as 100 mm². Thus, 1 cm² = 100 mm². Similarly, 1 m² = 10 000 cm².

EXERCISE 31 (Oral)

State the areas of the following figures; remember to say what units your answer is in:

1 A rectangle 7 cm by 4 cm
2 A rectangle 9 m by 6 m
3 A rectangle 11 mm by 5 mm
4 A rectangle 3 km by 2 km

5 A square of side 4 m

6 The net of a cube of edge 2 cm (see Fig. 8)

7 What is the width of a rectangle whose length is 4 cm and area 12 cm²?

8 What is the length of a rectangle, if its area is 7 cm² and its width 14 mm?

9 What is the side of a square whose area is 81 m²?

10 Is 1 cm² the same as 1 cm square? Is an area of 2 cm² the same area as 2 cm square?

Perimeter The perimeter of a figure means the distance all round it. In the case of a field this means the total length of the fence enclosing it. The perimeter of a rectangle is thus twice the length + twice the width; or we can add the length and width together first and then double the answer. If the perimeter is P units, the length l units, and the breadth b units, then

$$P = 2 \times l + 2 \times b.$$

We shall find later that we generally write $2l$ instead of $2 \times l$, and $2b$ instead of $2 \times b$, leaving out the multiplication sign. So the formula for the perimeter is

$$P = 2l + 2b.$$

Example 1 *A room is 16 m long and 10 m wide. Find its perimeter and the area of the carpet required to cover the floor.*

$$\text{Perimeter} = (2 \times 16 + 2 \times 10) \text{ m}$$
$$= (32 + 20) \text{ m} = 52 \text{ m}.$$
$$\text{Area} = (16 \times 10) \text{ m}^2$$
$$= 160 \text{ m}^2.$$

Example 2 *A rectangular lawn 80 m long and 32 m wide has a gravel path 4 m wide all round it. Find the area of the path (see Fig. 16).*

Method 1. The area of the grass $= 80 \times 32$ m²
$$= 2560 \text{ m}^2.$$

Now the length of the whole rectangle formed by the lawn and the path $= (80 + 4 + 4)$ m

$$= 88 \text{ m.}$$

The width $= (32 + 4 + 4)$ m

$$= 40 \text{ m.}$$

$\therefore$ the total area $\quad = 88 \times 40 \text{ m}^2$

$$= 3520 \text{ m}^2.$$

$\therefore$ the area of the path $= (3520 - 2560) \text{ m}^2$

$$= 960 \text{ m}^2.$$

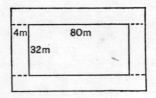

Fɪɢ. 16

Method 2.   The path can be divided up into two rectangles, each 88 m by 4 m, together with two more rectangles, each 32 m by 4 m.

$\therefore$ the area of the path

$$= (2 \times 88 \times 4 + 2 \times 32 \times 4) \text{ m}^2$$
$$= (704 + 256) \text{ m}^2$$
$$= 960 \text{ m}^2.$$

EXERCISE 32

Find the area and perimeter of each of the rectangles in Nos. 1–5.

1 A rugger pitch 110 m long, 65 m wide
2 A piece of paper 16 cm by 12 cm

3 A tennis court 26 m long, 12 m wide

4 A carpet 8 m by 3 m

5 A field 121 m long, 80 m wide

6 A rectangular block is 6 cm long, 3 cm wide and 2 cm high. Find the total area of all the six faces.

7 A room is 7 m long, 5 m wide, 4 m high. Find the total area of the four walls and the area of the ceiling.

8 An open tank has a base 3 m by 2 m, and the sides are $1\frac{1}{2}$ m high. Find the total area of the outside surface.

9 A rectangle has an area of 56 m² and it is 8 m long. Find its width and perimeter.

10 A picture 20 cm by 16 cm is mounted on a card, with a margin 4 cm wide all round. Find the area of the margin.

11 The width of a rectangle is 7 cm and the perimeter is 38 cm. Find the length of the rectangle and its area.

12 The perimeter of a square is 48 m. Find its area.

13 A rectangle is $3x$ m long and 7 m wide. Find its area and perimeter. (Remember that $3x$ means $3 \times x$.)

14 A rectangle has an area of $2x^2$ mm² and it is $2x$ mm long. Find its width and its perimeter.

15 The perimeter of a square is $4x$ cm. What is its area?

16 A tennis court is 26 m long and 12 m wide, and there is an extra space 5 m wide to give a run-back at each end, and a space $1\frac{1}{2}$ m wide all along each side. Find the length of netting required to go all round the ground.

17 A photograph 10 cm by 8 cm is mounted on a piece of cardboard which is 16 cm by 12 cm. Find the area of the margin round the photograph.

8. VOLUME OF A CUBOID

Volume If the measurements of a solid are given in centimetres, we obtain the **volume** by seeing how many cubic centimetres it contains.

A **cubic centimetre** is the volume inside a cube which has an edge 1 cm. (See Fig. 17.) We write this as 1 cm³.

Volume of a cuboid If a rectangular block is 5 cm long, 4 cm wide and 3 cm high, we could divide up the volume into three layers of small cubes, each small cube being a cubic centimetre (see Fig. 18). There would evidently be 5×4 of these small cubes in each layer. The total number of small cubes is thus $5 \times 4 \times 3$, or 60, and the volume of the block is said to be 60 cubic centimetres, or 60 cm³.

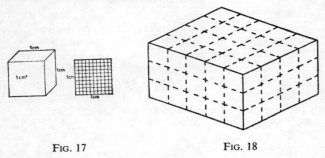

FIG. 17   FIG. 18

If the measurements were given in metres, it would be better to measure the volume in cubic metres, a cubic metre being the volume inside a cube whose edge is 1 m. Similarly we have a cubic millimetre. Whatever the units used, the method adopted above gives the same rule for the volume:

$$\textbf{Length} \left(\begin{array}{c} \textbf{m} \\ \textbf{in cm} \\ \textbf{mm} \end{array} \right) \times \textbf{Breadth} \times \textbf{Height} = \textbf{Volume} \left(\begin{array}{c} \textbf{m}^3 \\ \textbf{in cm}^3 \\ \textbf{mm}^3 \end{array} \right)$$

We can put this rule into a formula, as we did when we found the area of a rectangle. Suppose l units is the length, b units the breadth, and h units the height, then the volume V cubic units is given by the formula

$$V = l \times b \times h.$$

The volume of a cube whose edge is 5 cm is, by this rule, $(5 \times 5 \times 5)$, or 125, cubic centimetres, and this is written as 125 cm³. Remember that we wrote $(5 \times 5 \times 5)$ as 5^3, which was read '5 cubed'. Obviously,

$$1 \text{ m}^3 = 100 \times 100 \times 100 \text{ cm}^3 = 1\,000\,000 \text{ cm}^3;$$
$$1 \text{ cm}^3 = 10 \times 10 \times 10 \text{ mm}^3 = 1000 \text{ mm}^3.$$

Example 1 *Find the volume of a cuboid 8 cm by 7 cm by 3 cm.*

$$\text{Volume} = 8 \times 7 \times 3 \text{ cm}^3$$
$$= 168 \text{ cm}^3.$$

EXERCISE 33 (Oral)

State the volumes of the following cuboids, saying in what units your answer is measured:

1 6 m long, 5 m wide, 3 m high
2 10 cm by 6 cm by 5 cm
3 6 mm long, x mm wide, x mm high
4 8 m long, 6 m wide, 4 m high
5 3 cm long, a cm wide, 2 cm high
6 x cm long, x cm wide, 4 cm high
7 A cube with edge 2 mm
8 A cube with edge x cm
9 A cube with edge 3 cm
10 What is the edge of a cube whose volume is 64 cm³?
11 What is the height of a rectangular block which is 5 m long, 3 m wide, and has a volume 30 m³?

Capacity For everyday use, but not in order to express high precision measurements, the unit of capacity is the **litre,** which is 1000 cubic centimetres. Since 1 cubic centimetre of water weighs 1 gramme, a litre of water weighs 1000 grammes or 1 kg.

The **millilitre** (ml), which is a thousandth part of a litre, can thus be taken as equivalent to the cubic centimetre.

EXERCISE 34

1 Find in cubic metres the volume of air in a room 6 m long, 4 m wide and 3 m high.

2 Find the number of cubic centimetres of wood in a piece of timber 96 cm long, 6 cm wide and 5 cm thick.

3 Find how many cubic metres of water are required to fill a swimming bath 18 m long, 11 m wide, if the depth of the water is everywhere 2 m.   Find also the number of litres.

4 A room is 8 m long and 5 m wide, and it contains 140 m³ of air.   Find the height.

5 A tank is 3 m long, 2 m wide and 1 m deep.   Find how many litres it holds, and the weight of this quantity of water.

6 Express (i) 2500 cubic centimetres in litres, (ii) 0·03 litres in cubic centimetres.

Use of decimals in areas and volumes   Suppose we require the area of a rectangle 3·6 cm by 2·8 cm.

The length is 36 mm and the width is 28 mm.
The area = length × breadth = 36×28 mm²
= 1008 mm² = 10·08 cm².

$$
\begin{array}{r}
36 \\
28 \\
\hline
72 \\
288 \\
\hline
1008 \\
\hline
\end{array}
$$

This shows that it is not necessary to put the length and breadth in millimetres if they contain decimals of a centimetre. The rule on p. 44

area = length × breadth

still holds good if the length is 3·6 cm and the breadth is 2·8 cm. The product of these gives the area in square centimetres.

The same is true if the length and breadth are mixed numbers, containing fractions.

A similar argument shows that the rule

volume = length × breadth × height

for a cuboid can still be applied if the dimensions are not whole numbers, but contain decimal or other fractions.

Example 2 *Find the volume of a rectangular block* 4·8 *m long,* 2·3 *m wide and* 1·6 *m high.*

$$\text{Volume} = 4{\cdot}8 \times 2{\cdot}3 \times 1{\cdot}6 \text{ m}^3$$
$$= 17{\cdot}664 \text{ m}^3.$$

```
   48
   23
   96
  144
 1104
   16
 1104
 6624
17664
```

EXERCISE 35

(Miscellaneous examples on areas and volumes)

1 Express in cm² (i) 50 mm², (ii) ½ m².

2 Express in m² (i) 495 cm², (ii) 1 km².

Find the areas of the rectangles in Nos. 3–6:

3 5·4 cm by 3·6 cm, in cm²
4 8·5 m by 4·6 m, in m²
5 4·05 m by 135 cm, in m²
6 3·5 m by 25 cm, in cm²

Find the volumes of the cuboids in Nos. 7–9:

7 6·5 cm by 3 cm by 1·5 cm, in cm³
8 3·5 m by 2·4 m by 50 cm, in m³.
9 2 m long, 50 cm wide, 30 mm high, in cm³

10 A path is 200 m long and 1·6 m wide. Find the volume of gravel needed to cover it to a depth of 5 cm.

11 Find in cm² the area of Fig. 19, in which all the angles are right angles.

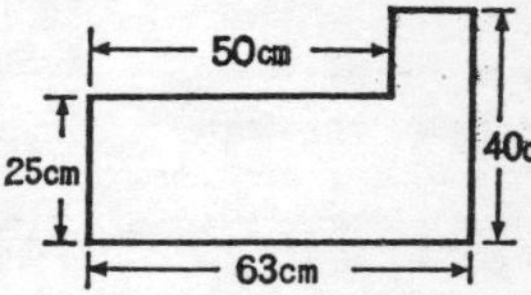

12 A carpet 5 m long and 3 m wide is placed in a room which is 7·5 m long and 4·75 m wide. Find the area of the uncovered part of the floor.

FIG. 19

13 A classroom is 9·6 m long, 8·4 m wide and 3 m high. Find how many pupils can be accommodated in the room if each is allowed 5 m³ of air space.

14 Find in cm² the area of Fig. 20, in which all the angles are right angles.

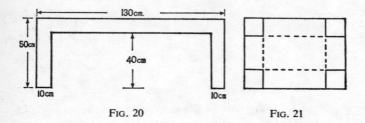

FIG. 20   FIG. 21

15 A sheet of cardboard (see Fig. 21) is a rectangle 24 cm by 16 cm. Equal squares of side 4 cm are cut out of each corner, and a tray is formed by folding along the dotted lines. Find in cm³ the capacity of the tray.

16 Find the weight of a rectangular block of stone measuring 2 m by 1 m by 40 cm, given that the stone is 2½ times as heavy as water.

17 Find the length of a rectangle whose area is 38·7 cm² and breadth 4·5 cm.

18 A tank is 2·5 m long and 1·8 m wide. How much does the water level rise if 540 litres of water are poured in?

19 A rectangular tank 2 m long and 1·62 m wide contains water to a depth of 75 cm. The water is transferred to an empty tank which is 1·5 m long and 1·2 m wide. Find the depth of the water.

———————

The remaining questions in this Exercise require a knowledge of the British Imperial system of lengths, areas and volumes, the table for which is as follows:

AREAS AND VOLUMES

Lengths	Areas	Volumes
12 inches= 1 foot	144 sq. in= 1 sq. ft	1728 cu. in= 1 cu. ft
3 feet= 1 yard	9 sq. ft= 1 sq. yd	27 cu. ft= 1 cu. yd
1760 yards= 1 mile	4840 sq. yd= 1 acre	

20 Find in acres the area of a field which is 550 yd long and 220 yd wide.

21 Find the volume of a cuboid 1 ft long, 9 in wide and 4 in high.

22 A rectangular field with an area of 30 acres is 880 yd long. Find its breadth and its perimeter.

23 How many cubic-inch blocks can be packed inside a rectangular box which is 2 ft long, 1 ft 3 in wide and 10 in high?

24 The floor of a room 24 ft by 16 ft has a border 2 ft wide all round which is to be stained. Find the area to be stained and the area of the rest of the floor.

25 Find the area of the walls of a room which is 25 ft long, 18 ft wide and 9 ft high.

26 Find the volume of air in a room 24 ft long, 16 ft wide and 9 ft high. Find also the area of the floor.

27 How many bricks, each 9 in long, $4\frac{1}{2}$ in wide and 3 in deep, are needed to build a wall 24 yd long, 15 ft high and 18 in thick?

28 A lawn 40 ft long and 32 ft wide is surrounded by a concrete path 3 ft wide. Find in ft² the area of the path.

29 A rectangular sheet of metal, 12 ft by 10 ft, has a rectangular piece 3 ft by 2 ft cut out of one corner. Find the area and perimeter of the portion of the sheet-metal which is left.

30 Find the total surface area of a rectangular block 6 in by $4\frac{1}{2}$ in by $2\frac{1}{2}$ in.

31 Find the total surface area of a rectangular block 5 ft 4 in by 3 ft 6 in by 2 ft.

32 A room 18 ft by 14 ft 6 in and 10 ft 6 in high is to have the walls distempered. If 110 ft² can be allowed for the windows and floor, find the area which is to be distempered.

9. UNITARY METHOD

Direct proportion

Example 1 *If* 4 *m of cloth cost* 180p, *what is the cost of* 11 *m?*

$$4 \text{ m cost } 180\text{p};$$

$$\therefore \quad 1 \text{ m costs } \frac{180}{4}\text{p};$$

$$\therefore \quad 11 \text{ m cost } \frac{180 \times 11}{4}\text{p} = 45 \times 11\text{p} = 495\text{p}.$$

Example 2 *If* 10 *eggs cost* 25p, *how many eggs can be bought for* 65p?

$$25\text{p buys } 10 \text{ eggs};$$

$$\therefore \quad 1\text{p buys } \frac{10}{25} \text{ eggs};$$

$$\therefore \quad 65\text{p buys } \frac{10 \times 65}{25} \text{ eggs}$$

$$= \frac{2 \times 65}{5} \text{ eggs} = 26 \text{ eggs}.$$

These are examples of what is called **unitary method,** because the second line of the argument deals with the cost of *one* metre or the number of eggs purchased by *one* penny.

Always word the first line so that it says what you are given as a complete sentence, with the quantity which you have to find at the right-hand end.

State the units in your answer (pence or eggs in the examples above).

EXERCISE 36 (Oral)

1 A car runs 150 km on 25 litres of petrol. How many kilometres will it run on 1 litre? How far on 15 litres?

2 5 tonnes of coal cost £45. What is the cost of 8 tonnes?

3 The bus fare for 4 km is 10p. Find the fare for 10 km at the same rate.

4 If 20 kg of potatoes cost 15p, find the cost of 8 kg.

5 A train travels 9 km in 6 min. How long does it take to travel 12 km at the same rate?

6 A man walks 24 km at a steady rate in 6 h. How far does he walk in 1 h? How far in x h?

7 If 12 tapers cost 6p, how many can be bought for 14p?

8 A train travels 120 m in 5 sec. How far does it travel in 3 sec? How far in t sec?

9 If 6 tennis balls cost 100p, how many can be bought for 150p?

10 If 8 loaves cost 72p, what is the cost of 20 loaves?

EXERCISE 37

1 A car travels 90 km in 95 min. Find the time to travel 36 km at the same rate.

2 If 9 kg of coffee cost 738p, find the cost of 7 kg.

3 A car uses 12 litres of petrol for a journey of 108 km. Find how many litres it uses for 81 km.

4 If 5 kg of cheese cost 280p, find how many kilogrammes can be bought for 196p.

5 A man walks $5\frac{1}{2}$ km in 66 minutes. How long does he take to walk 9 km? How long for x km?

6 A train travels 24 km in 25 min. How far would it travel in 40 min at the same rate?

7 If 200 g of tobacco cost 220p, find the cost of 90 g.

8 A car travels 15 km in 25 min. How far at this rate would it travel in 35 min? How far in x min?

9 If 120 Belgian francs equal £1, find the value of 84 francs.

10 If 40 cm³ of copper weigh 354 g, find the weight of 28 cm³.

11 If 1·6 cm³ of a substance weigh 3·64 g, find the weight of 10 cm³.

Inverse proportion

Example 3 *If* 8 *men can do a piece of work in* 5 *days, in how many days will* 10 *men do the work?*

8 men can do the work in 5 days;

∴ 1 man   „   „   5 × 8 days;

∴ 10 men   „   „ $\dfrac{5 \times 8}{10}$ days

= 4 days.

(Notice that 1 man does the work, not in $\frac{5}{8}$ days, but in 5 × 8 days.)

Example 4 *The stock of food in a camp would last* 12 *men for* 10 *days. How many men could live for* 8 *days on the same stock?*

For 10 days the food is enough for 12 men;

∴ „ 1 day   „   „   12 × 10 men;

∴ „ 8 days   „   „ $\dfrac{\overset{3}{12} \times 10}{\underset{2}{8}}$ men

= 15 men.

(Notice that for 1 day the food is enough, not for $\frac{12}{10}$ men, but for 12 × 10 men.)

Compare the argument in the following two cases:

(1) 5 m of cloth cost £8,

∴ 1 m   „   £$\frac{8}{5}$ (i.e. a *fifth* as much as 5 m).

(2) 5 men do a piece of work in 8 days,

∴ 1 man does it in 8 × 5 days (i.e. *five* times as long as 5 men).

(1) is called **direct proportion**. A *decrease* in the quantity at the beginning of the sentence leads to a *decrease* in that at the end, and an increase in one to an increase in the other.

(2) is called **inverse proportion**. A *decrease* in the quantity at the beginning of the sentence leads to an *increase* in that at the end, and an increase in one to a decrease in the other.

But there are many cases which are neither direct nor inverse proportion, and the unitary method must not be applied. For example, if a man weighs 64 kg at the age of 25, it does not follow that he will weigh 128 kg at the age of 50.

EXERCISE 38

This exercise contains examples of both direct and inverse proportion, as well as some where unitary method cannot be used (in which case you should say so, and not attempt to give any other answer).

1 At a speed of 56 km per hour a train takes 4 h for a journey. Find how long it would take at 64 km per hour.

2 If 3 men can do a piece of work in 10 days, how long would it take 5 men?

3 A boy saves £15 in 50 weeks. How long does it take him to save £6 at the same rate?

4 A boy weighs 50 kg when he is 14 years of age. What will he weigh when he is 21 years of age?

5 A boy runs 100 m in 12·4 sec. How long will he take to run a kilometre?

6 If 9 similar pumps, all working together, empty a tank in 20 min, how long would it take to empty the same tank with only 5 pumps working?

7 If 9 men earn altogether £42 in a day, how much will 15 men earn in a day at the same rate, if all the men are paid alike?

8 A certain sum of money is enough to pay the wages of 14 men for 16 days. How many men could be paid for 28 days at the same rate with the same sum?

9 If 5 cm³ of lead weigh 57 g, find the weight of a block of lead 10 cm long, 3 cm wide and 2 cm high.

10 A clock gains 54 sec in 12 days. How much will it gain in 22 days?

11 A golfer does the first 6 holes of an 18-hole course in 27 strokes. How many strokes does he take for the whole course?

12 When water is heated from freezing-point to boiling-point, its temperature rises by 180 Fahrenheit degrees or by 100 Celsius degrees. By how many Celsius degrees will the temperature rise if it rises through 54 Fahrenheit degrees? By how many Fahrenheit degrees will it rise if it rises through 65 Celsius degrees?

13 A ship takes 20 days for a certain journey if it steams at 12 nautical miles per hour. How long would it take for the same journey if it steamed at 15 nautical miles per hour?

14 On a certain map 5 cm represents a kilometre. What is the distance apart of two points which are 8·4 cm apart on the map?

15 If 27 men can do a piece of work in $11\frac{1}{3}$ hours, find how many men would be required to do the same work in 17 hours.

16 If £1680 is earned by 42 men in a certain time, how many men will earn £1760 at the same rate in the same time?

17 If 16 men dig a trench in 22 days, how long would it have taken 11 men to dig the same trench?

18 I have enough money to spend 210p a day for 25 days. How long will my money last if I spend 150p a day?

19 A swimming-bath can be filled in 8 hours by 6 similar pumps all working together. How many pumps working together are needed to fill the bath in 12 hours?

20 A haystack contains enough hay to feed 24 horses for 15 days. How long would the same hay last 20 horses? How long would it last $15x$ horses?

21 If I walk to the station at 7 km per h the journey takes 18 min. How long will it take if I run at 9 km per h?

10. FIRST NOTIONS IN ALGEBRA

Letters for numbers You have already met some cases where letters were used to represent numbers. For example, we said that if the length of a rectangle is l cm and the breadth b cm, the area is A cm², where $A = lb \times$, and the perimeter is P cm, where $P = 2l + 2b$. We must be careful not to say that the length of the rectangle is l, but to say l metres or l centimetres.

Again, we might say that, if one parcel weighs x kg and another y kg, the total weight is x kg $+ y$ kg, which we write $(x + y)$ kg, placing brackets round '$x + y$' to show that it is to be looked upon as a single number.

To take another illustration, if the thermometer read 48 degrees, and the temperature rose T degrees, the reading would then be $(48 + T)$ degrees. On the other hand, if the temperature fell T degrees, the reading would be $(48 - T)$ degrees.

As will be seen from these examples, the symbols $+$ and $-$ have exactly the same meanings when letters stand for numbers.

Multiplication If 4 articles cost 6p each, the total cost is 4×6 pence. Similarly, if 4 articles cost x pence each, the total cost is $4 \times x$ pence. This is usually written $4x$ pence, omitting the multiplication sign. Thus, $10a$ is a short way of writing $10 \times a$; $12y$ is short for $12 \times y$.

Examples

$$x \text{ metres} = 100x \text{ centimetres,}$$
$$b \text{ kilogrammes} = 1000b \text{ grammes,}$$
$$£z = 100z \text{ pence,}$$
$$m \text{ minutes} = 60m \text{ seconds.}$$

Notice the difference between 47 and $4x$. The former means, not 4×7, but 4 tens $+ 7$ units. Notice, too, that $4\frac{7}{8}$ means $4 + \frac{7}{8}$, not $4 \times \frac{7}{8}$.

Division Instead of $24 \div 6$, we can write $\frac{24}{6}$.

In the same way, $24 \div x$ is written as $\dfrac{24}{x}$.

Thus $\dfrac{5}{a}$ is another way of writing $5 \div a$; $\dfrac{y}{3}$ means $y \div 3$.

Examples

$$x \text{ pence} = £\frac{x}{100},$$

$$y \text{ millimetres} = \frac{y}{10} \text{ centimetres} = \frac{y}{1000} \text{ metres}.$$

The language of algebra When we use letters to stand for numbers, this is called **algebra.** Two symbols often used are:

the symbol $=$, meaning 'is equal to' (a *verb*);
the symbol $\therefore$, meaning 'therefore' (a *conjunction*).

With the aid of the signs and symbols mentioned before, statements can be made in the shortened language of algebra.

Example 1 *Write in the language of algebra: multiply the number* P *by* 4, *then take* 2 *away; the result is equal to* 34.

This becomes simply

$$4P - 2 = 34.$$

(Can you guess the number which P stands for?)

Example 2 *State in words the operations represented by* $\dfrac{3y-8}{5}$.

The operations are: multiply y by 3, take 8 away, and divide the result by 5.

EXERCISE 39

Write the following in symbols:

1 Twice y is equal to 8.
2 Five multiplied by P equals 40.
3 x multiplied by 3 equals 12.   **4** Take 2 away from x.
5 Take x away from 4; the result is equal to 1.
6 Add 4 to twice Q; the answer is 20.

7 From 4 times x take 5 times y.

8 Add 4 times x to 6, and then divide the result by 2.

9 Multiply x by 10, and add 5; the result equals 45.

10 Three times N gives the same answer as adding N to 10.

11 Divide x by 5; the result is equal to 9.

12 Twice x taken from 24 is equal to 6 times x.

13 P divided by 3 is equal to 6; therefore P is equal to 18.

14 Add 2 to three times x, and the result is 23; therefore x is equal to 7.

State in words the operations represented by:

15 $\dfrac{1+7x}{4}$ **16** $\dfrac{x^2-3}{5}$ **17** $\frac{1}{2}x+3$ **18** $\frac{1}{2}(x+3)$

Notation Many expressions in algebra can be written more simply if we deal with letters just as we should with numbers. For example, just as $8+8$ can be written as 2×8, and $8+8+8$ as 3×8, we say $P+P=2P$, $P+P+P=3P$, $P+P+P+P=4P$, and so on.

Examples

$$4x+3x=7x,$$
$$7y-2y=5y,$$
$$4\times 2x=2x+2x+2x+2x=8x,$$
$$6\times 3P=18P.$$

EXERCISE 40 (Oral)

Simplify:

1 $3x+x$	**2** $3x-x$	**3** $8y+4y$	**4** $9a+12a$
5 $3\times 5y$	**6** $2z\times 7$	**7** $9a-3a$	**8** $3\times 4x$
9 $2\frac{1}{2}x+3\frac{1}{2}x$	**10** $m+4m$	**11** $60b-10b$	**12** $4\times\frac{1}{2}x$

EXERCISE 41

1 How many milligrammes are there in L grammes? How many grammes in N mg?

2 A man is 40 years old now. How old will he be in T years' time?

3 A boy walks at 4 km per hour.   How far does he walk in H hours at this speed?

4 How many pence are there in £P?   How many pounds are there in Q pence?

5 There are 20 people in a bus, and y more get in.   How many are there now?

6 A farmer has x cows, and he buys 10 more.   How many has he then?

7 A sheet of stamps contains 12 rows with b stamps in each row.   How many stamps are there altogether?

8 If P is an even number, what are the two even numbers next above P?

9 From a stick x cm long, a portion y mm long is cut off. Find in millimetres what length is left.

10 A clock gains 30 sec a day.   How much does it gain in T days?

11 A bottle and cork together weigh 3 kg.   If the bottle weighs W kg, what does the cork weigh?

12 How many kilometres are there in x metres?   How many in y cm?

13 How many millimetres are there in x cm?   How many centimetres are there in y mm?

14 A man is P years old now.   How old was he 10 years ago?

15 How many tonnes are there (i) in w kg, (ii) in m grammes?

16 A train travels at a uniform speed of 50 km per h.   How many hours does it take to go 100 km?   How long to go y km?

17 A pile of exercise books is 12 cm high.   If there are N books, what is the thickness of each?

18 What is the volume of a cuboid 4 m long, 3 m wide and h m high?

19 A theatre-ticket costs 80 pence.   How many tickets can be bought for x pence?

20 A man has to walk 25 km.   How many hours will he take if he walks at a steady speed of v km per hour?

21 How many grammes are there (i) in $\frac{x}{4}$ mg, (ii) in $\frac{y}{5}$ kg?

22 A mixed school contains 300 pupils altogether. If there are B boys, how many girls are there?

23 How many times can a jug holding y litres be filled from a cask holding 30 litres?

24 Find an expression for the cost in pence of x kg of sugar at 7p per kg and y kg of tea at 23p per kg.

Further symbols   Indices are used in algebra in the same way as they are in arithmetic.   Thus,

x^2 (read as 'x squared') stands for $x \times x$,
x^3 (read as 'x cubed') stands for $x \times x \times x$,
x^4 (read as 'x to the fourth') stands for $x \times x \times x \times x$, and so on.

Just as the square root of 9 (that is, 3) is written $\sqrt{9}$, so the square root of x is written as $\sqrt{x}$.

The meaning of $4x$ has already been given as $4 \times x$;

$$\text{similarly, } 4x^2 \text{ stands for } 4 \times x^2.$$

Other examples:

$$5y^3 \text{ stands for } 5 \times y^3,$$
$$3xy \text{ stands for } 3 \times x \times y,$$
$$(4x)^2 \text{ stands for } 4x \times 4x, \text{ or } 16x^2.$$

Do not confuse x^2 with $2x$, or x^3 with $3x$.

Example 3   *If $a = 3$ and $b = 4$, find the values of:*

$$(i)\ 5ab, \quad (ii)\ (2a)^3, \quad (iii)\ \sqrt{9b}, \quad (iv)\ 7a^2b.$$

(i) $5ab = 5 \times 3 \times 4 = 60$.
(ii) $(2a)^3 = 2a \times 2a \times 2a = 6 \times 6 \times 6 = 216$;

$$\text{or } 8a^3 = 8 \times 27 = 216.$$

(iii) $\sqrt{9b} = \sqrt{36} = 6$.
(iv) $7a^2b = 7 \times 9 \times 4 = 252$.

EXERCISE 42

Find the values of the following expressions, if a stands for 2 and b stands for 3:

1 $3a$	**2** a^3	**3** $2b+5$	**4** $6a-4$
5 $\dfrac{2a}{5}$	**6** $1\frac{1}{3}b$	**7** $4ab$	**8** $\dfrac{a}{4}+\dfrac{b}{4}$
9 $\dfrac{a}{b}$	**10** $b+4a$	**11** b^2+a^2	**12** $3b-2a$
13 $\dfrac{6}{a}+\dfrac{6}{b}$	**14** $\dfrac{3ab}{6}$	**15** $\dfrac{3a}{2b}$	**16** $a\div\frac{2}{3}$
17 $b^2\times1\frac{1}{3}$	**18** $2b\div1\frac{1}{2}$	**19** $\dfrac{ab^2}{b}$	**20** $\dfrac{a}{b}\times\dfrac{2b}{a}$

Find the values of the following expressions, if $x=0$ and $y=4$:

21 $3xy$	**22** $2x+3y$	**23** $\dfrac{x}{y}$	**24** $\dfrac{y^2}{8}$	**25** x^2+y^2
26 y^2-x^2	**27** $\dfrac{y^3}{2}$	**28** $\dfrac{y+2}{3}$	**29** $\dfrac{x+y+8}{y}$	**30** $2y^2$

If P$=3$ and Q$=5$, find the values of the following:

31 $2PQ$	**32** $\dfrac{1}{P}+\dfrac{1}{Q}$	**33** $\dfrac{8P}{9}\times\dfrac{1}{4}$	**34** $\dfrac{P}{1}+\dfrac{Q}{5}$
35 $4P-2Q$	**36** $2+4P$	**37** $\dfrac{P+3}{3}$	**38** $\dfrac{2P+4}{Q}$
39 $\dfrac{2P}{Q}\times6\frac{2}{3}$	**40** P^3Q	**41** $P\times\dfrac{1}{Q}\times\dfrac{10}{27}$	**42** Q^2-2P
43 $2P^2Q$	**44** $\dfrac{Q}{P}+\dfrac{5}{6}$	**45** $\dfrac{PQ^2}{30}$	**46** $\dfrac{Q-P}{P}$
47 $\dfrac{12P}{8}$	**48** $\dfrac{3Q}{10P^2}$	**49** $1\frac{1}{5}Q\times1\frac{1}{3}P$	**50** $\dfrac{Q}{P}\div2\frac{2}{9}$

Addition and subtraction of terms Parts of an expression which are connected by $+$ or $-$ signs are called **terms**.

Thus, $3a + 2a$ contains the two terms $3a$ and $2a$. These are called **like terms**, because they can be collected together to make $5a$. Again, $5x - 3y$ contains the two terms $5x$ and $3y$. These are called **unlike terms**, because they cannot be collected together and replaced by a single term.

$2a + 3b - 1$ contains the three terms $2a$, $3b$, and 1, all unlike. This expression cannot be simplified at all, unless we know the values of the letters a and b.

$2ab$ consists of only *one* term; a and b are *factors*, not separate terms.

We can simplify an expression containing several terms by collecting together all the like terms, putting those with the same sign together.

Example 4 *Simplify:* (i) $3x - x + 4x + 2x - 5x$,
(ii) $8a + 7b - 4a - 2b + 5a - a - 3b$.

(i) $3x - x + 4x + 2x - 5x = 3x + 4x + 2x - x - 5x$
$$= 9x - 6x = 3x.$$

(ii) $8a + 7b - 4a - 2b + 5a - a - 3b$
$$= 8a + 5a - 4a - a + 7b - 2b - 3b$$
$$= 13a - 5a + 7b - 5b$$
$$= 8a + 2b.$$

EXERCISE 43

Simplify the following:

1 $a - a + a$ 2 $3x + x + x + x - x$ 3 $3a + 2a + a$

4 $5x - 4x$ 5 $b + b + b + b + b$ 6 $x + x + 3x$

7 $4x + 4x - 2x$ 8 $10y - y$ 9 $f - f + f + f - f$

10 $6g - 2g - 3g$ 11 $h + 2h + 3h + 4h$ 12 $a + 6a - 3a$

13 $3y + 2y - y - y$ 14 $7x - 2x + 3x - x - 4x$

15 $6p - 3p - p$ 16 $x + 5x - 2x + 3x$

17 $8y - 2y - 3y + 5y - 6y$ 18 $15a - 4a - 4a$

19 $2x + 8x - x + 3x - 6x$ 20 $5d + d + 3d - 2d$

21 $x + x + x - x - x + x + 3x$ 22 $5r + 6r - r - 3r$

23 $4y - y + 2y - 4y$ 24 $6b + 2b - 3b$

25 $6x + 5x - 4x + x + 3x - 7x$

Simplify the following whenever it is possible. (If no shorter form can be found, write 'No shorter form'.)

26 $x + 2y + 3x - 2x - 2y$ **27** $2a - b + 3b - a - b$
28 $5x + y + 3y + x$ **29** $a + b + c - a - b + c$
30 $7x - 2y - 1$ **31** $x + y + 2x + y$
32 $1 + 2x$ **33** $3a + 6c - 2a - b + c - 4b$
34 $1 + 2x + 3a - x - a$ **35** $5a + b + 2b - a$
36 $8x - 2y - 2 - 3x - y$ **37** $a + 2b + 3c$ **38** $ab + 2ab$
39 $ab + ba$ **40** $5x - 5$ **41** $3e + f - e + 4f - f$
42 $7x + 5 - 2x - 2$ **43** $9a - 2b - 3b - 4b$
44 $y + 2x + 1$ **45** $4x - 2y + 2y - x - 3$
46 $4 + 2x + 3y - 2 - x + 3y$ **47** $5a + 3b - 2a + b + 2$
48 $6x + y - 4x + y - y$ **49** $3x - 3$ **50** $3x - x$

11. THE PRISM AND THE PYRAMID

You will remember that we discussed the cube and the cuboid earlier in this book. The faces of these two solids are all rectangles and squares. The solids which we are now going to talk about also have plane faces, but not necessarily rectangular or square. They are the prism and the pyramid.

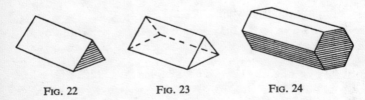

Fig. 22   Fig. 23   Fig. 24

Prism Fig. 22 represents a **three-sided prism**; Fig. 23 shows the same prism with dotted lines for the edges which are hidden. The ends of the prism are **triangles**.

Fig. 24 represents a **six-sided prism**. Its ends are called **hexagons**.

The cuboid is a prism whose ends are rectangles. The end of a prism is a plane figure bounded by straight lines. Such a figure is called a **polygon** (many sides). A polygon with

3 sides is called a **triangle**;
4 sides   „   **quadrilateral**;
5 sides   „   **pentagon**;
6 sides   „   **hexagon**;
8 sides   „   an **octagon**;
10 sides   „   a **decagon**.

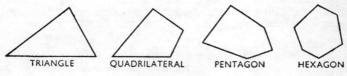

TRIANGLE   QUADRILATERAL   PENTAGON   HEXAGON

FIG. 25

Pyramid Another solid whose faces are polygons is the **pyramid**. The name is thought to be derived from the Egyptian word *piremus*, which meant *high*.

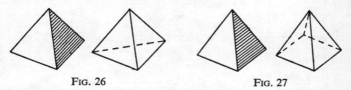

FIG. 26   FIG. 27

Each of the four faces of the pyramid in Fig. 26 is a triangle. Another name for this pyramid is the **tetrahedron** (four faces). Fig. 27 shows a pyramid on a square base.

How to draw a pyramid A sketch of a pyramid on a square base is made by first drawing the base as it would appear from the side. (See Fig. 28, where the base is ABCD.) Mark the centre of the base, O, which will be the point where AC crosses BD, and through this point draw a line to

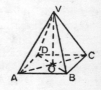

FIG. 28

represent the vertical height of the pyramid. Mark the vertex V of the pyramid on this line, and join to A, B, C and D. Try to avoid choosing V so that VA passes very nearly through D. Use dotted lines for edges which are not visible.

EXERCISE 44

1 Make a freehand sketch of a pyramid on a square base.

2 Make a freehand sketch of a cube, each of whose edges is 4 cm. Letter the bottom face ABCD, and let the vertical edges be AE, BF, CG, DH. Mark the centre O of the face EFGH, and join it to A, B, C, D. What is the solid OABCD? What is its vertical height?

Nets of the prism and the pyramid The net of a triangular prism (i.e. the figure you will have to cut out in thin cardboard to make the prism) is shown in Fig. 29. Fig. 30 is the net of a tetrahedron, and Fig. 31 is that of a pyramid on a square base.

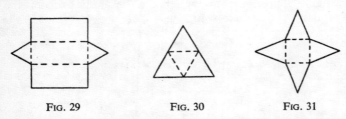

FIG. 29   FIG. 30   FIG. 31

Later we shall construct these nets accurately, but before we can do so we must learn how to handle our mathematical instruments properly. If the net is not neatly and carefully drawn, the model will look untidy when it is made.

The chief mathematical instruments are the ruler, set square, compasses and protractor. You will already be familiar with the use of the ruler for drawing a straight line and for measuring lines in centimetres and millimetres. In the next section we shall explain the use of the set square and compasses.

12. SET SQUARE AND COMPASSES

Use of the set square   The set square is used for drawing a line at right angles to another line.   Such a line is called a **perpendicular.**   If we need a perpendicular to a line AB at a particular point P in the line, we can place the set square as in Fig. 32.   But it is difficult to draw the perpendicular right to the corner of the set square, and a better way is as follows:

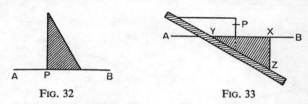

FIG. 32   FIG. 33

To draw a perpendicular to a line   Suppose we have a line AB, and we want to draw a perpendicular to AB through a point P.   Place a set square in the position XYZ (see Fig. 33), so that XY lies along AB.   Place a ruler along YZ.   Holding the ruler firm, slide the set square along the ruler until the edge XZ passes through P.   Then draw the perpendicular through P to the line AB.   Do not draw it just to the line, but continue it a short distance beyond.

Fig. 33 shows the point P not lying on the line AB, but the method can also be used when P lies on the line.

When P lies on the line AB, we talk of **erecting a perpendicular at P to AB**; when P does not lie on AB, we talk of **dropping a perpendicular from P to AB.**

Use of compasses   Compasses are used:

(i) for transferring a length from one place on the paper to another (dividers also are often used for this purpose);

(ii) for drawing a circle, or part of a circle, with its centre at a given point and with a given radius.

Definitions   A **circle** is the path traced out by a point which moves so that its distance from a fixed point (called the **centre**) is a fixed length (called the **radius**). When you draw a circle with compasses, the point where the steel end of one leg rests is the centre, and the pencil point traces out the circle. Sometimes the word 'circle' means the space inside the curve, and so the curve is often spoken of as the **circumference** of the circle.

Any portion of the circumference is called an **arc** of the circle. The straight line joining any two points on the circumference of the circle is called a **chord**. If the chord passes through the centre of the circle, it is called a **diameter**. The two arcs into which a diameter divides the circumference are called **semicircles**.

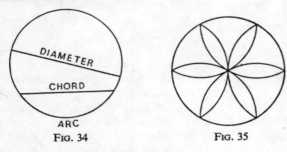

DIAMETER

CHORD

ARC

Fig. 34   Fig. 35

EXERCISE 45

1 Draw a straight line AB on your paper and mark a point P on the line. Use the set square to draw a perpendicular through P to AB.

2 Repeat No. 1, but mark P about 4 cm from AB.

3 Draw a straight line AB 5 cm long, and use the set square to make a square ABCD.

4 Draw a rectangle PQRS with length 9 cm and breadth 7 cm.

5 Mark any point O on your paper, and draw a circle with centre at O and with a radius of 4 cm. Draw any chord AB of the circle (not a diameter), and with the set square drop a perpendicular from O to AB. Measure the two parts of AB.

6 Draw a circle with radius 4 cm, and copy the pattern shown in Fig. 35. Each of the six points on the complete circle is the centre of an arc, and the arcs all have a radius 4 cm.

7 Copy the pattern shown in Fig. 36. The large circle should have radius 4 cm, and the dotted diameters are at right angles to one another. The small circles have their centres half-way along the radii, and the radius of each small circle is 2 cm.

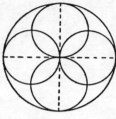

FIG. 36

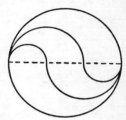

FIG. 37

8 Copy Fig. 37. The radius of the large circle should be 6 cm and two of the semicircles have a radius 2 cm and the other two semicircles a radius 4 cm.

9 Copy Fig. 38. Start by drawing a circle of radius 4 cm and mark any point A on the circumference. With centre A and radius 4 cm, draw an arc to cut the circle at B. With

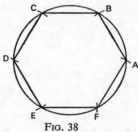

FIG. 38

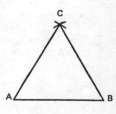

FIG. 39

centre B and radius 4 cm, draw an arc to cut the circle at C, and so on. ABCDEF is called a **regular hexagon**.

10 Draw a line AB 5 cm long. With centre A and radius 5 cm, draw an arc as in Fig. 39, and with centre B and radius 5 cm, draw an arc to cut the first arc at C. Join C to A and B. ABC is called an **equilateral triangle**.

13. MULTIPLICATION AND DIVISION IN ALGEBRA

Multiplication   We have seen that $5 \times 2x = 10x$.
In the same way,

$$5 \times 2 \times 3x = 30x,$$
$$3ab \times 8 = 24ab,$$
$$3y \times 4y = 3y \times 4 \times y$$
$$= 12y \times y = 12y^2,$$
$$3a \times 2b = 6ab,$$
$$6a \times 2a = 12a^2,$$
$$2a \times 3b \times 4 = 6ab \times 4 = 24ab.$$

EXERCISE 46

Express as a single term:

1 $2x \times 3$	**2** $2x \times 3x$	**3** $2x \times 3y$	**4** $6x \times 4x$
5 $6a \times 4b$	**6** $3n \times 4n$	**7** $(3x)^2$	**8** $3 \times 2x \times 4$
9 $7 \times 4y$	**10** $2x^2 \times 3y$	**11** $3d \times 4e$	**12** $4u \times 3 \times u$
13 $9a \times a$	**14** $2p \times 3r \times 5$	**15** $3a^2 \times 2b^2$	**16** $4p \times 2q$
17 $3a \times 4b \times 2c$	**18** $2P \times R \times 7$	**19** $(10a)^2$	**20** $10b \times 2$

Division   We can divide both numerator and denominator of a fraction by the same factor, exactly as in arithmetic.

Thus

$$\frac{12a}{3} = \frac{4a}{1} = 4a,$$

and

$$\frac{12a}{3a} = \frac{12}{3} = 4.$$

This is the same as saying that $12a \div 3 = 4a$, and $12a \div 3a = 4$.

Similarly,

$$\frac{10xy}{5} = 2xy,$$

$$\frac{10xy}{5y} = 2x,$$

and

$$\frac{12a^2}{3a} = 4a.$$

EXERCISE 47

Simplify:

1 $14x \div 7$	**2** $16a \div 4a$	**3** $12p \div 6$
4 $12q \div q$	**5** $15ab \div 5ab$	**6** $32x \div 8x$
7 $9a^2 \div 3a^2$	**8** $12a^2b \div 4ab$	**9** $18c \div 9$
10 $24xy^2 \div 12y$	**11** $48xy \div 12$	**12** $21z^2 \div 7z$
13 $16p \div 8$	**14** $27x^2 \div 3x$	**15** $22x^2 \div 11x$
16 $4ab \div a$	**17** $26d^2 \div 13$	**18** $12ax \div 6x$
19 $20a \div 2a$	**20** $25p^2 \div 5p$	**21** $\dfrac{15m^2}{3m^2}$
22 $\dfrac{18xy}{9y}$	**23** $\dfrac{28p^2q}{7q}$	**24** $\dfrac{5 \times 8y}{4y}$
25 $\dfrac{2x \times 3y}{6}$	**26** $\dfrac{6 \times 14a}{7a}$	**27** $\dfrac{16abc}{8c}$
28 $\dfrac{8a^2}{16a}$	**29** $\dfrac{(2y)^2}{2}$	**30** $\dfrac{(3x)^2}{9x}$

EXERCISE 48

Write the following in simpler forms:

1 $N \times 4 \times 2$	**2** $a \times 0$	**3** $2P \times 1$	**4** $3 \times x \times 4$
5 $x^2 \times 3 \times 5$	**6** $2ab \times 3a$	**7** $4x^2 \div x$	**8** $\dfrac{x}{x}$
9 $3y \times \dfrac{2}{3}$	**10** $\dfrac{1}{2}$ of $4a$	**11** $\dfrac{3 \times 4x}{15}$	**12** $2a^2 \times 3b$
13 $ab \times ab$	**14** $x \times 2x \times x \times 2x$	**15** $x \times a \times a \times x \times a$	
16 $3xy \times 2y$	**17** $6x \div 3$	**18** $6x \div 6x$	**19** $ab \times bc$
20 $5x - 5 + x$	**21** $6 \times 6a \times b$	**22** $\dfrac{ax}{bx}$	**23** $4x + 3y + x$
24 $3 \times a \times 2b$	**25** $\dfrac{a}{a^2}$	**26** $4N \div 1$	**27** $2x^2 \times 2x$
28 $\dfrac{b \times 27b}{3}$		**29** $abc \times ab$	**30** $\dfrac{3y \times 12}{4}$

31 $7x - 7 + 2x - 2$ **32** $\dfrac{x}{2} \div 12$ **33** $\dfrac{9x}{3x}$

34 $\dfrac{4}{2p}$ **35** $r^2 h \div \dfrac{1}{3}$ **36** $\dfrac{2}{3}$ of $3a^3$

EXERCISE 49 (Miscellaneous)

Give the answers to this exercise in their shortest forms.

1 A motorist drives at a steady speed of 50 km per hour. How far does he go in $\dfrac{2x}{5}$ h?

2 Express $\dfrac{3x}{4}$ metres in cm, and $150y$ cm in metres.

3 Find the area and perimeter of a rectangle $3x$ cm by $2x$ cm.

4 A cuboid has edges 6 cm, $3a$ cm and $2a$ cm. Find (i) its volume in cubic centimetres, (ii) the sum of the lengths of its edges in centimetres.

5 Find the total cost in pence of x kg of butter at 40p per kg and $\frac{1}{2}x$ kg of margarine at 36p per kg.

6 An open tank is 3 m long, $4x$ m wide and 2 m deep. Find (i) the volume, (ii) the total area of the four walls and the bottom.

7

Find (i) the area, (ii) the perimeter of each of the figures in Nos. 7–9, where all the corners are right angles and the dimensions are all in centimetres.

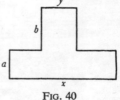

FIG. 40

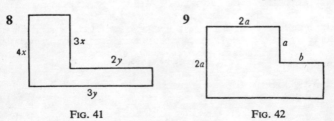

FIG. 41   FIG. 42

10 Find the area of a square whose side is $\frac{a}{3}$ cm.

11 Find the volume of a cube whose edge is $\frac{a}{4}$ mm.

12 A rectangular lawn is 10 m long and x m wide, and a rectangular flower-bed 6 m long and $\frac{x}{3}$ m wide is cut in it. Find the area of the flower-bed and of the grass.

13 Find how many hours it takes me to walk $\frac{7x}{4}$ km at $5\frac{3}{5}$ km per hour.

14 A man has £x and spends $20x$ pence. Find how much he has left (i) in pence, (ii) in £.

15 Express in grammes: (i) $30a$ mg, (ii) $\frac{b}{500}$ kg, (iii) $\frac{c}{2500}$ tonnes.

16 A man takes a daily paper costing $2\frac{1}{2}$p per day and a Sunday paper costing 5p per copy. He also pays 4p per week for delivery. Find his newspaper bill for T weeks (i) in pence, (ii) in £.

17 The area of a rectangular carpet is 27 m². If the length is $\frac{3x}{2}$ m, find the breadth.

18 Find in centimetres the height of a pile of $12n$ books, if each book is $\frac{n}{6}$ cm thick.

14. ANGLES

Right angle Suppose one hand of a clock is pointing to 12. When it has moved until it is pointing to 3, we say that it has turned through a **right angle**. When it is pointing to 6, it has turned through two right angles; when it is pointing to 9, through three right angles; and when it points to 12 again we say that it has turned through four right angles, or a complete turn.

Similarly, if you stand facing North, turning through one right angle brings you to East; turning through two right angles brings you to South; through three right angles to West; and when you have turned through four right angles you will be facing North again.

'Right turn' and 'left turn' mean that you are to turn through one right angle. 'About turn' means two right angles. 'Half right turn' means turn right, through half a right angle.

EXERCISE 50

State in right angles, or fractions of a right angle, the angles through which you turn in Nos. 1–10. 'Clockwise' means in the same direction as that in which the hands of a clock move; 'counter-clockwise' means the opposite direction to this.

1 From E. to SE., clockwise
2   ,,   SE. to SW.,   ,,
3   ,,   N. to SW.,   ,,
4   ,,   N. to SW., counter-clockwise
5   ,,   N. to E.,   ,,
6   ,,   N. to NW., clockwise
7   ,,   W. to N., counter-clockwise
8   ,,   N. to SE., clockwise
9   ,,   NW. to E., counter-clockwise
10   ,,   NW. to SE., clockwise

Fig. 43

In Nos. 11–15, state the final direction if you start by facing North and turn through:

11 1 right angle clockwise
12 3 right angles counter-clockwise
13 $1\frac{1}{2}$ right angles counter-clockwise
14 $\frac{1}{2}$ right angle clockwise
15 $2\frac{1}{2}$ right angles counter-clockwise

16 Through what angle, in right angles or fractions of a right angle, does the minute-hand of a clock turn in: (i) 1 h, (ii) 15 min, (iii) 5 min, (iv) 10 min, (v) $2\frac{1}{4}$ h, (vi) x h?

Angles and how to name them If you are standing at O and facing in the direction OA, the amount of turning which you have to make before you are facing in the direction OB is called the **angle** between OA and OB. It is written ∠AOB (read 'angle AOB').

O is called the **vertex** of the angle, OA and OB are called the **arms** of the angle. When we write ∠AOB, the middle letter is the vertex and the two outside letters are points, one on each arm. It is not necessary for the arms OA and OB to be the same length; the size of the angle depends only on the amount of turning from one arm to the other, and not on the lengths of the arms.

In Fig. 44, the shortest way to turn from OA to OB is counter-clockwise. You could also turn *clockwise* from OA

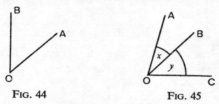

FIG. 44   FIG. 45

and eventually face in the direction OB. By ∠AOB we always mean the smallest amount of turning, whichever the direction may be.

If there is only one angle at O we can call it the angle O. But this must not be done in Fig. 45, where there are three angles, namely ∠AOB, ∠BOC and ∠AOC. An angle is often denoted by a small letter placed in it, and the angle marked by a circular arc. In Fig. 45, ∠AOB is called x and ∠BOC is called y.

If a right angle is divided into 90 equal parts, each part is called a **degree**. An angle of 45 degrees (or half a right angle) is written 45°. A complete turn is 360°.

For very accurate work, the degree is further sub-divided into 90 minutes, and each minute into 60 seconds. We therefore have:

1 right angle = **90 degrees** (90°),
1 degree   = **60 minutes** (60′),
1 minute   = **60 seconds** (60″).

Notice that seconds and minutes of angle measurement resemble seconds and minutes of time. The early Babylonians in the sixth century B.C. are supposed to have been the first people to divide the complete turn into 360°.

Use of the protractor The number of degrees in an angle is measured by a **protractor.**

To measure an angle, place the protractor so that the centre O is at the vertex of the angle, and either OX or OY along one arm. Then see under which graduation the other arm of the angle lies. In Fig. 46 the angle AOC is 43°.

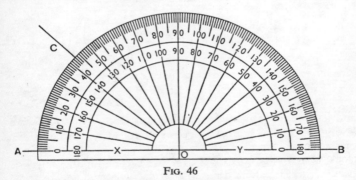

FIG. 46

Be careful to take the correct set of numbers. The outer set (0, 10, 20 . . .) is the one to take if we are measuring ∠AOC, but the inner set (0, 10, 20 . . .) if we are measuring ∠BOC, which is 137°.

To make an angle of any given size at a point P in a line AB, place the protractor with the centre O at P, and the 0–180 line of the protractor along AB. Make a very small dot at the edge of the protractor against the necessary graduation, at Q, say. Take the protractor away, and join QP. Be sure to see whether it is ∠APQ or ∠BPQ which is the angle required. Common sense is the best guide.

Kinds of angles

An angle less than a right angle is called an **acute** (sharp) **angle**.

An angle bigger than a right angle but less than two right angles is called an **obtuse** (blunt) **angle**.

Angles bigger than two right angles but less than four right angles are called **reflex** (bent back) **angles**.

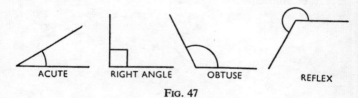

ACUTE   RIGHT ANGLE   OBTUSE   REFLEX

FIG. 47

EXERCISE 51

(*Numerical*)

1 Express in degrees: (i) 3 right angles, (ii) $\frac{1}{3}$ of a right angle, (iii) $1\frac{1}{2}$ right angles, (iv) $\frac{2}{5}$ of a right angle, (v) n right angles.

2 Express in right angles: (i) 180°, (ii) 45°, (iii) 225°, (iv) 60°, (v) 120°, (vi) 270°, (vii) x°.

3 Through how many degrees does the minute-hand of a clock turn in (i) 10 min, (ii) $\frac{1}{2}$ h, (iii) 5 min, (iv) 20 min, (v) $\frac{3}{4}$ h, (vi) $5t$ min?

4 Through how many degrees does the hour-hand of a clock turn in (i) 1 h, (ii) $\frac{1}{2}$ h, (iii) $1\frac{1}{2}$ h, (iv) t h?

(*Drawing and measurement*)

5 One angle of your set square is, of course, a right angle. Measure the other two angles with a protractor, and add together the numbers of degrees in all the three angles.

6 Using a ruler, draw on your paper a fairly large triangle, any shape you like, and measure the number of degrees in each angle. Make a list of the sizes of the angles, and add them together.

7 Draw a straight line AB on your paper, and mark a point P on the line somewhere near the middle. Using a protractor, draw a line PX, through P, so that ∠APX is 58°. Measure ∠XPB.

8 Repeat No. 7, but make ∠APX 41°.

9 „ „ ∠APX 134°.

10 Draw two straight lines AB and CD, crossing at O as in Fig. 48. Measure all the four angles at O, and write down the number of degrees in each angle.

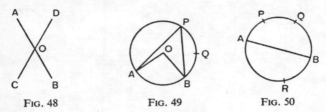

FIG. 48   FIG. 49   FIG. 50

11 Draw a circle with radius 4 cm and let O be the centre. Mark any two radii OA, OB so that ∠AOB = 70° (see Fig. 49). Mark any point P on the circle, as in the figure; join PA and PB, and measure ∠APB.

Now take a second point Q on the circle, and measure ∠AQB. Do you notice anything about your answers?

12 Draw a circle with any convenient radius. (Do not make the circle too small.) Draw any diameter AB, thus dividing the circle into two semicircles. Mark any three points P, Q and R, all lying on the circle, as in Fig. 50, and join each of these points to A and B. Estimate the numbers of degrees in the angles APB, AQB, ARB, and test by measurement.

(These angles are called 'angles in a semicircle'. Can you make a general statement about angles in a semicircle?)

13 Draw a circle with radius 4 cm and mark any two points A, B on it. Mark three other points P, Q, R on the circle and all on the same side of the chord AB, as in Fig. 51. Join each of these points to A and B, and make a list of the sizes of the angles APB, AQB, ARB.

(These angles are said to be 'in the same segment of the circle'. Can you make a general statement about angles in the same segment of a circle?)

14 Draw a circle with a radius 4 cm and draw any quadrilateral ABCD, as in Fig. 52, with its four vertices all lying on the circle. Make a list of the sizes of the angles A, B, C, D.

What do you notice about $\angle A + \angle C$, and about $\angle B + \angle D$?

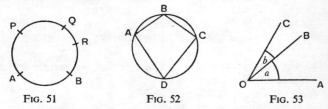

Fig. 51   Fig. 52   Fig. 53

(A quadrilateral like the one you have drawn is called a 'cyclic quadrilateral'. Can you make a general statement about the opposite angles of a cyclic quadrilateral?)

Addition and subtraction of angles In Fig. 53 there are two angles, AOB and BOC, with the same vertex O and with OB an arm of each angle. If $\angle AOB = a$ degrees and $\angle BOC = b$ degrees, it is obvious that $\angle AOC = (a+b)$ degrees, for the amount of turning from OA to OB, followed by the amount of turning from OB to OC, is the same as the amount of turning from OA to OC. This is written

$$\angle AOB + \angle BOC = \angle AOC, \text{ or } a + b = \angle AOC.$$

In the same way, $\angle AOC - \angle BOC = \angle AOB$.

Two angles like $\angle AOB$ and $\angle BOC$ are called **adjacent angles,** as they lie next to one another.

If in Fig. 53 the two angles AOB and BOC are equal, OB is said to **bisect** $\angle AOC$, or to be the **bisector** of $\angle AOC$.

Adjacent angles on a straight line Fig. 54 shows a straight line COA, and another straight line OB meeting it at O. Angles AOB and BOC are denoted by a and b, as in the figure.

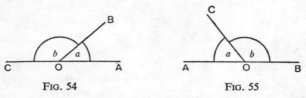

FIG. 54   FIG. 55

Since the total amount of turning from OA to OC is two right angles, it is clear that $a+b=2$ right angles.

The two angles AOB, BOC in Fig. 54 are called **adjacent angles on a straight line,** and the statement just made means that:

The sum of adjacent angles on a straight line is two right angles.

Two angles whose sum is two right angles are called **supplementary angles.** If we represent one of the two by x degrees, we can represent the other by $(180-x)$ degrees.

If we wanted to test whether AOB was a straight line in Fig. 55, we should see if $(a+b)$ made two right angles.

Vertically opposite angles Imagine two rods AB and PQ, as in Fig. 56, crossing one another at X and hinged at that point, rather like a pair of scissors. When XP lies along XA, XQ will lie along XB. The angles AXP and BXQ in the figure must be equal, because they both represent the angle through which PXQ must be turned before the scissors close up. The angles AXP, BXQ are called **vertically opposite angles,** because they have the same vertex X and are on opposite sides of it. Angles AXQ, PXB are another pair of vertically opposite angles. We see, then, that:

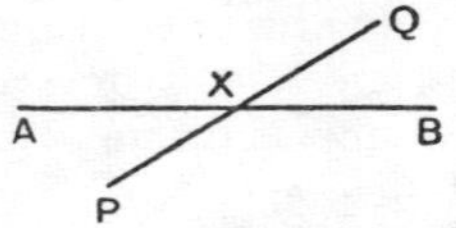

FIG. 56

If two straight lines intersect, the vertically opposite angles are equal.

EXERCISE 52

Where several questions use the same figure, you should draw a separate figure for each question, but do not waste time drawing accurate ones.

1 In Fig. 57, if $x = 42$, find y.
2 In Fig. 57, if $x = 37$, find y.

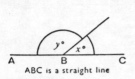

ABC is a straight line

Fig. 57

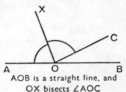

AOB is a straight line, and
OX bisects ∠AOC

Fig. 58

3 In Fig. 57, if $y = 130$, find x.
4 In Fig. 58, if ∠BOC = 30°, calculate ∠AOC and ∠AOX.
5 In Fig. 58, if ∠AOX = 62°, calculate ∠BOC.
6 Copy Fig. 58, and draw another line OY bisecting ∠BOC. If ∠BOC = 36°, calculate ∠COX and ∠COY. What do you notice about ∠XOY?
7 In Fig. 59, if $x = 38$, state the sizes of all the other angles of the figure.
8 In Fig. 59, if OA is the bisector of ∠POX and OB is the

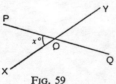

Fig. 59

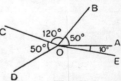

Fig. 60

bisector of ∠YOQ, and ∠POX = 40°, calculate ∠s POA, POY and YOB, and hence show that AOB is a straight line.
9 In Fig. 60, calculate ∠DOE. Are AOC and BOD straight lines? Is COE a straight line? Give reasons in each case.

10 In Fig. 59, if $\angle POX = x°$, how many degrees are there in each of the other angles?

11 In Fig. 57, if $y = 2x$, find what numbers x and y stand for.

12 In Fig. 57, if $y = 3x$, find what numbers x and y stand for.

13 In Fig. 58, if $\angle AOX = a°$, find in terms of a the numbers of degrees in angles AOC and COB.

14 In Fig. 61, find x.

Fig. 61

15. PROPERTIES OF PARALLELS

Parallel lines   You will already be familiar with the idea of parallel lines as lines in one plane which are everywhere the same distance apart; two of the lines ruled on a page of your exercise book, for example, or the two rails on a straight stretch of railway; the top and bottom edges of the door, the two edges of your ruler, the opposite sides of a rectangle. All these are examples of **parallel lines,** i.e. lines in one plane which do not meet however far they may be produced (or continued) in either direction; and they have the property that they are everywhere the same distance apart.

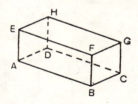

Fig. 62 shows a cuboid. Notice how it is lettered. The base is ABCD, the top is EFGH, and these faces are joined by edges AE, BF, CG, DH.   The lines EF and AB are parallel.   So also are EF and HG.   The lines EH and AB do not meet, but they are not parallel, because they are not in the same plane.   There are any number of lines through E which do not meet AB, but only one of these is parallel to AB, namely EF; and we call EF *the parallel* through E to AB.

Fig. 62

EXERCISE 53 (Oral)

State whether the following pairs of lines in Fig. 62 are parallel:

1 BF, DH	**2** AB, EG	**3** EF, DC
4 EF, BC	**5** HG, AC	**6** HG, AB
7 EG, AC	**8** AE, CG	**9** AD, FG
10 CG, DH		

Corresponding angles Suppose you are at A and another person is at B, due North of you. If you both start by facing North, and both turn through the same angle, say 30°, clockwise, you will then both be again looking in the same direction, and therefore the lines AX, BY in Fig. 63 will be parallel. The line NBA is called a **transversal,** cutting the parallel lines at A and B. The angles NBY, BAX are called **corresponding angles.** Notice that the lines AX, BY are parallel only if these corresponding angles are equal.

FIG. 63

To draw a parallel to a given line through a given point

Let the given line be PQ and the given point O.

Place your set square in the position ABC (see Fig. 64), with the longest edge AB along the given line PQ. Put your ruler with the edge along AC. Holding the ruler firmly on the paper, slide the set square along the ruler until it reaches the position XYZ, with the longest edge XY passing through the given point O where the parallel

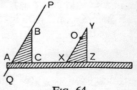

FIG. 64

is required. Rule along XY, and this will be parallel to PQ because you have made the corresponding angles BAC, YXZ equal.

Compare Figs. 65 and 66. There are four pairs of corresponding angles in both figures, namely:

    PQD, QRB; PQC, QRA; DQR, BRS; CQR, ARS.

But whereas in Fig. 65 the lines AB, CD are not parallel and no two corresponding angles are equal, in Fig. 66 the lines AB, CD are parallel and every pair of corresponding angles are equal.

Arrows are generally used to indicate that lines are parallel, as in Fig. 66. The fact is written as 'AB ∥ CD'.

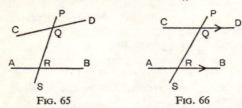

    Fig. 65   Fig. 66

Alternate angles   Referring again to Fig. 66, the angles PQD, CQR are vertically opposite angles, and are therefore equal. Hence if $\angle$PQD is equal to $\angle$QRB, we know that $\angle$CQR must equal $\angle$QRB. These two angles, CQR and QRB, are called **alternate angles.** Another pair of such angles are DQR and QRA. They are called alternate because they are between the lines AB, CD and are on opposite sides of the transversal PQRS. We have thus found another test for the lines AB, CD to be parallel, namely, that either pair of alternate angles should be equal.

You may find it helpful at first to think of alternate angles as the angles at the corners of a letter Z.

Interior angles on the same side of the transversal   Look again at Fig. 66.

Since PQR is a straight line, $\angle$PQD + $\angle$DQR = 180°.

But $\angle$PQD = $\angle$QRB, as these are corresponding angles for the parallel lines AB, CD.

    ∴ $\angle$QRB + $\angle$DQR = 180°.

This pair of angles, QRB and DQR, both have the line QR

as one of their arms, and they are called **interior angles on the same side of the transversal.** They are sometimes called *conjoined* or *allied* angles. Another pair of such angles are QRA and CQR. The third test we have found for the lines AB, CD to be parallel is that the sum of the interior angles should be 180°.

Summary We will now collect up all the facts we have found about the angles formed when a transversal cuts two parallel lines.

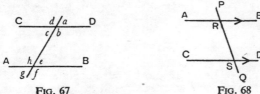

Fig. 67   Fig. 68

If AB is parallel to CD (see Fig. 67), then

$$\left.\begin{array}{l} a=e \\ b=f \\ c=g \\ d=h \end{array}\right\} \text{Four sets of corresponding angles equal.}$$

$$\left.\begin{array}{l} b=h \\ c=e \end{array}\right\} \text{Two sets of alternate angles equal.}$$

$$\left.\begin{array}{l} b+e=180° \\ c+h=180° \end{array}\right\} \text{Two sets of interior angles supplementary.}$$

To test whether AB and CD are parallel, we have to find either

    one pair of corresponding angles equal,

or one pair of alternate angles equal,

or one pair of interior angles whose sum is 180°.

EXERCISE 54

1 In Fig. 68, name four pairs of corresponding angles, two pairs of alternate angles, and two pairs of interior angles.

2 In Fig. 68, if ∠ARP = 64°, fill in on your own freehand figure the number of degrees in each of the other angles.

3 In Fig. 68, if ∠PRB = 102°, state the numbers of degrees in ∠CSR, ∠CSQ, ∠ARS.

4 In Fig. 68, if ∠PRB is represented by $x°$, how would you represent all the other angles in the figure?

5 In Fig. 69, if $a = 27$ and $b = 56$, calculate ∠BCX, ∠XCD, ∠BCY.

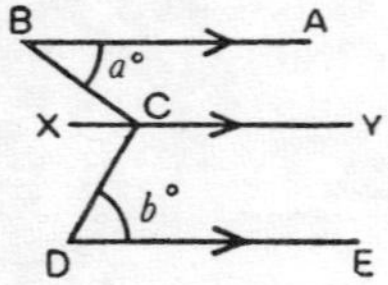

FIG. 69

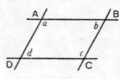

FIG. 70

6 In Fig. 69, if $a = 31$ and $b = 59$, calculate ∠BCD.

7 In Fig. 69, if ∠BCY = 151° and ∠DCY = 103°, calculate a and b.

8 In Fig. 69, if ∠BCD = 80° and $b = 48$, calculate a.

9 In Fig. 69, express ∠BCD in terms of a and b.

10 In Fig. 70, if $a = 124°$, $b = 54°$, $c = 126°$ and $d = 56°$, which lines are parallel, and why?

11 In Fig. 70, if AB ∥ DC and AD ∥ BC, and $b = 61°$, calculate a, c and d.

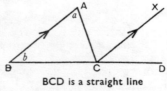

BCD is a straight line

FIG. 71

12 In Fig. 71, if $a = 50°$ and $b = 35°$, calculate ∠XCD, ∠ACX and ∠ACB.

13 In Fig. 71, if ∠A = 55° and ∠B = 28°, calculate ∠ACD.

14 In Fig. 71, if ∠ACD = 95° and $a = 62°$, calculate b.

15 In Fig. 71, express ∠ACD in terms of a and b.

16 In Fig. 72, if $p = 25°$ and $q = 63°$, calculate a, b and c.

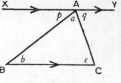

17 In Fig. 72, if $b = 34°$ and $c = 70°$, calculate p, q and a.

18 In Fig. 72, what is the value of $p + a + q$? Hence find the value of $a + b + c$.

FIG. 72

16. ANGLE-SUM OF TRIANGLE AND POLYGON

If ABC is any triangle, and we extend the side BC to D in the direction from B to C, this is called 'producing BC to any point D'.

Now draw CX, through C, parallel to BA. This means that you are to go from C to any point X in the same direction as from B to A (*not* from A to B). We now have Fig. 73.

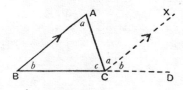

FIG. 73

$\angle$XCA $= \angle$BAC, for these are alternate angles for the parallels BA, CX. Call them both a.

$\angle$XCD $= \angle$ABC, for these are corresponding angles for the parallels BA, CX. Call them both b.

If we represent $\angle$ACB by c, we have three angles a, b, c at the point C on a straight line BCD, and their sum is 180°.

But these same angles a, b, c are the angles of the triangle ABC.

This shows that the three angles of a triangle add up to 180°, and the reasoning is just the same whatever the shape of the triangle or the sizes of the angles. We have found that

The angle-sum of a triangle is 180° or two right angles.

EXERCISE 55

1 In Fig. 74, if ∠BAC = 70° and ∠ABC = 30°, find ∠ACB.

2 In Fig. 74, if ∠BAC = 54° and ∠ACB = 42°, find ∠ABX.

3 If two angles of a triangle are 90°, 60°, find the third angle.

4 If two angles of a triangle are 108°, 46°, find the third angle.

5 In Fig. 74, if ∠ABX = 106° and ∠A = 67°, find ∠ACY.

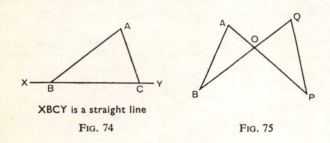

XBCY is a straight line

FIG. 74   FIG. 75

6 If two angles of a triangle are equal and the third angle is 36°, find all the angles of the triangle.

7 If one angle of a triangle is 130°, and the other two angles are equal to one another, find the number of degrees in each of them.

8 Can a triangle have its angles 42°, 68°, 60°? Give a reason for your answer.

9 If the three angles of a triangle are all equal, how big are they?

10 In Fig. 74, if ∠ABX = 135°, ∠ACY = 120°, calculate ∠A.

11 In Fig. 75, AOP and BOQ are straight lines. If ∠B = 27°, ∠P = 30° and ∠A = 49°, calculate ∠Q.

12 In Fig. 75, if ∠B = 25°, ∠P = 25° and ∠POQ = 93°, calculate ∠A and ∠Q.

13 In Fig. 76, BI bisects ∠ABC and CI bisects ∠ACB. If ∠ABC = 42° and ∠ACB = 114°, calculate ∠BIC.

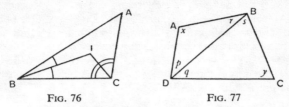

FIG. 76   FIG. 77

14 In Fig. 77, ABCD is a quadrilateral with a diagonal BD drawn. If $x = 140°$, $p = 26°$, $q = 45°$, $y = 60°$, calculate r and s.

Add together all the angles x, y, p, q, r, s. What do you notice about the sum of angles ABC, BCD, CDA, DAB?

15 In Fig. 77, what is the value of $x + p + r$? What is the value of $y + q + s$? What answer does this give for ∠DAB + ∠ABC + ∠BCD + ∠CDA?

Definitions The terms *acute angle* and *obtuse angle* were defined on page 79. Since the angle-sum of a triangle has now been shown to be 180°, it follows that, if one angle of a triangle is a right angle or an obtuse angle, then both the other two angles must be acute.

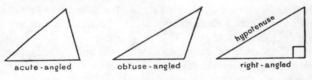

acute-angled   obtuse-angled   right-angled

FIG. 78

An **acute-angled triangle** has all three angles acute.

An **obtuse-angled triangle** has one of its angles obtuse.

A **right-angled triangle** has one of its angles a right angle. The side opposite the right angle is called the **hypotenuse.**

If ABC is a triangle, the angle A is said to be **included** between the sides AB and AC.

We have already defined a polygon as a plane figure bounded by straight lines. If none of its angles are reflex (i.e. greater than 180°) the polygon is said to be **convex**. A corner of a polygon is called a **vertex** (plural **vertices**). A **regular polygon** has all its sides equal and all its angles equal. In that case a circle can be drawn through all its vertices.

In naming a polygon, go round the vertices in order. In Fig. 79 the quadrilateral on the left is ABCD; that on the right is not ABCD, but ABDC.

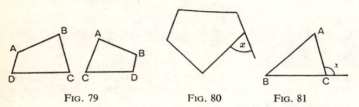

Fig. 79   Fig. 80   Fig. 81

If one side of a polygon is produced, the angle so formed is called an **exterior angle** of the polygon. The ordinary angles are often called **interior angles.** In Fig. 80, the angle marked *x* is an exterior angle of the polygon. In Fig. 81, the angle marked *x* is an **exterior angle of the triangle.**

Property of the exterior angle of a triangle. You will remember that, when we proved that the sum of the angles of a triangle is 180°, we formed an exterior angle by producing one side (see p. 89, Fig. 73). The exterior angle was then shown to consist of two parts, which were the same as the other two angles of the triangle.

In Fig. 81, therefore, $x = \angle A + \angle B$; or in words:

If one side of a triangle is produced, the exterior angle is equal to the sum of the two interior opposite angles.

Exterior angles of a polygon Suppose that the sides of a polygon ABCDEF are produced in order, i.e. as shown in Fig. 82. The exterior angles in that figure are called *a*, *b*, *c*, *d*, *e*, *f*.

If you think of the polygon as a field, and you walk along AB, the angle through which you turn when you get to B is *b*.   If you then walk along BC until you get to C, you turn through the angle *c*, and then you will be walking along CD.   Continuing in this way until you reach A,

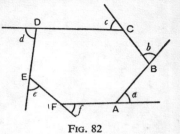

Fig. 82

you finally turn through the angle *a*.   You will then be walking along AB again, and so must have turned through a complete revolution, or 360°.

Hence $\qquad a+b+c+d+e+f=360°.$

We have here used a polygon with six sides, but the argument would be just the same however many sides there were.   Hence:

If the sides of a polygon are produced in order, the sum of the exterior angles is 360°.

To find the angle of a regular polygon   If the polygon is regular, all its interior angles are equal.

∴ all its exterior angles are equal, since at every vertex the interior angle + the exterior angle = 180°.

But the sum of all the exterior angles = 360°.

We therefore find the exterior angle by dividing 360° by the number of sides; and the interior angle can then be found by subtracting the exterior angle from 180°.

For example, the exterior angle of a regular pentagon (5 sides)
$$=\frac{360°}{5}=72°.$$

∴ the interior angle = 180° − 72° = 108°.

Example 1   *Find the interior angle of a regular polygon with 9 sides.*

The sum of all the 9 exterior angles = 360°.

∴ each exterior angle $=\dfrac{360°}{9}=40°.$

∴ each interior angle = 180° − 40° = 140°.

EXERCISE 56

Find the marked angles in Figs. 83–85.

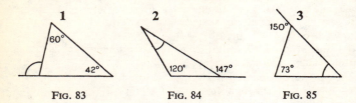

1	**2**	**3**
60° / 42°	120° / 147°	150° / 73°
FIG. 83	FIG. 84	FIG. 85

4 Find (i) the exterior angle, (ii) the interior angle of a regular octagon (8 sides).

5 Repeat No. 4 for a regular decagon (10 sides).

6 Find the interior angle of a regular hexagon (6 sides).

7 Find the interior angle of a regular polygon with 20 sides.

8 If each exterior angle of a regular polygon is 30°, how many sides has the polygon?

9 If a regular polygon has n sides, how could you represent each exterior angle?

10 Draw accurately a regular pentagon with each side 5 cm. (First find the number of degrees in the interior angle; start with AB 5 cm, make the necessary angle at B, cut off BC equal to 5 cm, and so on.)

11 Draw a regular octagon with each side 4 cm.

12 Complete the table below showing the exterior and interior angles of regular polygons with 3, 4, 5, 6, 8, 10 sides:

No. of sides	Name of polygon	Exterior angle	Interior angle
3	Triangle		
4	Square		
5	Pentagon		
6	Hexagon		
8	Octagon		
10	Decagon		

13 Use Fig. 86 to prove the following fact:

The sum of the angles of a quadrilateral is four right angles.

FIG. 86

FIG. 87

14 Use Fig. 87 to find the sum of the angles of any pentagon (whether regular or not).

15 By joining one vertex of a hexagon to three other vertices, find the sum of the angles of a hexagon.

16 In Fig. 88 ABCDE is a pentagon, and any point O is marked inside it. O is then joined to each vertex, thus forming five triangles.

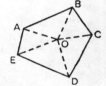

FIG. 88

(i) What, in right angles, is the sum of the angles of these five triangles?

(ii) What is the sum of the five angles at O?

Deduce the sum of the angles of the pentagon, and compare your answer with the one you obtained in No. 14.

17 Use the method of No. 16 to find the sum of the angles of a hexagon, and compare your answer with the one you obtained in No. 15.

18 Use the method of No. 16 to find an expression, in right angles, for the sum of the angles of a polygon with *n* sides. Test your answer by putting *n* equal to 3, 4, 5, 6 in turn, and seeing if you obtain the results you have found already.

17. CONSTRUCTION OF TRIANGLES

Construction of triangles There are three sides and three angles in a triangle, but it is not necessary to be told all these six measurements in order to be able to draw a triangle of a particular size. Try to decide for yourself how many measurements you think you would need in order to draw a triangle.

We shall take a few different selections of the six measurements (usually called the **data**), and see whether they are sufficient to give a definite triangle. We shall in this way discover what data are necessary to fix the shape and size of a triangle.

To construct a triangle, given two sides and the angle included between those sides.

Example 1 *Construct* △ABC *in which* AB = 5·4 *cm*, AC = 3·2 *cm and* ∠A = 40°.

First draw any straight line, and cut off from it a part AB equal to 5·4 cm.

Make an angle of 40° at A with the protractor.

With centre A and radius 3·2 cm, use your compasses to make an arc to cut at C the arm of the angle.

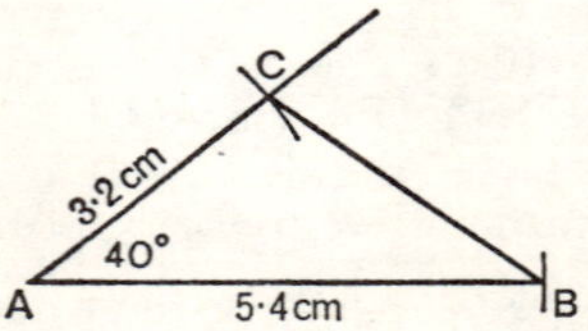

Join BC.

Then ABC is the required triangle.

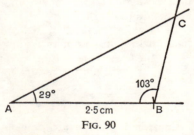

FIG. 89

To construct a triangle, given a side and two angles.

Example 2 *Construct* △ABC *in which* AB = 2·5 *cm*, ∠A = 29° *and* ∠B = 103°.

Draw a straight line and cut off from it a part AB equal to 2·5 cm.

Make at A an angle of 29° and at B an angle of 103°.

Let the arms of these angles intersect at C.

Then ABC is the required triangle.

FIG. 90

In order to construct △ABC given AB, ∠A and ∠C, we should first add together ∠A and ∠C, and subtract their sum from 180°, thus obtaining the size of ∠B. The rest of the work would then be as in the example above.

To construct a triangle, given the three sides.

Example 3 *Construct* △ABC *in which* AB = 2·2 *cm*, BC = 1·8 *cm*, CA = 2·9 *cm*.

Draw any straight line, and cut off from it a part AC equal to 2·9 cm.

With centre A and radius 2·2 cm, draw an arc.

With centre C and radius 1·8 cm, draw an arc to cut the first arc at B.

Join BA, BC.

Then ABC is the required triangle.

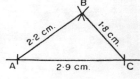

FIG. 91

It is best to draw the longest side first. Notice that the triangle is possible only if the sum of two of the sides is greater than the third side; for if this were not so, the two arcs would not cut.

To construct a triangle, given two sides and an angle opposite to one of them.

Example 4 *Construct* △ABC *in which* AB = 6 *cm*, ∠A = 35° *and* BC = 4·5 *cm*.

From any straight line, cut off a part AB equal to 6 cm.

Make angle BAX equal to 35°.

With centre B and radius 4·5 cm, draw an arc to cut AX at C_1 and C_2.

There are two possible positions, C_1 and C_2, of the vertex C.

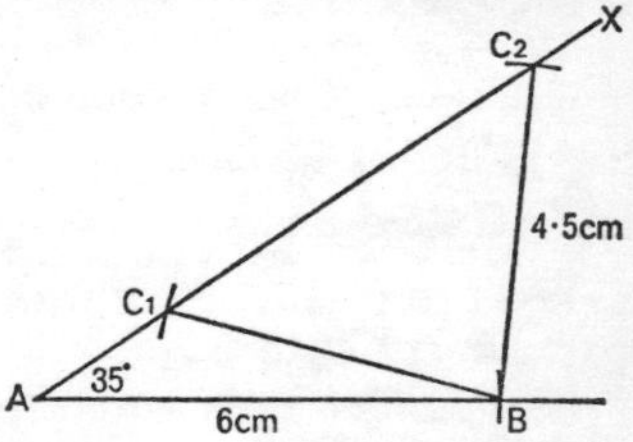

FIG. 92

There are thus two triangles, ABC_1 and ABC_2, in both of which AB = 6 cm, ∠A = 35° and BC = 4·5 cm.

Example 5 *Construct* △ABC *in which* AB = 6 *cm*, ∠A = 35° *and* BC = 7·5 *cm*.

Proceed as in Example 4. The arc with centre B and radius 7·5 cm cuts AX (or AX produced backwards) at two points C_1, C_2, as in Fig. 93. But C_2 is not a possible position of the vertex C, as it makes ∠BAC₂ equal to 145° instead of 35°.

Example 6 *Construct △ABC in which AB=6 cm, ∠A=35° and BC=2 cm.*

Proceed as in Example 4. The arc with centre B and radius 2 cm does not cut AX at all.

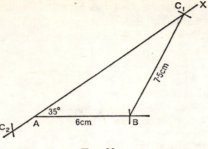

FIG. 93

There are therefore no possible positions of the vertex C, and no triangles can be drawn with the required measurements.

The ambiguous case Examples 4, 5 and 6 show that, when we are given two sides and an angle opposite to one of them, these facts do not always fix the shape and size of the triangle uniquely. On account of the doubt or ambiguity involved, this case of the construction of triangles is known as the **ambiguous case**.

Construction of right-angled triangle

Example 7 *Construct △ABC in which AB=6 cm, ∠A=90° and BC=7·5 cm.*

From any straight line, cut off a part AB equal to 6 cm.

Make angle BAX equal to 90°.

With centre B and radius 7·5 cm, draw an arc to cut AX (or AX produced backwards) at C₁ and C₂.

There are two possible positions, C₁ and C₂, of the vertex C; but the figure will be symmetrical about the line AB, and the two △s ABC₁, ABC₂ will obviously be equal in every respect. See Fig. 94.

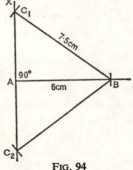

FIG. 94

Quadrilaterals Although, as we have seen, we can draw a triangle if we know the lengths of the three sides, in the case of a quadrilateral it is not sufficient to know the lengths of the four sides. If we imagine four strips of cardboard of different lengths, AB, BC, CD, DA, made into a quadrilateral ABCD by joining the ends, it is obvious that the figure can change its shape, and the quadrilateral is not fixed. Some additional piece of information, such as the length of AC or the size of angle ABC, is necessary to fix the quadrilateral.

When drawing a quadrilateral, you should begin with a lettered sketch of the required figure, without troubling to make the lines and angles the proper size. Mark the given measurements on your sketch, and try to find some triangle in the figure which you can draw accurately. When drawing a triangle, too, it is often helpful to start with a freehand sketch and mark the dimensions on it.

EXERCISE 57

In this exercise the capital letters A, B, C denote the sizes of the angles of the triangle, and the small letters a, b, c denote the lengths of the sides opposite the corresponding capital letters. See Fig. 95.

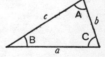

In Nos. 1–14, construct (when possible) △ABC from the given measurements. If there are two possible triangles, draw both; if there is no solution, say so.

FIG. 95

1 $a = 5$ cm, $c = 4$ cm, B $= 48°$. Measure b.

2 $a = 2 \cdot 8$ cm, $b = 5 \cdot 2$ cm, C $= 120°$. Measure c.

3 $a = 6 \cdot 3$ cm, $c = 8 \cdot 1$ cm, B $= 35°$. Measure b.

4 $c = 4.6$ cm, A = 34°, B = 41°.   Measure a.

5 $a = 4.2$ cm, A = 48°, B = 30°.   Measure c.

6 $b = 5.1$ cm, B = 114°, C = 36°.   Measure c.

7 $a = 3$ cm, $b = 4.5$ cm, $c = 3.5$ cm.   Measure B.

8 $a = 5.3$ cm, $b = 6.8$ cm, $c = 3$ cm.   Measure A.

9 $b = 4$ cm, $c = 6$ cm, B = 40°.   Measure a.

10 $a = 2$ cm, $c = 5$ cm, A = 40°.   Measure b.

11 $a = 7.8$ cm, $c = 5$ cm, A = 140°.   Measure b.

12 $a = 8$ cm, B = 30°, $b = 4$ cm.   Measure c.

13 $a = 3$ cm, B = 30°, $b = 4$ cm.   Measure c.

14 $c = 7$ cm, A = 25°, $a = 3$ cm.   Measure b.

In Nos. 15–19, draw the quadrilateral ABCD to the given measurements:

15 AB = 4.8 cm, AD = 4.8 cm, BD = 7.3 cm, BC = 5.5 cm, CD = 3.9 cm.   Measure AC.

16 AB = 5.4 cm, AD = 3.9 cm, ∠BAD = 76°, CD = 4.2 cm, BC = 4.1 cm.   Measure AC.

17 BC = 3.4 cm, ∠CBA = 90°, ∠BCD = 135°, BA = 3.7 cm, CD = 5 cm.   Measure AD.

18 CD = 4.5 cm, ∠BCD = 105°, BC = 3.5 cm, ∠ADC = 100°, ∠ABC = 84°.   Measure AB.

19 AB = 5.2 cm, AC = 5.9 cm, AD = 3.8 cm, BD = 7.1 cm, CD = 2.8 cm.   Measure BC.

18. FORMULAE

Use of brackets Just as we put several objects in a parcel and tie it up with string, so we use brackets in mathematics to show that the contents are to be taken together.

Thus, $(x+3)$ means the number obtained by adding 3 to x,
$6(5+2)$ means $6 \times (5+2)$, or 6×7,
$a(x+3)$ means $a \times (x+3)$.

Similarly $(x-y) \div 4$ means that y is to be subtracted from x, and the result divided by 4. This could also be written $\frac{1}{4}(x-y)$, or $\frac{x-y}{4}$. In this last form no brackets are needed round the top line, as the line separating the top from the bottom of the fraction serves the same purpose as brackets would do.

It is easy to see numerically that $6(2+3)$ is the same as $(6 \times 2)+(6 \times 3)$, and more generally that

$$p(x+y)=px+py,$$
$$p(x-y)=px-py.$$

These facts are illustrated geometrically in the figures below.

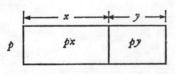

FIG. 96

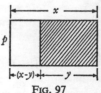

FIG. 97

In Fig. 96, the rectangle $(x+y)$ cm long and p cm wide has an area of $p(x+y)$ cm². But it can be divided into two rectangles with areas px cm² and py cm².

In Fig. 97, the rectangle x cm long and p cm wide, which has an area px cm², has a shaded area py cm² removed. This leaves a rectangle $(x-y)$ cm long and p cm wide, and therefore an area $p(x-y)$ cm². Thus, $px-py=p(x-y)$.

Example 1 *Simplify* $2(4a-3)+3(a-1)$.

$$2(4a-3)+3(a-1) = 8a-6+3a-3$$
$$= 8a+3a-6-3 = 11a-9.$$

EXERCISE 58 (Oral)

Find the values of the following:

1 $3(5+7)$ **2** $(3\times5)+7$ **3** $(12\div6)\times2$ **4** $12\div(6\times2)$

5 $3+5(8-2)$ **6** $3+(5\times8)-2$ **7** $(3+5)\times(8-2)$

8 $3(8-5)+2$ **9** $(3\times8)-(5+2)$ **10** $16-(2+3)-(4-1)$

11 8 pencils are each x cm long, and 1 cm is cut off each. Give an expression for the new total length of all the pencils.

12 A jam-jar weighs w kg empty, and holds 2 kg of jam when full. Give an expression for the weight of 5 full jars of jam.

13 If 200 g of coffee are packed in a tin which weighs x grammes empty, what is the weight of 3 tins of coffee?

Remove brackets from the following:

14 $2(3x-y)$ **15** $7(2a-3b)$ **16** $3x(x-1)$

17 $4(x^2-x+1)$ **18** $a(2x-t)$ **19** $5a(2a-4b)$

20 $6(4p+2q+1)$ **21** $2x(a+3b)$ **22** $8(3x-2)$

23 $5(a+4)+2$ **24** $a+b(c+d)$ **25** $4x(1-8x)$

Give the answers to Nos. 26–32 with brackets removed.

26 How many mm are there in $(x+2y)$ cm?

27 How many pence are there in £$(a-b)$?

28 How many km are there in $(4+x)$ metres? How many cm are there?

29 A cuboid is 5 cm long, 3 cm wide and $(x-2)$ cm high. Find the volume in cubic centimetres.

30 Water is poured into a rectangular tank 8 m long, 5 m wide and 4 m high, until the water level is x m from the top of the tank. What is the depth of the water? What is the volume of the water?

31 Express in symbols: subtract 3 from $7a$, multiply the result by 5, and then add 4.

32 Express in symbols: add $3x$ to $4y$, take away 2, and divide the result by 6.

Evaluate, with as little calculation as possible:

33 $(19 \times 647) + (19 \times 353)$ **34** $(23 \times 483) - (23 \times 283)$

35 $\left(\dfrac{22}{7} \times 73\right) - \left(\dfrac{22}{7} \times 66\right)$ **36** $\left(\dfrac{1}{25} \times 537\right) + \left(\dfrac{1}{25} \times 1963\right)$

Formulae and their construction We have already met one
or two formulae. For example, A=lb is a formula for the
area of a rectangle, and V=lbh is a formula for the volume of a
cuboid.

We are now going to make up some more formulae. A
simple way will often be to think first of a numerical case.
Thus the formula for the time t hours to travel d kilometres at
v kilometres per hour can be found by putting $d=15$, $v=5$,
when t is obviously 3. This suggests that the formula is $t=\dfrac{d}{v}$.

EXERCISE 59

1 A rectangle x cm wide and $3x$ cm long has a perimeter
P cm. Find a formula expressing P in terms of x.

2 Two angles of a triangle are $x°$ and $y°$. If the third angle
is $z°$, find a formula for z in terms of x and y.

3 The angles of a triangle are $x°$, $y°$ and $2y°$. Find a
formula for x in terms of y.

4 What is the sum of the exterior angles of a polygon?
If the polygon is regular and has n sides, find a formula for the
number of degrees in each exterior angle.

5 A piece of elastic is 30 cm long when unstretched, and it
stretches 1 cm for each 20 gramme weight hung on the end.
Find a formula for the length, l cm, when a weight W grammes
is hung on the end.

6 If the sum of the lengths of the edges of the cuboid in Fig. 98 is E cm, find a formula for E in terms of x and y.

7 If the volume of the cuboid in Fig. 98 is V cm³, find a formula for V in terms of x and y.

8 If the sum of the areas of all the faces in Fig. 98 is A cm², find a formula for A in terms of x and y.

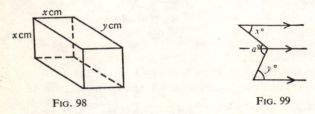

FIG. 98   FIG. 99

9 In Fig. 99, find a formula for a in terms of x and y.

10 A boy can swim at u km per hour if there is no current. If there is a stream flowing at v km per hour, find the speed of the boy if he swims (i) with the stream, (ii) against the stream. Find also a formula for the time in hours to swim x km downstream and then x km up-stream.

11 Two sides of a triangle are each x cm long, and the third side is y cm long. The whole perimeter is 10 cm. Find a formula for y in terms of x.

12 A rectangular block is a cm high, $2a$ cm wide, $\frac{3}{4}a$ cm long. The volume is V cm³. Find a formula for V in terms of a.

13 Find an expression for the area of wood needed for a match-box and its cover if the length is $3x$ cm, breadth $2x$ cm and depth x cm.

14 The housewife's rule for cooking a turkey is to allow 30 min for each kg weight and then add on 15 min extra. If the time for a turkey weighing W kg is T min, find a formula for T in terms of W.

15 In Fig. 100, ABC is a straight line.   Find (i) a formula for y in terms of x, (ii) a formula for x in terms of y.

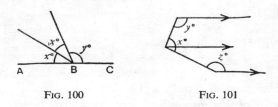

FIG. 100   FIG. 101

16 In Fig. 101, find a formula for x in terms of y and z.

17 If £$a = b$ pence, find a formula for a in terms of b.

18 A grocer mixes x kg of tea at 80p per kg with y kg at 72p per kg.   Find the cost in pence of $(x + y)$ kg of the mixture.
If the cost per kg of the mixture is C pence, find the formula for C.

19 In a certain house the charge for electricity consists of a standing charge of £1 per quarter (however much electricity is used) together with a charge of 2p per unit of electricity used.   If the householder uses x units in a quarter, construct a formula for the total charge in pence for the quarter.

Substitution in a formula   We can obtain a special result from a general formula by substituting in the formula.

For example, if we are told that the sum, S degrees, of the angles of a polygon of n sides is given by the formula

$$S = 90(2n - 4),$$

it is an easy matter to find S for any particular value of n.

Thus, if $n = 5$, we have

$$S = 90(2 \times 5 - 4)$$
$$= 90(10 - 4) = 90 \times 6 = 540.$$

∴ the angles of a five-sided polygon make 540°.

EXERCISE 60

1 When the staircase of a house is being built, the rise and tread are often connected by the formula $R = \frac{1}{2}(60 - T)$, where R cm is the rise and T cm the tread. Calculate the rise if the tread is (i) 14 cm, (ii) 28 cm.

2 When a stone is dropped from the top of a cliff, it is known that $s = 4 \cdot 9t^2$, where s metres is the distance fallen in t sec. Find how far the stone falls in 3 sec.

3 The load that may safely be supported by a steel rope of diameter d cm is L tonnes, where $L = \frac{32d^2}{25}$. Find the safe load for a steel rope of diameter $1\frac{1}{2}$ cm.

4 The sum of the interior angles of a polygon of n sides can be shown to be $90(2n - 4)$ degrees. Find the sum of the angles if the polygon has (i) 4, (ii) 6, (iii) 10 sides.

5 The area A cm² of a circle of radius r cm is given by the formula $A = \frac{22}{7}r^2$. Find the area of a circle of radius $3\frac{1}{2}$ cm.

6 A bag weighs b grammes when empty, and x marbles, each weighing m grammes, are put into it. Find a formula for the total weight in grammes of the bag and the marbles, and from your formula find the weight when $b = 250$, $x = 5$, $m = 80$.

7 The volume of a cylinder is $\frac{22}{7}r^2h$ cm³, where r cm is the radius of the end and h cm is the height. Find the volume of a cylinder of height 14 cm and radius $2\frac{1}{2}$ cm.

8 The number of years E which the insurance companies expect a man to live if he is x years old now is given by the formula $E = \frac{2}{3}(80 - x)$. Calculate how many years a man can expect to live if his present age is (i) 20, (ii) 62.

9 If a batsman scores altogether r runs in x innings, and was n times not out, his average is $\frac{r}{x - n}$ runs. Find his average if he scores 336 runs in 18 innings, being twice not out.

10 The total area of the curved surface and the two ends of a cylinder of radius r cm and height h cm is $\frac{44}{7}r(r+h)$ cm². Find in cm² the total surface area of a cylinder of radius 3 cm and height 11 cm.

11 The area of cinders required for a circular running-track is $\frac{22}{7}(R+r)(R-r)$ m², where R metres is the radius of the outer edge and r metres that of the inner edge of the track. Calculate the area of cinders required for a track in which the outer radius is 120 m and the inner radius 113 m.

12 The surface area A cm² of a ball whose radius is r cm is given by the formula $A=\frac{88}{7}r^2$. Find the surface area of a ball of radius $3\frac{1}{2}$ cm.

19. EQUATIONS (I)

Working a formula backwards On p. 105 we used the formula $S=90(2n-4)$ to find the sum of the angles of a polygon with 5 sides. The question we now have to ask ourselves is: can we work the formula the other way round; or in other words, can we find the value of n if we know that of S?

Let us suppose that $S=1800$, so that $90(2n-4)=1800$.

Since the numbers $90(2n-4)$ and 1800 are equal, they will still be equal if both are divided by 90.

$\therefore 2n-4=20$.

Now add 4 to both sides,

$$2n-4+4=20+4,$$
or $$2n=24.$$
$$\therefore n=12.$$

Example 1 *In Ex.* 60, *No.* 1, *the formula connecting the rise R cm and the tread T cm for each step of a staircase was given as* $R = \frac{1}{2}(60 - T)$. *Find T if* $R = 25$.

We know that $\frac{1}{2}(60 - T) = 25$.

Since the numbers $\frac{1}{2}(60 - T)$ and 25 are equal, they will still be equal if they are both doubled.

Now $2 \times \frac{1}{2}(60 - T) = 60 - T$, and $2 \times 25 = 50$.

$$\therefore \ 60 - T = 50.$$
$$\therefore \ T = 10.$$

Example 2 *Express by an equation the statement: I think of a number, I then double it, and take 5 away; the result is* 17.

Suppose the number I thought of is x.

Doubling it makes $2x$.

Taking 5 away leaves $2x - 5$.

$$\therefore \ 2x - 5 = 17.$$

This form of writing the statement is called an **equation,** and x is called the **unknown.** The process of finding what number x stands for is called **solving the equation.**

What we do when we solve an equation is to find what we call a **root** of the equation, i.e. a value of the unknown which makes the two sides of the equation the same. The equations we are now to consider will have only one root, but later we shall meet equations with more roots than one. We can always test whether the value obtained for a root is correct by substituting it in the original equation and seeing if the two sides are equal.

An equation is like a pair of scales with objects or weights in the left-hand pan balancing those in the right-hand pan. Obviously, if the scales balance to start with, they will still balance if we do the same thing to each. With an equation we can do any of the four following things:

1 **Add the same number to each side.**
2 **Subtract the same number from each side.**
3 **Multiply both sides by the same number.**
4 **Divide both sides by the same number.**

For example, the equation obtained above, in Ex. 2, was

$$2x - 5 = 17.$$
$$\therefore\ 2x - 5 + 5 = 17 + 5, \text{ adding 5 to both sides.}$$
$$\therefore\ 2x = 22.$$
$$\therefore\ \frac{2x}{2} = \frac{22}{2}, \text{ dividing both sides by 2.}$$
$$\therefore\ x = 11.$$

$\therefore$ the number I thought of must have been 11.

Check. Twice 11 is 22, and when 5 is taken away the result is 17, so 11 is the correct number.

Example 3 *I think of a number, divide it by 3 and add* 10. *The result is* 16. *What was the number I thought of?*

Let x be the number.

Then $\dfrac{x}{3} + 10 = 16.$

$\therefore\ \dfrac{x}{3} + 10 - 10 = 16 - 10$, subtracting 10 from both sides.

$\therefore\ \dfrac{x}{3} = 6.$

$\therefore\ \dfrac{x}{3} \times 3 = 6 \times 3$, multiplying both sides by 3.

$x = 18.$

$\therefore$ the number was 18.

Check. $18 \div 3 = 6$, and $6 + 10 = 16$, so 18 was the correct number.

If the terms with the unknown in them occur on the right-hand side and not on the left, begin by reversing the equation; thus,

$$15 = 5x.$$
$$\therefore\ 5x = 15.$$
$$\therefore\ x = 3, \text{ on dividing both sides by 5.}$$

When you are checking your answer, substitute the value obtained in the original equation, i.e. in the equation *before* you simplified it in any way.

EXERCISE 61

Write as equations the statements in Nos. 1–12, and then solve them, explaining your reasoning as in the worked examples above.

1 I think of a number, subtract 8 from it. The result is 21. Find the number.

2 I think of a number, double it, and add 5. The result is 11. Find the number.

3 I think of a number, halve it, and subtract 3. The answer is 7. Find the number.

4 I think of a number, multiply it by 3, and add 6. The answer is 30. Find the number.

5 I think of a number, multiply it by 3, add 4, and take away the number I first thought of. The result is 22. Find the number.

6 I think of a number and multiply it by 4; the result is the same as if I added 24 to the original number. Find the number.

7 I think of a number, x. How would you represent (i) the next integer above x, (ii) the next integer below x?

These three are called 'consecutive integers'. Find three consecutive integers whose sum is 96.

8 Find the even number which, when added to the even number next above it, makes 58. (If the first even number is represented by x, how can you represent the even number next above x?)

9 I think of a number, divide it by 5, and add 6. The answer is 11. Find the number.

10 I think of a number, add 5 to it, and multiply the result by 4. The answer is 48. Find the number.

11 I think of a number, multiply it by 4, and take away 24. The result is the same as the number I first thought of. Find the number.

12 I think of a number, multiply it by 3, and add 7. The result is 40. Find the number.

Solve the equations in Nos. 13–30.

13 $2x=0$ **14** $\frac{y}{5}+4=7$ **15** $3x-3=15$

16 $\frac{3t}{10}=6$ **17** $x+2\frac{1}{2}=9$ **18** $z-3\cdot6=8\cdot2$

19 $5=n-4$ **20** $29=7p+8$ **21** $2x-4=6+x$

22 $4=4+3v$ **23** $5+2y=23$ **24** $\frac{r}{3}-2=4$

25 $\frac{1}{2}x+5=13$ **26** $2=2+y$ **27** $5\frac{1}{2}=t+1\frac{1}{4}$

28 $8y+6=30$ **29** $\frac{x}{4}-2=3$ **30** $12=2+\frac{x}{5}$

Solve the following problems by forming equations:

31 In a triangle ABC the angle A is $x°$, and the angles B and C are each four times angle A. Find the three angles of the triangle.

32 The sum of the angles of a polygon of n sides is $(2n-4)$ right angles. Find the number of sides if the sum of the angles is 14 right angles.

33 A man, who is x years old now, has a son aged 5. In 7 years the father will be 4 times as old as his son will be then. How old is the father now?

34 The result of adding 42 to a certain number is the same as the result of multiplying the number by 8. Find the number.

35 The perimeter of a rectangle is 44 cm. If the breadth is x cm and the length $(x+2)$ cm, find the length and the breadth.

36 A rod 30 m long is broken into two pieces, one of length x m and the other of length $(x-4)$ m. Find x.

37 I walked for x hours at a steady speed of $5\frac{1}{2}$ km per hour and then cycled for the same number of hours at a steady speed of $15\frac{1}{2}$ km per hour. I had then travelled 49 km altogether. Find x.

38 The perimeter of a square is 22 cm. Find its side.

39 In Fig. 102, find x.

40 One side of a rectangle is 4 times another. The perimeter is 17 cm. Find the length of the shorter side.

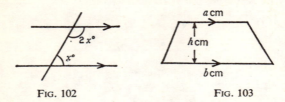

FIG. 102   FIG. 103

41 A formula for the area of the trapezium shown in Fig. 103 is $A = \frac{1}{2}h(a+b)$, where a cm and b cm are the lengths of the two parallel sides, h cm is the distance between them, and A cm^2 is the area. Calculate the value of b if $A = 39$, $h = 6$ and $a = 4$.

42 £430 is to be divided between 3 brothers, so that the middle one gets £x, the eldest twice as much, and the youngest £50 less than the middle brother. Find how much they should each get.

43 The volume, V cm^3, of gas in a cylinder is connected with the pressure, P grammes weight, by the formula $PV = 500$. Find the pressure when the volume is 25 cm^3.

44 If F° Fahrenheit is the same temperature as C° Celsius, it is known that $F = 32 + \dfrac{9C}{5}$. Find what Celsius temperature is the same as 176° Fahrenheit.

20. TRIANGLES AND QUADRILATERALS

In this section we shall discuss some special kinds of triangles and quadrilaterals, and find some of their properties.

Isosceles triangle   A triangle which has two sides equal is called an **isosceles triangle** (*iso-sceles* means '*equal legs*'). The third side is called **the base,** and the vertex opposite the base is called **the vertex.** The angle at the vertex is the **vertical angle,** and the angles at the ends of the base are the **base angles.**

Suppose ABC is an isosceles triangle, in which AB=AC. Draw the bisector of ∠BAC, and let this bisector meet the base at D, as in Fig. 104.

It will be obvious from the figure that

Fig. 104

$$\angle B = \angle C,$$
$$BD = CD,$$

and ∠s ADB, ADC are right angles.

These results will be proved later (see Example 1, p. 174).

For the present we shall assume the following facts about an isosceles triangle:

If two sides of a triangle are equal, the base angles are equal.

The bisector of the vertical angle of an isosceles triangle bisects the base at right angles.

Conversely,

If two angles of a triangle are equal, then the sides opposite those sides are equal.

Equilateral triangle A triangle which has all three sides equal is called an **equilateral triangle.**

From what you have learned about an isosceles triangle, it is obvious that all the three angles of an equilateral triangle are equal, and therefore each angle is $\frac{1}{3}$ of 180°, or 60°.

Each angle of an equilateral triangle is 60°.

EXERCISE 62

1 The vertical angle of an isosceles triangle is 62°. Find the base angles.

2 One base angle of an isosceles triangle is 73°. Find the vertical angle.

3 In Fig. 105, if ∠B = 54°, calculate ∠CAD.

4 In Fig. 105, if ∠CAD = 128°, calculate ∠C.

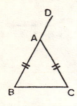

Fɪɢ. 105

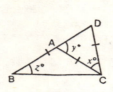

Fɪɢ. 106

5. In Fig. 106, if $z = 34$, calculate y and x.

6 In Fig. 106, if $x = 20$, calculate y and z.

7 In Fig. 106, if $y = 62$, calculate x and z.

8 In Fig. 107, AB = AC and CB = CD. If ∠A = 42°, calculate ∠ABC and ∠ACD.

9 In Fig. 107, AB = AC and CB = CD. If ∠A = 36°, show that DA = DC.

10 In the triangle ABC, AB = AC and ∠C = 72°. The bisector of the angle C meets AB at X. Prove that CX = AX and that CB = CX.

Fɪɢ. 107

11 In Fig. 108, if ∠AOX = 20° and ∠BOX = 50°, calculate ∠APO, ∠BPO and ∠APB.

12 In Fig. 108, if ∠AOX = 18° and ∠BOX = 70°, calculate ∠APB and ∠AOB.

13 In Fig. 108, if ∠APO = 15° and ∠BPO = 35°, calculate ∠AOB, ∠APB.

14 In Fig. 108, if ∠APO = x° and ∠BPO = y°, find an expression, containing x and y, for the number of degrees in ∠AOB.

Fɪɢ. 108

15 The base angles of an isosceles triangle are each x°. Find the vertical angle in terms of x.

16 The vertical angle of an isosceles triangle is $x°$. Find the base angles in terms of x.

17 A base angle of an isosceles triangle is $x°$, and the vertical angle is three times a base angle. Find the value of x.

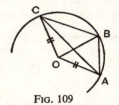
FIG. 109

FIG. 110

18 In Fig. 109, OA = OB = OC. If ∠AOB = 60° and ∠BOC = 80°, calculate ∠s OAB, OCB and OAC. Hence calculate the three angles of △ABC.

19 In Fig. 110, O is the centre of the circle and AB is a diameter. If ∠APO = $x°$ and ∠BPO = $y°$, write down the numbers of degrees in the angles of △APB. Hence prove that $x + y = 90$.

Parallelogram In Fig. 111, we have two pairs of parallel lines crossing one another. The quadrilateral so formed is called a **parallelogram** (a word which can be shortened in writing to ||gram or parm.).

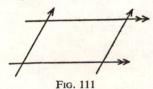
FIG. 111

A **parallelogram** is a quadrilateral with both pairs of opposite sides parallel. The lines joining opposite vertices are called **diagonals**.

Certain properties of the parallelogram will be proved later in this book (see Example 2, p. 176). At present we shall assume that:

The opposite sides of a parallelogram are equal.

The opposite angles of a parallelogram are equal.

In Fig. 112, both diagonals of the parallelogram are drawn, intersecting at O. We shall assume that OA = OC and OB = OD; in general,

The diagonals of a parallelogram bisect each other.

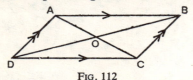

FIG. 112

The rectangle and the square are special forms of the parallelogram in which the angles are right angles. They therefore possess all the properties of the parallelogram (as well as some other properties). For example, the diagonals of a rectangle bisect each other.

Rhombus A parallelogram with all its sides equal is called a **rhombus** (Fig. 113).

The rhombus has all the properties of the parallelogram, but other important ones as well.

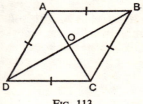

FIG. 113

It will be proved later that the diagonals of the rhombus cut at right angles, i.e. in Fig. 113, the four angles at O are all right angles. Also BD bisects the angles ABC, ADC, while AC bisects the angles BAD, BCD.

A rhombus has the following properties, in addition to those of a parallelogram:

(a) all the sides are equal,

(b) the diagonals cut at right angles,

(c) the diagonals bisect the angles.

A **trapezium** is a quadrilateral which has only one pair of opposite sides parallel, as in Fig. 114.

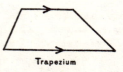

Trapezium

FIG. 114

EXERCISE 63

1 Construct a parallelogram ABCD in which AB = 6 cm, BC = 4·8 cm and ∠B = 40°.   Measure BD.

2 Draw a parallelogram ABCD in which AB = 3·4 cm, BC = 4·4 cm and the diagonal AC = 7 cm.   Measure BD.

3 Draw a rhombus PQRS in which PQ = 4 cm and ∠P = 49°. Measure PR.

4 Construct a parallelogram ABCD in which the diagonal AC = 7·6 cm, the diagonal BD = 5·2 cm, and the angle between the diagonals = 70°.   (Begin with an angle of 70°, and step off the halves of the diagonals along the arms of the angle.) Measure AB and BC.

5 Construct a parallelogram ABCD in which AC = 6·4 cm, BD = 2·8 cm and BC = 3·6 cm.   (Begin by drawing △BOC, O being the point where the diagonals intersect.)   Measure AB.

6 Draw a rectangle with sides 4·8 cm and 3·2 cm.   Measure the diagonal.

7 Draw a rhombus with diagonals 5·2 cm and 3·8 cm. (Start with a right angle, and measure off the halves of the diagonals along the arms.)   Measure a side of the rhombus.

8 Draw a parallelogram ABCD in which AB = 7·1 cm, AD = 3·3 cm and ∠B = 64°.   Measure AC.

9 Draw a rectangle in which the diagonals are 6 cm long and the angle between them is 30°.   Measure the sides of the rectangle.

10 Draw a trapezium ABCD in which AB = 3·8 cm, BC = 3·2 cm, AC = 5·8 cm, CD is parallel to BA and CD = 6·7 cm.   Measure AD.

11 Draw a rectangle PQRS, given that PQ = 3·6 cm and the diagonal PR = 4·2 cm.   Measure PS.

12 Draw a parallelogram ABCD, given that AB = 3·8 cm, AD = 4 cm, AC = 4·6 cm.   Measure BD.

13 Draw a rhombus ABCD in which the diagonal AC = 5 cm and ∠BAD = 40°. (Begin with AC, and find ∠s BAC, BCA.)   Measure AB.

21. RULER AND COMPASSES CONSTRUCTIONS

Angles and lines can be bisected, and parallels and perpendiculars drawn, without using a set square or a protractor or the graduations on the edge of the ruler. The methods are called 'ruler and compasses' methods, as they require only the ruler (as a straight edge) and a pair of compasses. These 'ruler and compasses' constructions will now be explained. They are very neat and quick, and they will give you some useful practice in handling geometrical instruments. As a general rule, however, set squares should be used for drawing parallels and perpendiculars.

Neatness and accuracy are very important in these constructions. Use a hard pencil with a good point. When you draw an arc of a circle with a suitable radius, take as big a radius as you conveniently can. Avoid letting the lines and arcs cut at very small angles. Do not make the arcs too small, and do not rub out any construction lines.

CONSTRUCTION 1

To copy a given angle.

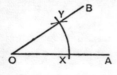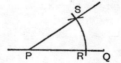

FIG. 115

Suppose AOB is a given angle, and we wish to make at P, on the line PQ, an angle equal to ∠AOB.

With centre O and any radius, draw an arc to cut OA at X and OB at Y.

With centre P and the same radius, draw an arc to cut PQ at R.

With centre   and radius equal to XY, draw an arc to cut this arc at S. Join PS.

Then ∠SPR is the required angle.

CONSTRUCTION 2

To bisect a given angle.

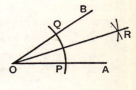

Let AOB be the given angle.
With centre O and any radius, draw an arc to cut OA at P and OB at Q.
With centres P and Q in turn and any suitable radius (the same in each case), draw arcs to cut at R.
Join OR.
Then OR is the required bisector.

Fig. 116

CONSTRUCTION 3

Through a given point to draw a straight line parallel to a given straight line.

Suppose we want to draw a line through P parallel to AB.

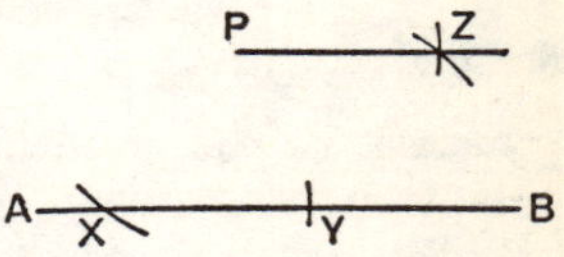

With centre P and any suitable radius, draw an arc to cut AB at X.

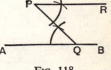

With centre X and the same radius, draw an arc to cut AB at Y.

With centre Y and the same radius, draw an arc.

Fig. 117

With centre P and the same radius, draw an arc to cut the last arc at Z.   Join PZ.

Then PZ is parallel to AB.

An alternative method is shown in Fig. 118, where P is joined to any point Q in AB, and an angle QPR is copied equal to the alternate angle AQP.

Fig. 118

CONSTRUCTION 4

To find the mid-point of a given straight line.

To draw the perpendicular bisector of a given straight line.

Let AB be the given straight line.
With centre A and any suitable radius (bigger than half AB), draw two arcs, one on each side of AB.

With centre B and the same radius, draw two arcs to cut the first two arcs at X and Y.

Join XY, and let it cut AB at O.
Then O is the mid-point of AB, and XY is the perpendicular bisector of AB.

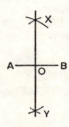

FIG. 119

CONSTRUCTION 5

To erect a perpendicular to a given straight line at a point in the line.

Let AB be the given line and P a point in it.

With centre P and any radius, draw arcs on each side of P to cut AB at X and Y.

With centre X and any radius, draw an arc.

FIG. 120

With centre Y and the same radius, draw an arc to cut the last arc at Q.

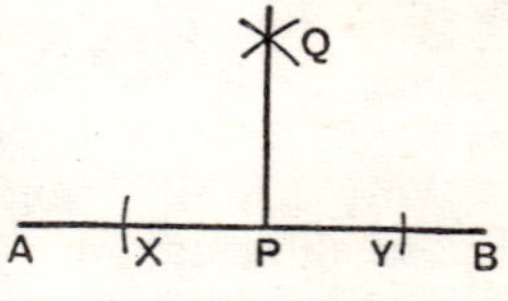

Join PQ.

Then PQ is the perpendicular to AB at P.

Note. This is the same as bisecting ∠APB, an angle of 180°, by the method of Construction 2.

CONSTRUCTION 6

To draw a perpendicular to a given straight line from a point outside the line.

Let AB be the given straight line and P the given point.

With centre P and any suitable radius, draw an arc to cut AB at Q and R.

With centres Q and R in turn and any suitable radius (the same for both), draw arcs to cut at X.

Join PX.

Then PX is perpendicular to AB.

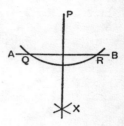

Fig. 121

CONSTRUCTION 7

To construct some special angles.

An angle of 60°.

Suppose we want to make an angle of 60° at A, with AB as one arm of the angle.

With centre A and any radius, draw an arc to cut AB at P.

With centre P and the same radius, draw an arc to cut the first arc at Q.

Join AQ.

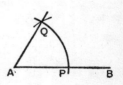

Fig. 122

Then ∠QAB = 60°.

For △AQP has been made equilateral, and so each angle is 60°.

An angle of 30° is obtained by constructing an angle of 60° as above, and then bisecting it.

An angle of 45° is obtained by constructing an angle of 90° as in Construction 5, and then bisecting it.

CONSTRUCTION 8

To draw a straight line parallel to a given straight line and at a given distance from it.

Let AB be the given straight line and *a* cm the given distance.

Mark any point P in AB, and erect the perpendicular PQ to the line AB.

Along PQ mark off PR equal to *a* cm.

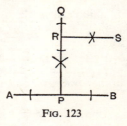

FIG. 123

Erect at R the perpendicular RS to PQ (or draw the parallel through R to AB).

Then RS is the required parallel.

An alternative method is shown in Fig. 124, in which any two points P and Q are taken in AB, and arcs are drawn with radius *a* cm and these points as centres in turn. A ruler is then placed so that its edge touches

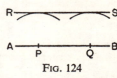

FIG. 124

both arcs. The first method is generally considered the better.

EXERCISE 64

The set square should not be used in this Exercise, and the protractor should be used only when necessary.

1 Construct an equilateral triangle with each side 4 cm. Draw and measure the perpendicular from a vertex to the opposite side (called an **altitude** of the triangle).

2 Construct a square with each side 4·6 cm. Measure the diagonal.

3 Construct a trapezium ABCD in which AB = 5·8 cm, ∠A = 60°, AD = 2·6 cm, DC is parallel to AB and DC = 2·6 cm. Measure BC.

4 Construct an isosceles triangle ABC in which AB=AC, BC=3·7 cm, and the length of the perpendicular from A to BC is 4·6 cm.   Measure AB.   (Begin with the base BC, and draw its perpendicular bisector.)

5 Construct a regular octagon (8 sides) with each side 3 cm.   (What is the exterior angle of a regular octagon?)

6 Construct a parallelogram ABCD in which AB=3·6 cm, the diagonal AC=4·8 cm and ∠BAC=30°.   Measure BD.

7 Draw a triangle ABC in which BC=5·2 cm, ∠B=36° and ∠A=32°.   Find the mid-points of the three sides of the triangle, and join each mid-point to the opposite vertex.

(These lines are called **medians.**   What do you notice about the three medians of a triangle?)

8 Draw a triangle ABC in which AB=7 cm, ∠A=62°, ∠B=47°.   Construct the perpendicular bisectors of AC and BC, and let them cut at O.   With centre O and radius equal to OA, draw a circle.   What do you notice about this circle?

9 Draw a triangle ABC in which AB=4 cm, BC=6 cm, AC=8 cm.   Construct the bisector of ∠A, and let it cut BC at X.   Measure BX and XC.

10 Draw a circle with any radius you like, and draw any chord AB.   Construct the perpendicular bisector of AB. Through what point do you think that the perpendicular bisector of any chord always passes?

11 Draw a triangle ABC in which AB=12 cm, AC=9 cm, BC=6·4 cm.   Construct the bisectors of any two angles of the triangle, and let these bisectors cut at I.   Draw a perpendicular from I to AB, and let P be the foot of this perpendicular. With centre I and radius IP, draw a circle.   What do you notice about this circle?   Measure IP.

12 Draw a triangle with sides 5·6 cm, 5·2 cm and 3·8 cm. Construct perpendiculars from each vertex to the opposite side. What do you notice about these three lines?

22. CONSTRUCTION OF MODELS OF SOLIDS

You have already made models of the cube and cuboid by first making accurate drawings of their nets, and should now be able to go on to the construction of more difficult models. There are usually several different ways of drawing the net of a solid, and you should try to invent them for yourself. The importance of accuracy in drawing the net will become very obvious when you come to the stage of making up the model and gumming it together. The exercises which follow give you full details how to draw the nets and where it is most convenient to have the flaps along the edges. Keep your models when you have made them.

You will need the following equipment, besides your geometrical instruments: a zinc plate, a cutting knife, a safety ruler, some sheets of thin cardboard in assorted colours, a bottle of gum or quick-drying cement.

Construct the net accurately on the cardboard, and cut along the continuous lines. Place the ruler along the dotted lines, and score lightly with the cutting knife, but do not press hard enough to cut through. The net will then fold up neatly to make the model. Consider carefully before you gum the flaps in what order you are going to fix them, as it is sometimes difficult to press down the last flap.

EXERCISE 65

Make cardboard models from the nets described in Nos. 1–10.

1 Draw the net of a cube whose edges are all 3 cm long (see Fig. 9, p. 41), and make a model of the cube.

2 Draw the net of a cuboid, 4 cm by 3 cm by 1·5 cm (see Fig. 10, p. 41), and make a model of the cuboid.

3

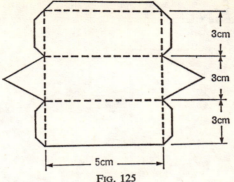

Fig. 125

Triangular prism   The ends are equilateral triangles of side 3 cm.

4

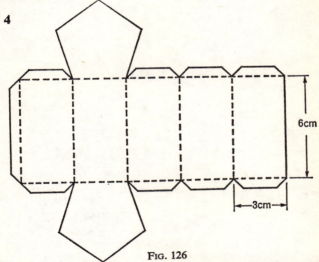

Fig. 126

Pentagonal prism   The ends are regular pentagons, side 3 cm.
(Remember that the angles of a regular pentagon are 108°.)

5 Draw the net of **a hexagonal prism** of length 6 cm and with its ends regular hexagons of side 3 cm. (Use Fig. 126 as a hint, and remember that the angle of a regular hexagon is 120°.) Make a model of the prism.

6

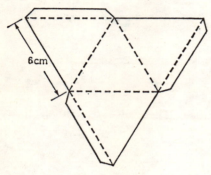

Fig. 127

Regular tetrahedron, with each edge 6 cm long.

7

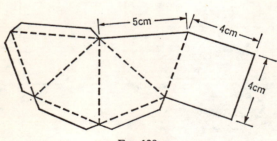

Fig. 128

Pyramid on a square base: each edge of the base is 4 cm and each of the slant edges is 5 cm.

8

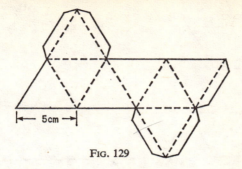

FIG. 129

Regular octahedron; the 8 faces are equilateral triangles of side 5 cm.

9

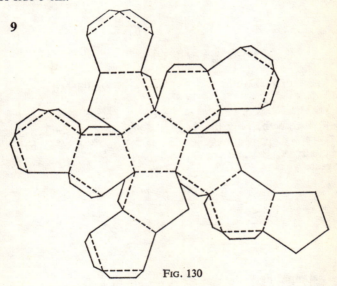

FIG. 130

Regular dodecahedron; the 12 faces are all regular pentagons of side 4 cm.

10

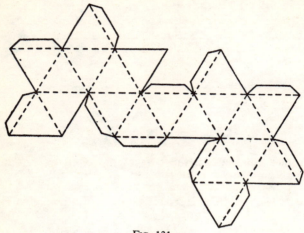

Fɪɢ. 131

Regular icosahedron; the 20 faces are all equilateral triangles, of side 4 cm.

11 The solids of which you have made models in Nos. 1, 6, 8, 9, 10 are the only five **regular solids,** that is, solids whose faces are congruent regular figures. Copy the table below, where F, V, E stand for the numbers of faces, vertices, and edges:

	F	V	E
Tetrahedron	4	4	6
Cube	6		
Octahedron	8		
Dodecahedron	12		
Icosahedron	20		

By comparing V + F and E, try to deduce a formula connecting these numbers. It is called **Euler's Formula,** after the eighteenth-century Swiss mathematician.

23. DECIMALS (II)

Approximations   When we say that the length of a line is
4·6 cm, we mean that the length is nearer to 4·6 cm than to
4·5 cm or 4·7 cm.   The length of a line cannot be measured
exactly;   any answer we give is an approximate one, but it
must be reliable as far as it goes.   More careful measurement
might show that the length was 4·62 cm.   This means that the
length is nearer to 4·62 cm than to 4·61 cm or 4·63 cm.   It lies
between 4·615 cm and 4·625 cm.

The result 4·6 cm is said to be **correct to one decimal place.**
The result 4·62 cm is said to be **correct to two decimal places.**
The word 'correct' is often left out, and we say the length is
4·62 cm to two decimal places.

To obtain an answer to any particular number of decimal
places, we must always take the working to one more place of
decimals than is actually required.   If this extra figure is
less than 5, ignore it;   if the extra figure is more than 5, make
the figure before it one more.   If the extra figure is 5, the
modern practice is to round off the number so as to make the
last figure even.   The reason for this is that, if the extra figure
5 is repeatedly used to make the figure before it one more,
there is a cumulative tendency in a long calculation in the same
direction, causing the final answer to be too big or too small,
depending on the calculation.

Examples   The numbers

$$4·618,\quad 4·614,\quad 4·615,\quad 4·625,$$

corrected to two decimal places, become

$$4·62,\quad 4·61,\quad 4·62,\quad 4·62.$$

Fractions expressed as decimals   Some fractions are exact
decimals.   For example,

$$\tfrac{1}{2}=0·5,\quad \tfrac{1}{4}=0·25,\quad \tfrac{1}{8}=0·125,\quad \tfrac{3}{4}=0·75.$$

But if we try to express $\tfrac{1}{3}$ as a decimal, we get

$$3 \,\lfloor\, \overline{1·00000} \ldots$$
$$\overline{0·33333} \ldots$$

However many 0's we add, the division by 3 never comes to an end, and we get a succession of 3's in the answer. This is called a **recurring decimal,** and is written 0·3̇ (read 'nought point 3 recurring').

Similarly, $\frac{1}{6} = 0·16̇$, $\frac{2}{3} = 0·6̇$.

To two places of decimals, $\frac{2}{3}$ is 0·67; to three places of decimals, it is 0·667.

As far as possible, you should avoid expressing fractions as decimals if they recur.

Significant figures are the figures in a number, apart from any 0's which occur either before the first or after the last figure to show where the decimal point comes.

Consider the following numbers, all with the significant figures 576:

$$5760, \quad 576, \quad 5·76, \quad 0·00576.$$

Correct to two significant figures, these would be

$$5800, \quad 580, \quad 5·8, \quad 0·0058.$$

Correct to one significant figure, they would be

$$6000, \quad 600, \quad 6, \quad 0·006.$$

Similarly, correct to two significant figures 5740 becomes 5700, 5750 becomes 5800, 5650 becomes 5600.

Limits of error　　If a line is stated to be 3·6 cm long, correct to two significant figures, we know that the exact length is between 3·55 cm and 3·65 cm, and the maximum error is ±0·05 cm (meaning +0·05 or −0·05). If the length is stated to be 3·67 cm, correct to three significant figures, we know that the exact length is between 3·665 cm and 3·675 cm, and the maximum error is ±0·005 cm.

Example 1 *Two lengths are given, to three significant figures, as 2·63 cm and 4·75 cm. What are the greatest and least possible values of their true sum?*

The greatest possible value of the sum is (2·635 + 4·755) cm = 7·39 cm.

The least possible value is (2·625 + 4·745) cm = 7·37 cm.

Example 2 *What are the greatest and least possible answers if 9·48 is subtracted from 12·96, both numbers being correct to two decimal places?*

$$\text{Greatest difference} = 12·965 - 9·475 = 3·49.$$
$$\text{Least difference} = 12·955 - 9·485 = 3·47.$$

Example 3 *The sides of a rectangle are measured to be 4·6 cm and 2·2 cm, both to the nearest millimetre. Find the area, giving the answer with an appropriate degree of accuracy.*

The length lies between 4·55 cm and 4·65 cm.
The width lies between 2·15 cm and 2·25 cm.
The least possible area is $4·55 \times 2·15$ cm² = 9·7825 cm.²
The greatest possible area is $4·65 \times 2·25$ cm² = 10·4625 cm².

∴ the area lies between 9·7825 and 10·4625 cm.²
The area may therefore be said to be 10 cm², or, more accurately, $10·12 \pm 0·34$ cm².

Notice that we are not entitled to say that the area is $4·6 \times 2·2$, or 10·12, cm².

EXERCISE 66

Express the following numbers correct to (i) one, (ii) two, (iii) three decimal places:

| **1** 14·5625 | **2** 8·638 | **3** 27·486 | **4** 0·0708 |
| **5** 2·755 | **6** 5·2399 | **7** 0·0375 | **8** 2·4845 |

Express as decimals, correct to three places:

9 $\frac{1}{7}$ **10** $\frac{5}{11}$ **11** $\frac{7}{6}$ **12** $\frac{5}{9}$ **13** $\frac{3}{7}$

State the number of significant figures in the following:

| **14** 4·267 | **15** 0·004267 | **16** 403700 | **17** 0·415 |
| **18** 4005 | **19** 12·8 | **20** 285·6 | **21** 0·990 |

22 Give each of the numbers in Nos. 14–21 correct to one significant figure less than are there given.

In Nos. 23–25, state the limits between which the exact values lie, if the approximate values are:

23 3·72   **24** 0·609   **25** 7000 to three significant figures.

26 If the sides of a triangle are measured as 5·9 cm, 4·8 cm and 3·6 cm, each to the nearest millimetre, find the limits between which the perimeter must lie.

27 The length and breadth of a rectangle are measured, each to two significant figures, and found to be 8·7 cm and 3·2 cm. What are the greatest and least possible values of the area in cm²?

28 The weight of 1 cm³ of mercury is stated to be 13·6 g, to three significant figures. Between what limits does the weight of 30 cm³ lie?

29 If the length of the circumference of a circle is divided by the length of the diameter, the result is known to be 3·14159265, correct to nine significant figures. Find by how much this number differs from $3\frac{1}{7}$, giving the answer to three significant figures.

24. SCALE DRAWING

Points of the compass You will no doubt know the points of the compass already, at any rate North, South, East, West, and North-east, North-west, South-east, South-west. The direction NNE. bisects the angle between N. and NE. The direction ENE. bisects the angle between E. and NE. Similarly for NNW., WNW., and so on.

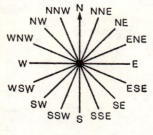

FIG. 132

Bearings The **bearing** of a point A from an observer is the direction in which the observer has to face if he looks towards A. There are two methods of giving a bearing:

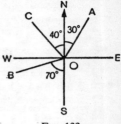

(i) In Fig. 133 the bearing of A from O is said to be N. 30° E. or 30° East of North. It means that you are to face north and then turn through an angle of 30° towards the east.

FIG. 133

Similarly, OB is S. 70° W. or 70° W. of S.
         OC is N. 40° W. or 40° W. of N.

Directions should always be measured eastwards or westwards from the north or from the south; never from east or west. For example, OA should not be called E. 60° N.

(ii) The bearing is given in terms of the angle, described clockwise, which the direction makes with the north line. For example, in Fig. 133, OA is on a bearing of 30° (usually written to save errors as 030°), OB is on a bearing of 250° (i.e. 180° + 70°), OC is on a bearing of 320° (i.e. 360° − 40°).

The north line from which the angle is measured may be the True North (i.e. a line pointing towards the geographical North Pole) or the Magnetic North (i.e. the direction indicated by a magnetic compass) or the Grid North (i.e. the direction of the grid lines on a map).

EXERCISE 67

State the bearings (by both methods) of the following directions:

1 Face N., turn through 40° clockwise.
2   „   S.,   „   40°   „
3   „   E.,   „   32° counter-clockwise.

4 Face W., turn through 16° clockwise.
5 „ SW.,   „   20°   „
6 „ N.,   „   118° counter-clockwise.
7 „ S.,   „   27° clockwise.
8 „ W.,   „   56° counter-clockwise.
9 „ E.,   „   135° clockwise.
10 „ NE.,   „   84°   „
11 Find the angle between N. 40° E. and S. 13° E.
12   „   „   N. 18° W. and N. 41° E.
13   „   „   N. 10° W. and S. 70° E.
14 Find the angles between (i) N. and NNE., (ii) ENE. and ESE., (iii) SE. and WNW.

Maps When a surveyor makes a map of a district the figure formed by the lines on his map is the same *shape* as that formed by the roads which the lines represent, but of course it is not the same *size*. In the same way an architect's plan of a house is the same shape as the house, but very much smaller. We say that it is drawn 'to scale'. The picture thrown on the screen at a cinema is the same shape as the picture on the film, but much larger.

Suppose a map is drawn to the scale of 1 cm to the km, and suppose that A and B are two places which are actually 1 km apart. They will be represented on the map by two points a centimetre apart. The fraction

$$\frac{\text{AB on the map}}{\text{AB on the ground}}$$

will be $\frac{1 \text{ cm}}{1 \text{ km}}$, or $\frac{1}{100\,000}$. This fraction will be the same whatever the distance AB may be; it expresses the fact that every length on the map is $\frac{1}{100\,000}$ of the corresponding length on the ground. This fraction is called the **Representative Fraction** of the map, shortened to R.F.

When an architect makes a plan of a building to the scale of 1 cm to 1 m, the R.F. is $\dfrac{1 \text{ cm}}{1 \text{ m}}$, or $\dfrac{1}{100}$. Every line on the plan is $\dfrac{1}{100}$ of the true measurement on the building.

The standard Ordnance Survey scale is $\dfrac{1}{25\,000}$, i.e. 1 cm to 250 m, or 4 cm to 1 km. A provisional series of maps in colour has been produced for almost the whole of Great Britain. The sheets cover an area 10×10 km, with grid lines at intervals of 1 km.

Scale drawing When you are making an accurate scale diagram, start by making a rough sketch and mark on it the lengths you are given. Choose a suitable scale, and state what it is. Do not write anything on the accurate drawing except letters marking points, as in your sketch. Do not rub out any construction lines. Use your set squares whenever it is quicker to do so. If you are asked for some particular length, the answer you give should be the actual length required, and not the scaled length.

EXERCISE 68

1 Find the R.F. of maps drawn to the scales of (i) 1 cm to 500 m, (ii) 1 cm to 10 km, (iii) 4 cm to 1 km.

2 If on a map the distance between two towns is 6·8 cm, and the scale of the map is 1 cm to 2 km, what is the actual distance between the towns? What would the distance be on a map whose scale was (i) 1 cm to 5 km, (ii) 1 cm to 15 km?

3 The scale of a map is 1 cm to 5 km. What is the actual distance between two towns which are 1·8 cm apart on the map? What is the distance on the map between two places which are actually 12 km apart?

4 A plan is drawn on a scale of 1 cm to 2 m. What distance is represented by a length 6·3 cm on the plan? What is the length of a line on the plan which represents an actual distance of 7·8 m?

5 A steamer travels due north for 10 km, then NE. for 12 km, then SE. for 8 km. Draw a plan, taking a scale of 1 cm to 5 km, and find how far the finish is from the starting point, measured in a direct line. What is the bearing of the finish from the starting point?

6 A straight road runs due east and west. A village P is 6 km north of the road, and another village Q is 18½ km SE. of P. Draw a map on a suitable scale, and find the distance of Q from the road.

7 A village P is 3 km east of another village Q, and a village R is 6 km south of Q. Draw a map to the scale of 1 cm to 1 km, and find the distance in a straight line between P and R. Find also the bearing of P from R. What is the bearing of R from P?

8 A is 6½ km due north of B, and B is 9½ km west of C. Find, by drawing, the distance and bearing of A from C. (Scale: 1 cm to 1 km.)

9 A, B and C are three church-towers; B is 5 km due N. of A, and C is 8 km NW. of A. Draw a map on the scale of 1 cm to 1 km, and find the distance and bearing of C from B.

10 Q is 27 km from P on a bearing of 060°; R is 19 km from P on a bearing of 340°. Draw a map to the scale of 1 cm to 5 km, and find the distance and bearing of R from Q.

11 In Fig. 134, A and B are two points 600 m apart on a straight road, and T is a tree. Draw a plan, and find from it the distance of the tree from B, and also the shortest distance of the tree from the road.

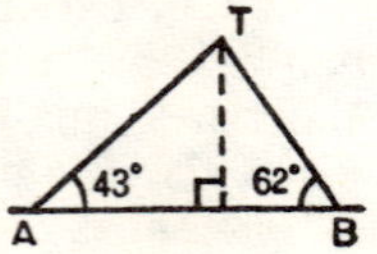

12 Draw a plan of a rectangular field 410 m long and 240 m wide, and find the length of a diagonal of the field.

Fig. 134

13 A gun is 7·2 km from a straight road, and the range of the gun is 11·4 km. Find from a diagram what length of the road is under fire.

14 The legs of a pair of compasses are 10 cm long, and they are opened to an angle of 50°. Find from a scale drawing the distance between the compass points.

15 B is 31 km from A on a bearing of 150°; C is on a bearing of 190° from A and on a bearing of 250° from B. Find the distance of C from B. (Scale: 1 cm to 5 km.)

16 A is 50 km west of B, and C is due north of B. If C is 72 km from A, find the distance of C from B.

17 Bedford is 37 km from Cambridge on a bearing of 260°, and Peterborough is 51 km from Cambridge on a bearing of 335°. Find the distance and bearing of Peterborough from Bedford.

18 Croydon is 32 km in a direction N. 65° E. from Guildford; Tunbridge Wells is 38 km in a direction S. 48° E. from Croydon; Brighton is 43 km in a direction S. 39° W. from Tunbridge Wells. Find from a scale-diagram the distance and bearing of Brighton from Guildford.

19 A and B are two points 400 m apart on a straight road. C is a tree 250 m from A and 300 m from B. Find from a scale drawing the distance of the tree from the road.

20 A river with straight banks runs due north. A man stands on one bank and observes that the bearing of a tree on the other bank is 325°; after walking 130 m due north along the bank, he finds the bearing of the same tree to be 220°. Find from a drawing the breadth of the river.

Angles of elevation and depression Suppose in Fig. 135 that AB represents a tower, and that you are standing at P, on a level with the foot of the tower. If you point a telescope horizontally towards the tower, and tilt the telescope until it points to A, the top of the tower, then the angle APB through which you have

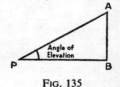

Fig. 135

elevated the telescope is called the **angle of elevation** of A as seen from P.

Now suppose you are standing on the top of a cliff at Q (see Fig. 136), and A is a boat on the sea. If you point a telescope horizontally in the direction of the boat, and tilt the telescope until it points to A, the angle AQB through which you have depressed the telescope is called the **angle of depression** of A as seen from Q.

Fɪɢ. 136

Notice that the angle of depression of A as seen from Q is the same as the angle of elevation of Q as seen from A; for these are alternate angles between the parallels BQ and AR in Fig. 136.

EXERCISE 69

1 A vertical flagstaff 19 m high stands in a level field. Find from a drawing the angles of elevation of the top and the middle point of the flagstaff from a point in the field 7 m from the foot of the flagstaff.

2 The angle of elevation of the top of a church spire from a point on the same level as the base of the spire and 300 m away is found to be 15°. Find the height of the spire.

3 From the top of a cliff 70 m high the angle of depression of a boat at sea is 29°. Find the distance of the boat from the foot of the cliff.

4 A house and a flagstaff stand on level ground. From a window in the house which is 5 m from the ground, the angle of elevation of the top of the flagstaff is 30°, and the angle of depression of the bottom of the flagstaff is 12°. Find the height of the flagstaff.

5 A man measures the angle of elevation of the top of a tower, which stands on level ground, to be 27°. He walks 35 m towards the tower, and finds the angle of elevation of the top of the tower to be 34°. Find the height of the tower.

6 The angles of depression of two buoys, which are in line with a ship, are observed from the top of the mast 27 m high to be 54° and 36°. Find the distance between the buoys.

7 A church stands on level ground. The angle of elevation of the top of the spire is measured from a point 2 m above the ground and 367 m from the spire, and found to be 17°. Find the height of the spire.

8 A flagstaff stands at the top of a hill which slopes at 14° to the horizontal. The angle of elevation of the top of the flagstaff is observed from a point A on the hill-side to be 32°; from a second point B on the hill-side, in a straight line between A and the flagstaff, the angle of elevation of the top of the flagstaff is found to be 39°. If AB=17 m, find the height of the flagstaff.

9 From the top of a tower the angle of depression of a point A on level ground below is 35°. On descending to a window in the tower at a depth 10 m below the top, the angle of depression of A is found to be 28°. Find the distance of A from the base of the tower.

Finding hidden treasure If you were told that some treasure lay buried in a field, and it was 10 m from a certain tree, how would you set about finding it? You would say that all points which were 10 m from the tree lay on a circle whose centre was the tree and whose radius was 10 m, and you would mark out this circle by means of a rope tied to the tree. See Fig. 137.

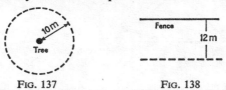

FIG. 137   FIG. 138

Now suppose that you were told that the treasure was 12 m from a straight fence which formed part of the boundary of the field. You would say that all points 12 m from the fence lay on a straight line parallel to the fence and 12 m away from it, and you would proceed to mark out this line. See Fig. 138.

In either case quoted above, you would have a lot of digging to do before you found the treasure. But if you were given *both* pieces of information, namely, that the treasure was 10 m from the tree and also 12 m from the fence, there would be only two places where it could possibly be. The two places are shown with crosses in Fig. 139.

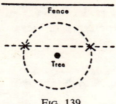

Fig. 139

If you find it difficult to guess the path on which all the possible positions of the treasure must lie, begin by marking any one point which answers to the description, then another possible point, then another, until the points begin to form some pattern.

As another hidden treasure example, suppose that the lines in Fig. 140 represent two roads, and we are told that the

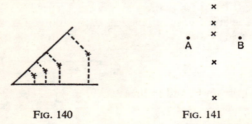

Fig. 140   Fig. 141

treasure is buried at a spot which is the same distance from one road as it is from the other. Remember that the distance of a point from a line means the length of the perpendicular drawn from the point to the line. A few possible positions of the treasure are marked in Fig. 140. Where do they all lie?

As another example, suppose A and B in Fig. 141 are two

trees, and we are told that the treasure is the same distance from one tree as from the other. Where do all the possible positions lie?

EXERCISE 70

In Fig. 142, PQ and PR represent two straight fences, at right angles, forming part of the boundary of a field. A is an ash tree, B a beech tree. In Nos. 1–8, state what pattern would be formed by all the possible positions of the treasure, if it was known to be:

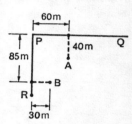

Fig. 142

1 20 m from A.

2 The same distance from PQ as from PR.

3 The same distance from A as from P.

4 10 m from the line joining A and B.

5 At equal distances from A and B.   **6** 15 m from B.

7 30 m from the fence PQ.

8 The same distance from PQ as from the line joining B and A.

Make a scale-drawing of Fig. 142 (on graph paper, if you have any). Mark with a cross the position (or positions) of the hidden treasure, if the information as to its whereabouts is given in Nos. 9–16.

9 80 m from P, and in line with A and B.

10 At equal distances from both fences PQ and PR, and in line with A and B.

11 As near as possible to the fence PR, and the same distance from A as it is from B.

12 40 m from A and 25 m from B.

13 40 m from B and 70 m from the fence PQ.

14 30 m from PR, and the same distance from PQ as from the line joining BA.

15 60 m from B, and the same distance from PQ as it is from PR.

16 55 m from B, and the same distance from P as it is from A.

25. PLAN AND ELEVATION (I)

Fig. 143 shows two vertical planes A and B, at right angles to one another, and a horizontal plane. The three planes resemble two walls and the floor of a room. A rectangular

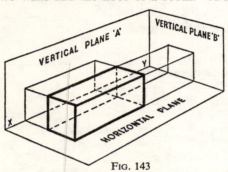

Fig. 143

block is placed on the horizontal plane with its edges parallel to the two vertical planes. If perpendiculars are now drawn from the corners of the block to one of the three planes, the figure thus obtained is called the **projection** on that plane. The projection on the horizontal plane is called the **plan;** in this instance the plan is simply the outline of the rectangular base of the block. The projection on the vertical plane A is called the **front elevation;** in this instance the front elevation is the rectangular side face of the block. The projection on the vertical plane B is called the **end** (or **side**) **elevation;** in our example it is the rectangular end of the block.

Now imagine the two vertical planes to be hinged along the vertical line in which they meet, and swing the vertical plane B about this hinge until it is in the same plane as the vertical plane A. Also imagine the vertical plane A to be hinged along the line (usually called the XY line) in which it meets the horizontal plane.   Swing the two vertical planes A and B (now the same plane) about this hinge until they are in the same plane as the horizontal plane.   The horizontal plane, the vertical plane A, and the vertical plane B are now all in one plane, and can be represented in the plane of your paper as in Fig. 144.

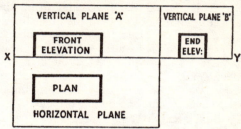

FIG. 144

Notice how the views are arranged in Fig. 144.   You must always use the lay-out shown here.   Of course you will not need to draw Fig. 143 first, but you will have it in your mind.

Example   *Draw the plan, front elevation and end elevation of a rectangular block 4 cm long, 2 cm wide and 1½ cm high, placed on the horizontal plane with its length parallel to the XY line.*

The drawing is shown in Fig. 145.   Start by drawing the

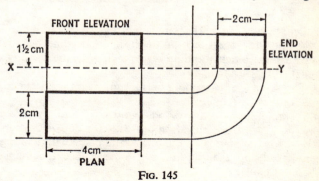

FIG. 145

XY line dotted across the paper, and a line perpendicular to it to represent the 'trace' of the vertical plane B (i.e. the line in which the vertical plane B meets the horizontal plane).

Study Fig. 145 carefully, and imitate it in your drawings in the exercise which follows. Notice the following points about the lines used in such drawings:

Outline. This should be sharp and firm, and should stand out a little more boldly than the other lines.

Construction lines. These should be faint, but clear, and should not be rubbed out in the finished drawing.

Dotted lines. These will be used in later examples to show hidden detail.

Dimension lines. These should be thin lines with an arrow at each end, and should be broken to receive the figures giving the length.

When you have had some practice in drawing plans and elevations, you will be able to look at a plan and elevation drawing and build up from it in your mind a picture of a solid object, such as is shown in Fig. 143.

EXERCISE 71

Draw the plan, front elevation and end elevation of the rectangular blocks in Nos. 1–3. In each case the block is placed on the horizontal plane, with four of its edges parallel to the XY line.

1 Length 4 cm, breadth 2 cm, height $1\frac{1}{2}$ cm; breadth parallel to XY, and the largest face on the horizontal plane.

2 The same block standing on its end, with the 2 cm edges parallel to the XY line.

3 The same block standing on its end, with the $1\frac{1}{2}$ cm edges parallel to the XY line.

4 A match-box measures 5·8 cm by 3·7 cm by 1·8 cm. Draw the plan, front elevation and side (or end) elevation of the box, when it stands on the horizontal plane with its longest edges parallel to the XY line and a large face touching the horizontal plane.

REVISION OF ELEMENTARY WORK
DRILL EXERCISES D 1-7
D 1.   Addition
Add the following columns and rows:

	1	**2**	**3**	**4**	**5**
6	572	316	189	447	203
7	37	495	647	308	75
8	793	86	778	539	173
9	869	662	58	704	729
10	683	520	886	745	128

	11	**12**	**13**	**14**	**15**
16	4189	8711	3990	2714	4119
17	1532	1837	6217	5427	1299
18	2953	9243	317	791	5518
19	1594	4819	5678	1432	6891
20	8306	8064	5704	4471	9876

D 2.   Subtraction
Subtract the second number from the first:

1 8964	**2** 6591	**3** 7594	**4** 1643	**5** 8663
5177	5186	4108	718	4329

6 98 631	**7** 77 140	**8** 63 179	**9** 55 284	**10** 99 442
6 793	53 988	36 795	44 220	86 887

11 973 776	**12** 679 543	**13** 598 321	**14** 985 276
640 724	635 972	482 116	846 237

D 3.   Multiplication
Multiply:

1 92, 76, 68, 27 by 4   **2** 45, 72, 48, 53 by 5
3 65, 47, 59, 21 by 6   **4** 53, 37, 74, 95 by 7
5 29, 55, 73, 81 by 8   **6** 48, 37, 62, 59 by 9
7 61, 47, 33, 634 by 11   **8** 97, 52, 117, 185 by 12
9 5897 by 3, 7, 9, 10   **10** 6399 by 5, 6, 8, 12

11 657×32 **12** 553×17 **13** 842×58

14 481×29 **15** 6296×31 **16** 5492×43

17 752×231 **18** 551×652 **19** 803×789

20 634×999 **21** 3628×417 **22** 7707×634

D 4. Division

Find the quotient and remainder:

1 $9252 \div 6$ **2** $2891 \div 7$ **3** $3416 \div 8$

4 $77\,162 \div 3$ **5** $69\,346 \div 12$ **6** $98\,989 \div 11$

7 $98\,712 \div 4$ **8** $7864 \div 8$ **9** $52\,866 \div 11$

10 $68\,390 \div 7$ **11** $7485 \div 9$ **12** $65\,785 \div 5$

13 $65\,471 \div 17$ **14** $45\,519 \div 13$ **15** $23\,187 \div 19$

16 $7140 \div 85$ **17** $67\,894 \div 23$ **18** $451\,897 \div 33$

19 $760\,354 \div 123$ **20** $427\,684 \div 75$ **21** $8\,050\,804 \div 632$

22 $1\,122\,334 \div 808$ **23** $18\,467 \div 504$ **24** $48\,600 \div 39$

25 $71\,765 \div 605$ **26** $23\,956 \div 59$ **27** $335\,582 \div 41$

D 5. Short Methods of Multiplication and Division

Use short methods to evaluate the following (e.g. to multiply by 25, multiply by 100 and then divide by 4):

1 2768×25

2 $31\,688 \times 125$ (multiply by 1000 and then divide by 8)

3 $46\,146 \times 25$ **4** 8775×250

5 $9\,025 \div 25$ $\left(\dfrac{9025}{25} = \dfrac{9025 \times 4}{25 \times 4} = \dfrac{\cdots\cdots}{100} \right)$

6 $52\,750 \div 125$ $\left(\dfrac{52\,750}{125} = \dfrac{52\,750 \times 8}{125 \times 8},\ \text{etc.} \right)$

7 248×99 $\{248 \times 99 = 248(100 - 1) = 24\,800 - 248\}$

8 7694×98 **9** 467×998

10 $28\,764 \times 25$ **11** $46\,993 \times 250$

12 $931\,500 \div 250$ **13** 7777×9999

14 4789×125 **15** $30\,850 \div 25$

D 6. Addition and Subtraction of Money

Add together:

£		£		£
1 14·38	**2**	11·64	**3**	23·86
4·87		18·53		6·90
21·71		7·59		18·54
6·36		6·40		5·27
7·28		8·71		19·06
4·57		1·93		6·82

£		£		£
4 12·76	**5**	18·10	**6**	13·54½
22·70½		6·81½		34·80
15·92		14·83		25·33½
2·71		8·28½		9·51
16·56½		26·49		15·32½
10·05		4·56½		7·87½

Subtract:

£		£		£
7 114·37	**8**	224·36	**9**	437·24
89·59		118·61		219·57½

£		£		£
10 326·32½	**11**	354·11	**12**	550·80
189·51½		238·62		241·59½

D 7. Multiplication and Division of Money

Multiply:

1 £4·37 × 5 **2** £3·92 × 6
3 £23·84 × 28 (Multiply by 4 and then by 7)
4 £36·51 × 18 **5** £53·64 × 30
6 £31·72 × 35 **7** £45·31 × 21

Divide the following, giving the answer correct to the nearest penny:

8 £314·57 ÷ 4 **9** £144·70 ÷ 12
10 £654·21 ÷ 9 **11** £5898·38 ÷ 10
12 £439·04 ÷ 8 **13** £107·35 ÷ 31
14 £43·69 ÷ 13 **15** £924·04 ÷ 17

REVISION PAPERS

PAPERS 1–10 (Elementary Work)

Paper 1

1 Divide 11 309 by 43, and multiply 427 by 999.

2 A man plants 4 potatoes to every square metre. He finds that the potatoes average 20 to the kilogramme. How many kilogrammes are required to plant 2400 m²?

3 How long would it take a train to travel 630 km at an average speed of 54 km per hour?

4 A man earns £15·42 in a week. Find how much he earns in a year of 52 weeks at the same rate.

5 Find the total weight of 4 boxes each 9·2 kg, 3 boxes each 18·1 kg, and 5 boxes each 11·3 kg.

Paper 2

1 What number must be multiplied by 38 to make 14 136?

2 Find the cost of 19 articles at £1·71 each.

3 A rectangular field is 265 m long and 102 m wide. Find the length of fencing needed to go all round it.

4 A man's pace is 80 cm. How many paces does he take in walking a kilometre?

5 The product of three numbers is 6422. Two of the numbers are 19 and 26. Find the third number.

Paper 3

1 A car runs 10 km to a litre of petrol. Find the cost of petrol for a journey of 600 km, when petrol costs 7p a litre.

2 How many pieces of string, each 10 cm long, can be cut off a length of 100 m?

3 What number, multiplied by 19, gives 4123?

4 How many minutes are there from 9.30 a.m. to 4.15 p.m. on the same day?

5 Multiply £204·80 by 48.

Paper 4

1 How far does a train travel in 15 h at an average speed of 72 km per hour?

2 What number must be added to 6843 to make 10 000?

3 A man starts with a salary of £950 a year, and he receives an increase of £35 a year after each year. What is his salary during his 20th year?

4 How many books 2 cm thick can be placed on a shelf which is 2·4 m long?

5 Divide £68·16 by 16.

Paper 5

1 How many times is 160p contained in £96?

2 Find the least number which must be added to 1276 to make the sum exactly divisible by 83.

3 Add together £67·35, £21·97 and £44·32.

4 If 13 tonnes of coal cost £106·08, what does a tonne cost?

5 Reduce 4 days 15 hr 22 min to minutes.

Paper 6

1 Find the value of $57 \times 28 \times 35$.

2 Divide £442·80 by 18.

3 A man takes 80 steps, each of 84 cm, every minute. How many minutes does he take to walk $10\frac{1}{2}$ km?

4 If eggs cost $1\frac{1}{2}$p each, how many shall I get for £1·17?

5 A boiler uses 28 kg of coke every day, and it is burning for 200 days in the year. Calculate the number of tonnes of coke used in a year.

Paper 7

1 A man earns £1120 a year. Find to the nearest penny how much he earns in a week.

2 Use short methods to evaluate (i) 8678×25, (ii) $123\,500 \div 125$.

3 Find the cost of 4 kg of tobacco at $1\frac{1}{2}$p per gramme.

4 Divide £78·66 by 23.

5 How many hurdles, each 2 m long, are needed to go all round a field 152 m long and 104 m wide?

Papers 8–10 *contain British Imperial units of length, weight and capacity.*

Paper 8

1 The greatest depth in the Atlantic Ocean is 4500 fathoms. Express this depth in miles and yards, if a fathom is 6 ft.

2 Reduce 3 tons 18 cwt 21 lb to pounds.

3 Subtract 2 yd 2 ft 10 in from 4 yd 1 ft 7 in.

4 How many $\frac{1}{4}$ lb packets can be made from 3 tons 1 cwt?

5 A man's pace is 30 in. How many paces does he take in walking a mile?

Paper 9

1 How many pint bottles can be filled from a 30-gallon cask, if 2 pints are wasted?

2 Reduce 448 928 oz to tons cwt lb.

3 How many books 1 in thick can be placed on a shelf 6 ft 8 in long?

4 Find the difference between the weight of 200 boxes each 2 lb 3 oz and the weight of 158 boxes each 2 lb 12 oz.

5 How many pieces of string, each 10 in long, can be cut off a length of 100 yd?

Paper 10

1 How many rails 42 ft long are needed for 7 miles of track containing two lines of rail?

2 Reduce 2 tons 5 cwt 30 lb to pounds.

3 Reduce 7872 ft to miles and yards.

4 Multiply 6 tons 3 cwt 56 lb by 12.

5 Find the cost of 8 lb of tobacco at 42p per oz.

PAPERS 11–15 (§1–8)

Paper 11

1 (i) Put into prime factors $12 \times 18 \times 14$.

(ii) Find the H.C.F. and L.C.M. of 88, 112, 504.

2 A cuboid rests with one edge on a horizontal table, and the opposite edge of the base is raised above the table. Make a freehand sketch of the cuboid.

3 A photograph 12 cm by 18 cm is mounted on a card, leaving a margin 4 cm wide all round. Find the area of the margin.

4 Give examples of the following: (i) a proper fraction, (ii) an improper fraction, (iii) a mixed number, (iv) an integer. Reduce to their lowest terms the fractions $\frac{90}{108}$ and $\frac{105}{120}$.

5 Evaluate $\dfrac{9 \cdot 45}{2 \cdot 7} + \dfrac{2 \cdot 76}{0 \cdot 23}$.

6 Express as denary numbers: 10110_2, 5432_6, 64_8, 1212_3.

Paper 12

1 (i) Simplify $2\frac{1}{12} + 1\frac{2}{9} + 1\frac{1}{6}$. (ii) Subtract $0 \cdot 964$ from $3 \cdot 27$.

2 Find the H.C.F. and L.C.M. of 484, 440, 550, 660.

3 (i) Write as decimals $31\frac{174}{1000}$ and $7\frac{6}{100}$.

(ii) Write as fractions $0 \cdot 03$ and $2 \cdot 67$.

(iii) Simplify $6\frac{3}{4} \times 1\frac{1}{6} \times 5\frac{1}{3}$.

4 Express 47_{10} as a number with the following bases: (i) 2, (ii) 3, (iii) 4, (iv) 5, (v) 8.

5 Make a sketch of the net of a cuboid $6 \cdot 0$ cm by $4 \cdot 5$ cm by $3 \cdot 0$ cm, and find the total area of the net.

6 One rod is 21 cm long and another is 12 cm long. Find the shortest length which contains each rod an exact number of times.

Paper 13

1 Put 540 225 into its prime factors, and hence find its square root.

2 Perform the calculations: (i) $342_5 + 213_5$, (ii) $310_5 - 121_5$, (iii) $124_5 \times 32_5$, (iv) $3343_5 \div 21_5$.

3 The L.C.M. of two numbers is $3^3 \times 5^2 \times 7 \times 11$ and their H.C.F. is 45. If one number is 4725, find the other.

4 Find the area and perimeter of a rectangle 110 m long and 70 m wide.

5 Simplify (i) $2\frac{1}{5} \times 1\frac{1}{4}$, (ii) $7\frac{2}{9} \div 4\frac{1}{3}$.

6 (i) Multiply 62·3 by 0·0048.
(ii) Divide 3·648 by 0·012.

Paper 14

1 Work out $\dfrac{1001011_2}{101_2} \times 1011_2$.

2 Find by the method of factors the square root of 245 025.

3 (i) Simplify $2\frac{1}{2} \times 1\frac{3}{4} \times \frac{8}{15}$.
(ii) Express as decimals the fractions $\frac{4}{5}$, $\frac{3}{20}$, $\frac{7}{8}$, $\frac{1}{25}$.

4 Evaluate (i) $4·18 + 17·49 + 12·2 + 0·94$.

$$\text{(ii)} \ \frac{6·3 \times 2}{1·12 \times 0·9}.$$

5 Find the total outside surface and the volume of a cuboid 8 cm by 6 cm by 2 cm.

6 Find the length of the longest measuring-rod which is contained exactly both in 60 cm and in 84 cm.

Paper 15

1 Simplify (i) $2\frac{1}{3} + 1\frac{5}{8} + 4\frac{1}{12}$, (ii) $1\frac{1}{2} \times 2\frac{3}{4} \div \frac{3}{16}$.

2 Perform the calculations: (i) $45_8 + 77_8$, (ii) $2163_8 \times 24_8$, (iii) $11472_8 \div 27_8$.

3 Express 2571_{10} as a binary numeral.

4 Find the H.C.F. and L.C.M. of 1575, 3675, 350.

5 (i) Multiply 27·1 by 0·72.

(ii) Divide 0·9309 by 0·107.

6 Find the area of the walls and the area of the floor of a room which is 12 m long, 9 m wide and 3 m high.

PAPERS 16–20 (§9–17)

Paper 16

1 A pyramid stands on a square base of side 4 cm and each slant edge is 5 cm long. Make a freehand sketch of the pyramid and its net.

2 Draw a triangle XYZ in which XY = 5·0 cm, $\angle X = 46°$ and $\angle Z = 33°$. Measure XZ.

3 The four angles of a quadrilateral are $x°$, $(x+6)°$, $(x+10)°$ and $(x+20)°$. Find x.

4 (i) Simplify $2a \times 3a^2$ and $30x^3 \div 6x$.

(ii) If $a = 1$, $b = 2$, $c = 5$, find the values of cab^2 and $3c(4b - 3a)$.

5 A man faces NE., and turns towards his right until he faces NW. State (i) in right angles, (ii) in degrees, the size of the angle through which he has turned.

6 Can a regular polygon be drawn such that each exterior angle is (i) 20°, (ii) 15°, (iii) 12°? If so, state the number of sides.

Paper 17

1 Draw a regular hexagon with each side 3·5 cm.

2 Simplify (i) $2 \times 2a^2 \times 3a^3$, (ii) $\dfrac{4x \times 3x^2}{12x^3}$, (iii) $\dfrac{6 \times 14y}{7y^2}$.

3 In Fig. 146, find x.

4 Calculate the interior angle of a regular ten-sided figure.

5 Draw a triangle ABC in which BC = 6·0 cm, $\angle A = 110°$ and $\angle B = 40°$. Measure AC.

6 If 18 men can do a piece of work in 24 days, how long will it take 12 men to do the same work, if they work at the same rate?

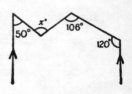

FIG. 146

Paper 18

1 In the triangle ABC, $\angle A = 68°$ and $\angle B = 54°$. The sides AB, AC are produced to X and Y respectively, and the bisectors of the angles CBX, BCY meet at P. Calculate $\angle$ BPC.

2 A cyclist riding at a uniform speed of 16 km per hour takes $2\frac{3}{4}$ hours to go a certain distance. Find how long he would take if he rode at 20 km per hour.

3 If $x = 0$, $y = 2$ and $z = 6$, find the values of (i) $3z - 5y$, (ii) $5y - xz$, (iii) $\frac{4y - z}{4}$, (iv) $xy^2 + yz^2$.

4 In Fig. 147, show that $x = a + b$.

5 Simplify   (i) $3x^2 \times 3x$,   (ii) $\frac{3x}{xy}$,   (iii) $a \times a \times 3 \times a \times 4a$.

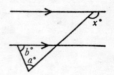

6 When the sides of a quadrilateral ABCD are produced in order, the exterior angles at B, C, D are 77°, 103° and 89° respectively. Find the angle BAD.

FIG. 147

Paper 19

1 In Fig. 148, find x.

2 ABCDEFGH is a regular octagon. If AB and DC are produced, calculate the angle at which they cut.

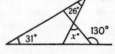

3 Prove that the sum of the interior angles of any five-sided figure is 540°.

FIG. 148

4 Simplify (i) $14x^3 \div 2x^2$, (ii) $\frac{3a^2 \times 9a}{15}$, (iii) $\frac{5a^2b}{3x} \div \frac{10ab^2}{27x}$.

5 Draw a triangle ABC in which AB = 8·0 cm, BC = 5·0 cm and CA = 4·6 cm. Using a set square, draw perpendiculars from A, B, C to the opposite sides, producing these sides when necessary.

6 Draw the net of a tetrahedron, each of whose edges is 3 cm long.

Paper 20

1 (i) Find the area of a square of side $\frac{a}{5}$ cm, and the volume of a cube of edge $\frac{a}{5}$ cm.

(ii) Express $2x$ cm in metres, and $250y$ cm in kilometres.

2 Simplify (i) $\dfrac{2x^3 \times 3y \times 7}{6y^2x}$, (ii) $\sqrt{36a^4}$.

3 What is the angle-sum of a quadrilateral? The angles of a quadrilateral in order are $x°$, $(x+5)°$, $(x+25)°$ and $(x+30)°$. Find the value of x, and show that one pair of opposite sides are parallel.

4 In Fig. 149, find x and y.

5 Find the interior angle of a regular polygon with 12 sides.

6 Draw a triangle ABC in which BC = 5·2 cm, $\angle B = 55°$ and $\angle A = 45°$.

Use the set square to draw through A a parallel to BC, and through C a parallel to BA. Let these lines meet at P, and measure CP.

Fig. 149

PAPERS 21–25 (§18–25)

Paper 21

1 From the top of a cliff 71 m above the sea the angle of depression of a boat at sea is 27°. Find by accurate scale drawing the distance of the boat from the foot of the cliff.

2 In Fig. 150, find x and y.

3 (i) Remove brackets and simplify $3(2x-1)+4(x+2)$.

(ii) Evaluate $\frac{1}{2}mv^2$ when $m=8$, $v=6$.

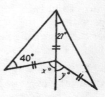

4 The weight of a body is stated to be $4·083 \pm 0·002$ grammes. What do you understand by this? Give the true weight correct to as many significant figures as you can.

Fig. 150

5 Solve the equation $15x - 5 = 6x + 13$.

6 Draw a parallelogram with diagonals 6·0 cm and 10·0 cm, and one side 5·7 cm.   Measure the other side.

Paper 22

1 Draw the plan, front and end elevation of a rectangular block 5·0 cm by 2·5 cm by 2·0 cm, placed on the horizontal plane with the 2·5 cm edges parallel to the XY line.

2 A piece of elastic is 24 cm long when unstretched, and every 1 kg weight hung at the end stretches the elastic 2 cm. Find an expression for the length in centimetres if a weight of W kg is hung at the end.

3 Solve the equation
$$5(x - 4) = 3x + 14.$$

4 In Fig. 151, BCD is a straight line; BX bisects $\angle$ABC and CX bisects $\angle$ACD.   Calculate the number of degrees in $\angle$BXC.

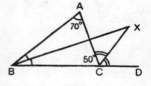

Fig. 151

5 The angle between a diagonal of a rhombus and a side is 22°. Calculate the angles of the rhombus.

6 Find the value of $ut + \frac{1}{2}at^2$ when $u = 10$, $t = 4$ and $a = 3$.

Paper 23

1 A flagstaff stands on the top of a tower.   At a point on the ground 18 m from the base of the tower, the angle of elevation of the top of the tower is observed to be 26°, and that of the top of the flagstaff is 39°.   By means of a scale drawing, find the height of the tower and the length of the flagstaff.

2 (i) One angle of a parallelogram is 65°.   What are the other angles?

(ii) The diagonals of a parallelogram ABCD cut at O.   If $\angle$AOB = 90° and AB = 4 cm, find the length of BC.

3 In Fig. 152, find x.

4 One number is 3 more than another. If the smaller number is doubled, the result is 14 more than the larger number. Find the two numbers.

5 Solve the equation $3x - 7 = 2x - 2$.

6 Draw a triangle ABC in which
$$AB = 4.7 \text{ cm}, \angle A = 37°, AC = 6.8 \text{ cm}.$$
Construct a line BD, meeting AC at D, such that $\angle ABD = \angle A$. Measure CD.

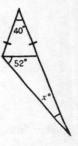

FIG. 152

Paper 24

1 ABC is an equilateral triangle. AB is produced to D, and BD = AB; CD is joined. Prove that $\angle ACD = 90°$.

2 Using ruler and compasses only, construct a triangle ABC in which $\angle A = 90°$, AC = 4.6 cm and BC = 7.8 cm. Measure AB.

3 Write the following numbers correct to (i) two, (ii) three significant figures: 0·005386, 4·966, 496·2, 0·05038.

4 Solve the equation $\dfrac{2x}{7} - 1 = 5$.

5 A speed of V km per hour can be shown to be the same as $\dfrac{250V}{9}$ cm per second. Find how many cm per second a train goes if it travels at 72 km per hour.

6 A boy cycled for x hours at an average speed of 20 km per hour, and then, after his bicycle broke down, he walked for $\frac{1}{2}x$ hours at 4 km per hour. Find an expression for the total distance he has travelled.

If the total distance travelled was 33 km, find the value of x.

Paper 25

1 Find the value of $\dfrac{PRT}{100}$ when P = 650, R = $2\frac{1}{2}$, T = 3.

2 Solve the equation $19 - x = 2x + 6$.

3 A man aged 45 has a son 16 years old. In how many years will the father be just twice as old as his son?

4 A tree in a field stands 16 m from a straight hedge. A treasure buried in the field is known to be 10 m from the hedge and 12 m from the tree. Make an accurate scale drawing, and mark with a cross the points at which you would dig to find the treasure.

5 The vertical angle of an isosceles triangle is 40°, and the length of the perpendicular from the vertex to the base is 5 cm. Construct the triangle, and measure its base.

PAPERS 26–30 (§1–25)

Paper 26

1 Using ruler and compasses only, construct angles of 75° and $67\frac{1}{2}$°.

2 Draw a triangle ABC in which AB = 6 cm, BC = 7 cm and CA = 8 cm. Construct the bisector of ∠ BAC, and measure the parts into which this bisector divides BC.

3 In Fig. 153, find the angles of △ PQR, if OP = OQ = OR.

4 At a village concert N people pay 18p each for admission, and 2N people pay 6p each. Find (i) in pence, (ii) in pounds, the total amount paid by all the 3N people.

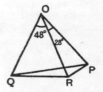

5 Solve the equation
$$5(x - 7) = 7 - x + 3(x - 5).$$

FIG. 153

6 Find the length of the shortest piece 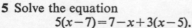 of wire which can be cut into equal pieces all 12 cm, or all 14 cm, or all 16 cm.

Paper 27

1 Evaluate (i) $735_8 \times 43_8$, (ii) $342_5 + 213_5$.

2 (i) Multiply 63·46 by 0·042.
(ii) Divide 0·5244 by 0·0019.

3 Express as fractions in their lowest terms: 0·08, 0·28, 0·05, 0·35, 0·8.

4 State without proof all the facts you know about the diagonals of: (i) a parallelogram, (ii) a rhombus, (iii) a rectangle, (iv) a square.

5 ABCD is a rectangular courtyard. AB = 60 m and BC = 35 m. A sundial is 15 m from AB and 10 m from BC. Using a scale of 1 cm to 10 m, draw an accurate plan, showing the position of the sundial.

6 In Fig. 154, ABCDE is a regular pentagon, and ABXY is a square. Calculate the numbers of degrees in the angles DBC, XBC, XBD.

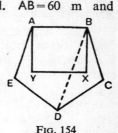

FIG. 154

Paper 28

1 Construct an isosceles triangle with base 4 cm and vertical angle 38°. Measure the equal sides.

2 ABCD is a rectangle whose diagonals cut at O. If $\angle CBD = 41°$, calculate $\angle AOB$ and $\angle ACD$.

3 The number 267 stands for 2 hundreds + 6 tens + 7 units. Write down in as short a form as possible the number which has x for the hundreds digit, y for the tens digit and z for the units digit.

4 A lawn 17 m long and 8 m wide is surrounded by a path $1\frac{1}{2}$ m wide. Find the number of cubic metres of gravel needed to cover the path to a depth of 6 cm.

5 Three men can do a piece of work in 10 h. How long would the same work take 5 men?

6 Put 17 424 into prime factors, and hence find its square root.

Paper 29

1 Evaluate (i) $4·8 + 3\frac{1}{2} + 0·6$, (ii) $\dfrac{2·7 \times 0·04 \times (0·1)^2}{0·3 \times 0·2}$.

2 Find (i) in cubic metres, (ii) in litres, how much water is required to fill a cistern $2\frac{1}{2}$ m long, $1\frac{1}{2}$ m wide, 1 m deep.

3 The foot of a ladder is 4 m from a wall, and the ladder reaches 8·3 m up the wall. Find from a scale drawing the angle which the ladder makes with the ground.

4 Sketch a general view of the object whose plan and front elevation are shown in Fig. 155.

5 ABCD is a parallelogram whose diagonals AC, BD cut at O; $\angle$ BAC = 26°, $\angle$ DAC = 37°, $\angle$ AOB = 110°. Calculate the numbers of degrees in the angles ABD, DBC, BCD.

6 Construct a rhombus with diagonals 5·4 cm and 4·4 cm. Measure a side.

Fig. 155

Paper 30

1 Simplify (i) $2x^2 \times 3xy \div 4y^2$, (ii) $3x^2 + 2x - 1 + 4x - x^2 - 3$.

2 A boy cycles for $2\frac{1}{2}$ hours at $3x$ km per hour, and then for 2 hours at $3\frac{1}{2}x$ km per hour. How far does he go altogether? If this total distance is 87 km, find the value of x.

3 (i) Express $\frac{175}{11}$ as a mixed number, and $8\frac{4}{9}$ as an improper fraction.

(ii) Perform the binary calculations $110101 - 11010$ and 110101×11010.

4 Simplify $3\frac{1}{7} - 2\frac{2}{3} + 1\frac{1}{2} + \frac{5}{6}$.

5 The diagonals of a parallelogram are 6·4 cm and 5·2 cm, and they intersect at an angle of 52°. Construct the parallelogram and measure its sides. (Use the fact that the diagonals of a parallelogram bisect one another.)

6 (i) Multiply 185·3 by 0·862. (ii) Find in cubic metres the capacity of a tank 3·6 m long, 2·2 m wide and 0·82 m deep.

SECTION B

26. GRAPHS OF STATISTICS

THE rainfall in centimetres for each month of a certain year at a town in West Africa is shown in the following table:

Jan	Feb	Mar	Apr	May	June	July	Aug	Sept	Oct	Nov	Dec
1·8	2·4	6·3	15·0	26·7	29·0	19·0	17·0	32·0	25·0	5·0	1·0

It is easier to see how the monthly rainfall varies if we draw a diagram like Fig. 156.

Rainfall Bar-chart

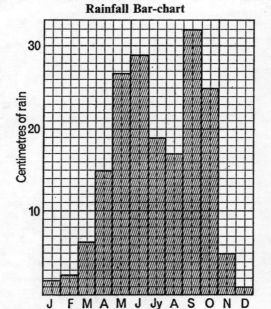

FIG. 156

161

Such a diagram is called a **bar-chart**. The months are marked at equal intervals along a line drawn across the page, and the rainfall in centimetres is marked along a line running up the page. Each of these lines is called an **axis** (plural, *axes*), and each axis is labelled. You will find that it saves time to use squared paper. Vertical bars are drawn, their heights indicating the rainfall for the various months. The bars are often drawn touching one another, although this is not really necessary, but they must all have the same width.

The bar-chart shows at a glance which were the driest and which were the wettest months of the year.

We will now take a rather different example. The following table gives the height of a boy at different ages.

Age in years	10	11	12	13	14
Height in centimetres	141·0	144·7	147·7	153·9	160·6

Age in years	15	16	17	18	19
Height in centimetres	166·0	174·2	177·8	179·0	180·0

These figures are illustrated in Fig. 157, where the bars of the previous example are omitted and only their tops marked.

Graph of Boy's Height

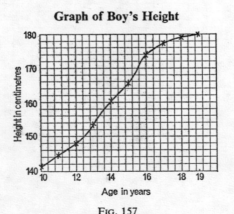

Fig. 157

When the points have been plotted, they are joined up by a smooth curve. The reason for this is that the points which lie between those plotted, even if not absolutely accurate, are at least a great help in estimating the boy's height at times between his birthdays. Such a diagram is called a **graph**.

Exercise. Read off from Fig. 157 the probable height of the boy at $12\frac{1}{2}$ and at $16\frac{1}{2}$.

Estimating values between the points which have been plotted is called **interpolation**. It can be done only when points between those plotted have any meaning and when the quantity represented changes gradually and continuously.

A graph or a bar-chart illustrates the manner in which two quantities are connected. The two quantities are called **variables**; thus in Fig. 156 the two variables are the month and the rainfall, while in Fig. 157 the two variables are the age and height of the boy. Of these two variables, you will usually find that you are able to choose the values of one variable, but the values of the other are then found by measurement or experiment or observation. In the case of the age and height of the boy, you could decide to measure his height every year, or every six months, or every month, and so *age* is the variable whose values (within reason) you select for yourself.

The variable whose values are chosen by you should always be measured along the axis which is drawn **across the page**. Later we shall call this variable the **independent variable**.

To make the graph clear and easy to understand, the following points should be observed:

1. Give the graph a title or heading.

2. Measure the quantity whose values are chosen (the independent variable) **along the axis drawn across the page; the quantity whose values are the result of observation or experiment, along the axis drawn up the page.**

3. Write along each axis what quantity is measured along it.

4. Choose as large a scale as you can get on your paper, and make sure that plotting and reading will be easy; thus, a centimetre may be taken to represent 1, 10, 100, 1000, etc., or 2, 20, 200, or 5, 50, 500; but do not take a centimetre to represent 7 or 3 or 4.

5. Mark the scales at regular intervals along both axes. If the unit is a fifth of a centimetre, say, there is no need to mark every unit. Every 5 or every 10 will do. If the scales are clearly marked, it is better not to write in words what scale is used, as this is unnecessary. Another point is that you need not start at 0; for example, in Fig. 157, the age starts at 10 and the height at 140 cm.

EXERCISE 72

Draw graphs or bar-charts (whichever is the more appropriate) to illustrate the following statistics:

1 The table below gives the average weight in kilogrammes of children at various ages:

Age in years	6	7	8	9	10	11	12	13	14
Weight in kg	19·5	21·3	23·1	25·6	28·3	31·5	35·4	39·9	45·3

2 Height of a sunflower at different ages:

Age in days	7	14	21	28	35	42
Height in cm	18	37	68½	94	133½	171½
Age in days	49	56	63	70	77	84
Height in cm	208½	231	251½	254	256½	257½

3 Population of the United Kingdom in millions:

Year	1871	1881	1891	1901	1911
Population in millions	27·4	31·0	34·3	38·2	42·0
Year	1921	1931	1941	1951	1961
Population in millions	44·0	46·0	—	50·2	52·7

There was no population census in 1941 on account of war-time conditions. Estimate from your graph the probable population in that year.

4 The number of people killed on the roads of Great Britain in the course of a year:

Year	1954	1955	1956	1957	1958	1959	1960
Road deaths	5010	5526	5367	5550	5970	6520	6970

Year	1961	1962	1963	1964	1965	1966	1967
Road deaths	6908	6709	6922	7820	7952	7985	7319

5 The temperature of a cooling body, taken every minute:

Minutes	0	1	2	3	4	5	6
Temperature (° C.)	90	74	60	47	38	31	27

6 Number of tons of coal used per day by a steamer going at different speeds:

Speed in knots	2	5	7	8	10	12	13	14
Number of tons	9	15	20	$22\frac{1}{2}$	32	45	60	80

7 Barometer readings taken every 4 h:

	Mid-night	4 a.m.	8 a.m.	Mid-day	4 p.m.	8 p.m.	Mid-night
Height in mm	752	754·2	750·7	753	748·5	748	753·8

8 Time of swing of a pendulum:

Length in cm	10	20	40	60	80	100	120	140
Time in sec	0·63	0·90	1·27	1·55	1·79	2·00	2·20	2·37

Estimate from your graph the time of swing of a pendulum 50 cm long, and the length of a pendulum whose time of swing is one second.

9 The times of sunset at London on the 15th of each month (Greenwich Mean Time):

Jan	Feb	Mar	Apr	May	June	July	Aug	Sept	Oct	Nov	Dec
4.18	5.13	6.04	6.56	7.45	8.19	8.12	7.24	6.16	5.08	4.11	3.52

10 A marble is rolled down a smooth groove cut in a sloping plank. The distances through which it has rolled in 1, 2, 3, . . . sec are:

Time in sec	0	1	2	3	4	5	6
Distance in cm	0	6	24	54	96	150	216

11 A piece of elastic, attached at one end, has various weights fastened in turn to the other end. The lengths of the elastic for different weights are as follows:

Weight in grammes	0	5	10	15	20	25	30	35
Length in cm	20	21·1	22·2	23·3	24·4	25·5	26·6	27·7

Find from your graph the length of the elastic when the weight is 18 g, and the weight when the length is 27 cm.

12 A patient's temperature was taken at intervals, as follows:

Time in hours	0	6	12	16	20
Temperature	103	100·4	101·2	102	103·5
Time in hours	24	30	36	42	48
Temperature	101	99·2	99·4	100·5	100

Travel graphs Suppose we want to draw a graph to show the distance from his starting-point of a man who walks at a steady rate of 5 kilometres per hour. The table of values is as follows:

Time in hours	0	$\frac{1}{2}$	1	$1\frac{1}{2}$	2	$2\frac{1}{2}$	3
Distance in kilometres	0	$2\frac{1}{2}$	5	$7\frac{1}{2}$	10	$12\frac{1}{2}$	15

Travel Graph

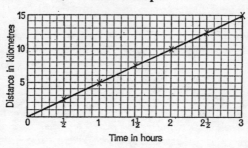

FIG. 158

When the points are plotted, you will notice that they lie on a straight line. Such a graph as Fig. 158 is called a **travel graph,** and the travel graph will always be a straight line if the speed is *uniform*, i.e. does not vary.

Travel Graph

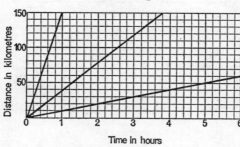

FIG. 159

Fig. 159 shows the travel graphs of a motor-boat travelling at 10 km per hour, a steamer at 40 km per hour, and an aeroplane at 150 km per hour. Find which is which.

Straight-line graphs A straight-line graph is obtained whenever equal increases in the quantity which is measured *across* the paper cause equal increases in the quantity which is measured *up* the paper. Thus, in Fig. 158, for every additional $\frac{1}{2}$ h measured along the time axis there is an additional $2\frac{1}{2}$ km measured along the distance axis. When we know beforehand that the graph is going to be a straight line, we need only plot two or three points.

Example *A spiral spring is hung from one end, and different loads are fastened to the other end. In each case the length of the spring is measured, and the results are tabulated as follows:*

Load in kg	0	5	10	15	20	25	30
Length in cm	10	12	14	16	18	20	22

Draw a graph to illustrate how the length of the spring depends on the load.

The graph is shown in Fig. 160.

Spiral Spring Graph

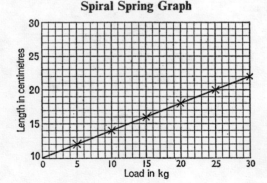

Fig. 160

Notice that equal increases in the load cause equal increases in the length of the spring. For example, every additional load of 5 kg causes the spring to stretch a further 2 cm.

EXERCISE 73

1 A man makes a journey, leaving home at noon. He travels partly on bicycle, partly on foot, and partly by motor coach. The travel graph is shown in Fig. 161.

Describe the journey in detail; give the different speeds, say how far he travels altogether, what time he reaches his destination, and what time he reaches home.

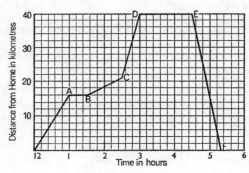

FIG. 161

Solve Nos. 2–8 graphically, by seeing where two travel graphs meet.

2 A man set out at noon to walk along a certain road at 5 km per hour. At 1.30 p.m. a boy started from the same place to cycle after him at 16 km per hour. Find when and where the cyclist overtook the man.

3 Two villages A and B are 12 km apart. A boy sets out from A at 10 a.m. to walk to B at a steady speed of 5 km per hour. Draw a travel graph of his distance from A.

At 11 a.m. another boys starts from B to walk to A by the same road at 6 km per hour. Draw a graph, on the same axes as before, showing his distances from A at various times. Hence find at what time the boys meet, and how far from A.

4 P and Q are two towns 60 km apart. A cyclist leaves P at noon to cycle to Q at 16 km per hour. At 1.0 p.m. a motorist travelling at 60 km per hour leaves P and travels to Q. He stays at Q half an hour, and then returns to P at the same speed as before. Find when the motorist passed the cyclist and at what distances from P.

5 A goods train leaves London at 9 a.m. and travels at 32 km per hour towards Brighton. It stops at Croydon, which is 16 km from London in the direction of Brighton, for 15 min, and then goes on at the same speed as before. An express on a separate track leaves London at 9.35 a.m. and travels towards Brighton at an average speed of 64 km per hour. When does the express overtake the goods train, and at what distance from London?

6 Mr. Smith walks for 45 min at 6 km per hour, rests by the roadside for 30 min, and then borrows a bicycle and cycles in the same direction as before at 20 km per hour. Mr. Jones starts from the same place as Mr. Smith, but 2 hours later, and motors along the same road at 60 km per hour. Find the distance he has motored when he overtakes Mr. Smith.

7 A goods train, travelling at a steady speed of 40 km per hour, passes a level crossing. Twenty minutes later an express travelling at 96 km per hour, in the same direction as the goods train, passes the same crossing. How far from the crossing will the goods train be when the express overtakes it?

8 A man sets out at noon along a certain road at 6 km per hour. Starting from a place on the same road 22 km away 30 min later, a boy cycles towards the man at 19 km per hour. How far does the cyclist go before he meets the man, and at what time does this occur?

9 Draw a graph for converting kilometres per hour into metres per second, up to 108 km per hour, given that 108 km per hour is the same as 30 m per sec. Express from your graph a speed of 69 km per hour in metres per sec, and a speed of 16 m per sec in kilometres per hour.

10 In an examination the marks run from 87 to 206, and it is necessary to reduce them so that they run from 0 to 100. Draw a straight-line graph which will do this, and read off the reduced marks of a boy who got 163 marks originally.

11 Given that the freezing point of water is 0° on the Celsius thermometer and 32° on the Fahrenheit thermometer, and that the boiling point of water is 100° Celsius and 212° Fahrenheit, draw a graph which can be used to convert from one scale to the other. From your graph find what temperature Celsius is the same as 100° Fahrenheit, and also what temperature Fahrenheit is the same as 78° Celsius.

27. CONGRUENCE

Congruent Triangles

Two triangles which have all the sides and angles of one equal to those of the other are called **congruent triangles.** The symbol $\equiv$ is used for 'is congruent to'; thus,

$$\triangle ABC \equiv \triangle PQR$$

means that one triangle would fit exactly over the other (though it might be necessary to turn one triangle over first before fitting it on the other). To make it clear which vertices correspond, we often write

$$\triangle s \; \frac{ABC}{PQR} \; \text{are congruent,}$$

to show that A corresponds to P, B to Q, C to R. BC and QR are called **corresponding sides,** as they are opposite **corresponding vertices;** so are CA and RP, and also AB and PQ.

But in order to see if the three sides and angles of one triangle are equal to those of another, it will not be necessary to measure all of them. Example 1, p. 96, showed how to construct a triangle, given two sides and the angle included between those sides. The information about the triangle ABC given in that example is evidently sufficient to enable you to draw a definite triangle. All such triangles will be exactly alike in every respect, apart, of course, from the errors due to inaccurate drawing. Not only would all the triangles have AB, AC and ∠A the same, but they would also have BC, ∠B and ∠C the same. Evidently two triangles with two sides of one equal to two sides of the other, and the angles enclosed by those sides equal, will have all the three sides and three angles of one equal to the three sides and three angles of the other. We have thus found a test for congruence:

Two triangles which have two sides of one equal to two sides of the other, each to each, and the included angles equal, are congruent.

It is important to notice that the angles which are equal must be **included** (or enclosed) between the two sides in each triangle. Fig. 162 shows two triangles which have two sides of one equal to two sides of the other, and an angle of one equal

FIG. 162

to an angle of the other, but the triangles are evidently not congruent. This fact was also shown in Examples 4–6, p. 97, where we found that, when we are given two sides and a non-included angle, these facts do not always fix uniquely the shape and size of the triangle. We conclude that two triangles are not necessarily congruent if they have two sides and a non-included angle of one equal respectively to two sides and a non-included angle of the other.

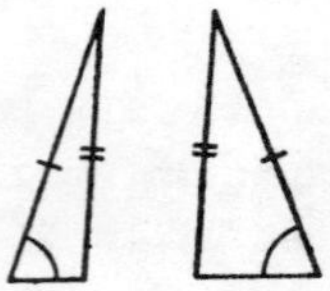

How to mark figures. Put the same mark on two lengths or two angles which are equal. Fig. 163 shows two triangles which are congruent. They are △s $\frac{\text{ABC}}{\text{PQR}}$.

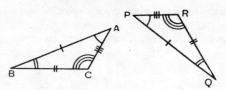

FIG. 163

Right angles can be marked in an obvious way, and arrows denote parallels.

Example 2, p. 96, showed the method of constructing a triangle, given a side and two angles. It is obvious from the construction that one side and *any* two angles fix the shape and size of the triangle, provided we are told whether the given side is opposite one of the angles or is an arm of both of them.

Hence we see that two triangles are congruent if they have two angles of one equal to two angles of the other, and one side of one equal to one side of the other, but the side must occupy the same position in both triangles; or, as we say, the side must *correspond*.

Fig. 164 shows how important it is that the side should be the

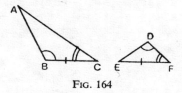

FIG. 164

corresponding side. Triangles ABC, DEF are not congruent, although ∠B = ∠D, ∠C = ∠F and BC = EF; because EF is opposite ∠D, but BC is not opposite ∠B.

It does not matter which two angles of one triangle are equal to two angles of the other, so long as the equal sides are corresponding sides. Thus our second test for congruence is:

If two triangles have two angles and a side of one equal to two angles and the corresponding side of the other, then the triangles are congruent.

In Example 3, p. 97, it was clear that the lengths of the three sides are sufficient information to fix the size and shape of the triangle, and we draw the conclusion that all triangles with these lengths as their sides will be congruent. In other words:

If two triangles have the three sides of one respectively equal to those of the other, then the two triangles are congruent.

Example 7, p. 98, showed that the measurements of the sides AB and BC, with the information that the angle A is a right angle, are enough to fix the triangle. Since the lengths of the hypotenuse (BC) and one other side (AB) of a right-angled triangle are sufficient to fix the triangle definitely, we conclude that

If two right-angled triangles have the hypotenuse and another side of the one triangle respectively equal to the hypotenuse and another side of the other triangle, then the two triangles are congruent.

Example 1 *Prove that, if two sides of a triangle are equal, then the base angles are equal. Prove also that the bisector of the vertical angle bisects the base at right angles.*

In Fig. 165, ABC is an isosceles triangle in which AB = AC. The bisector of ∠BAC is drawn, and meets the base BC at D.

We have to prove that

$$\angle B = \angle C,$$
$$BD = CD,$$

and $\angle$s ADB, ADC are right angles.

In the triangles BAD, CAD,

$$AB = AC \text{ (given)},$$
$$\angle BAD = CAD \text{ (construction)},$$

and AD is a side of both triangles.

Fig. 165

$\therefore \ \triangle s \ \begin{smallmatrix} BAD \\ CAD \end{smallmatrix}$ are congruent (two sides and the included angle equal).

$$\therefore \ \angle B = \angle C,$$
$$BD = CD,$$
and $\qquad \angle ADB = \angle ADC.$

Now $\angle ADB + \angle ADC = 180°$ (adjacent angles on a straight line).

$\therefore \ \angle ADB = 90°$ and $\angle ADC = 90°$.

Since we have shown that BD = CD and that AD is perpendicular to BC, it follows that AD is the perpendicular bisector of BC.

These facts about the isosceles triangle were stated on p. 113, without any proof being given at that stage. It was also stated that, if two angles of a triangle are equal, then the sides opposite those angles are equal. The proof depends on drawing the bisector of the vertical angle, as above, and showing that the triangles so formed are congruent. You should try to make up the proof of this as an exercise.

Example 2 *Defining a parallelogram as a quadrilateral in which both pairs of opposite sides are parallel, prove that* (i) *opposite sides are equal,* (ii) *opposite angles are equal.*

Suppose that ABCD is a parallelogram, with AB parallel to DC and AD parallel to BC, as in Fig. 166.
Join BD, and let the angles be as shown.

(i) Since AB and DC are parallel, $a_1 = a_2$ (alternate);
   ,,   AD ,,   BC   ,, $b_1 = b_2$ (alternate).

Thus in the $\triangle$s CDB, ABD,

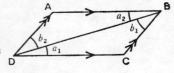

$$a_1 = a_2,$$
$$b_1 = b_2,$$

and BD is a side of both triangles;

Fig. 166

$\therefore \triangle$s $\begin{matrix} \text{CDB} \\ \text{ABD} \end{matrix}$ are congruent

(two angles and a corresponding side equal).

$$\therefore \text{BC} = \text{DA},$$
and $$\text{CD} = \text{AB}.$$

$\therefore$ opposite sides are equal.

(ii) In Fig. 166, we have shown that $a_1 = a_2$ and $b_2 = b_1$.

But $a_1 + b_2 = \angle\text{ADC},$
and $a_2 + b_1 = \angle\text{ABC}.$
$$\therefore \angle\text{ABC} = \angle\text{ADC}.$$

Similarly, by drawing the other diagonal AC, we could show that $\angle\text{BCD} = \angle\text{DAB}$.

(Alternatively, these angles could be deduced to be equal from the congruent triangles $\begin{matrix} \text{CDB} \\ \text{ABD} \end{matrix}$.)

$\therefore$ opposite angles are equal.

EXERCISE 74

State whether the triangles in Figs. 167–183 are congruent. If they are, write them with corresponding vertices, in the form △s $\frac{ABC}{PQR}$, and name the other equal sides and angles of the two triangles. If the triangles are not congruent, explain why they are not.

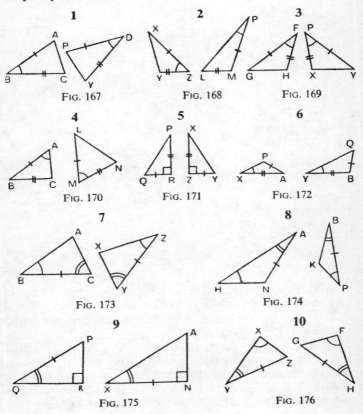

1 FIG. 167
2 FIG. 168
3 FIG. 169
4 FIG. 170
5 FIG. 171
6 FIG. 172
7 FIG. 173
8 FIG. 174
9 FIG. 175
10 FIG. 176

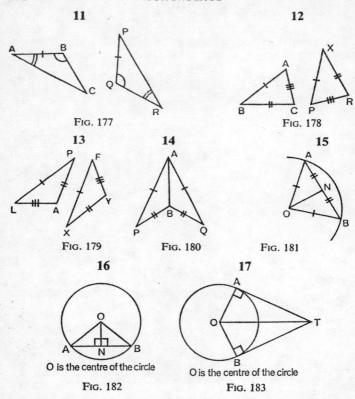

11

Fig. 177

12

Fig. 178

13

Fig. 179

14

Fig. 180

15

Fig. 181

16

O is the centre of the circle

Fig. 182

17

O is the centre of the circle

Fig. 183

18 P is any point on the bisector of the angle BAC; M and N are the feet of the perpendiculars from P to AB and AC. Prove that the triangles PAM, PAN are congruent, and deduce that PM = PN.

19 In Fig. 182, prove that AN = NB. (This proves that the foot of the perpendicular from the centre of a circle to a chord is the mid-point of the chord.)

20 In Fig. 183, prove that TA = TB. (This proves that the two tangents from the point T to the circle are equal in length.)

28. INTERCEPT AND MID-POINT THEOREMS

Suppose we have three parallel lines, and a line cutting them at P, Q, R as in Fig. 184.

A line such as PQR has already been called a **transversal.** The lengths PQ and QR, the parts of the transversal intercepted or cut off by the parallels, are called the **intercepts** made by the parallels.

Now suppose that the parallels are the same distance apart. This means that, if PL and QM are drawn, as in Fig. 184, perpendicular to the lines, then PL and QM will be equal.

In the triangles PLQ, QMR,

PL = QM (given),

∠PLQ = ∠QMR (rt. angles),

∠PQL = ∠QRM (corr. angles).

∴ △s $\begin{array}{c}PLQ\\QMR\end{array}$ are congruent.

∴ PQ = QR.

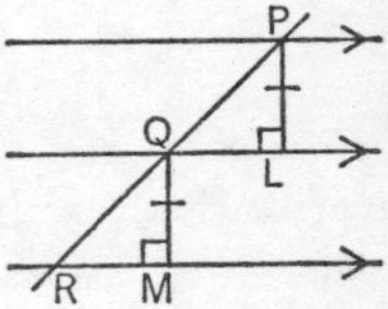

Fig. 184

It follows that, if the parallel lines are the same distance apart, then the intercepts made on this (and therefore on any other) transversal are equal.

Conversely, if the parallels cut off equal intercepts on *one* transversal, they must be the same distance apart, and the parallels must then cut off equal intercepts on any other transversal.

The argument could be extended to any number of parallels. In Fig. 185, where there are four parallels the same distance apart, the intercepts PQ, QR, RS are all equal.

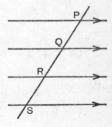

Fig. 185

This property of parallels is known as the **Intercept Theorem.** It provides us with a method of dividing a given line into any number of equal parts, without any measurement or calculation.

Example 1 *Divide the line AB into three equal parts.*

Make any angle at A, and cut off equal lengths AP, PQ, QR along the arm of the angle. (Any convenient length will do for these.)

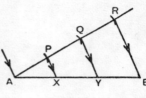

Join RB, and draw parallels through P and Q to RB.

Let these parallels meet AB at X and Y.

Fig. 186

Then AX, XY, YB are the required equal parts.

The parallel through A is added to show why the construction is correct. By making AP, PQ, QR all equal, we have four parallels all the same distance apart, and by the Intercept Theorem AX, XY and YB must all be equal.

A similar method may be used for dividing AB into any number of equal parts.

Mid-point Theorem

Suppose we have a triangle ABC, and P is the mid-point of AB.

Draw PQ parallel to BC, meeting AC at Q. Draw through A another parallel to BC.

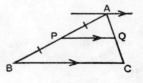

We thus have three parallels, and since AP = PB the parallels must be the same distance apart.

$$\therefore \text{AQ} = \text{QC.}$$

Fig. 187

It is thus clear that the line joining the mid-points of AB and AC is parallel to BC.

Now let R be the mid-point of BC.

From what has been said, it is evident that PQ is parallel to BC, and QR is parallel to AB.

The figure PQRB is therefore a parallelogram, for both pairs of opposite sides are parallel.

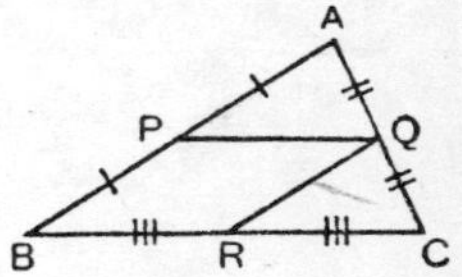

∴ PQ = BR (since opposite sides of a parallelogram are also equal).

∴ PQ = ½BC.

In the same way,

FIG. 188

$$QR = \tfrac{1}{2}AB \quad \text{and} \quad PR = \tfrac{1}{2}AC.$$

This property of a triangle is called the **Mid-point Theorem,** which states that

The line joining the mid-points of two sides of a triangle is parallel to the third side and is equal to one-half of it.

EXERCISE 75

1 In Fig. 189, AP = PB = 2 cm, BC = 3 cm and AC = 2·6 cm. Calculate the lengths of AQ and PQ.

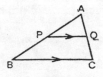

FIG. 189

2 In Fig. 189, AQ = QC = 1 cm, AB = 3·8 cm, BC = 4·4 cm. Find the lengths of PB and PQ.

3 In Fig. 189, AP = 2 cm, PB = 2 cm, AQ = 1 cm, PQ = 1½ cm. Find the lengths of AC and BC.

4 D is the mid-point of the side BC of △ABC, E is the mid-point of CA, and F the mid-point of AB. If AB=7 cm, BC=8 cm, CA=9 cm, find the lengths of DE, EF, FD.

5 In Fig. 190, AB=3 cm, EF=5 cm and BD=DF. Find the length of CD. (Hint: calculate DX and XC.)

6 In Fig. 191, AB=3 cm, EF=5 cm and BD=DF. Find the length of CD. (Hint: calculate CX and DX.)

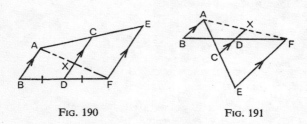

FIG. 190   FIG. 191

7 D, E, F are the mid-points of the sides BC, CA, AB of △ABC. If ∠A=70°, ∠B=60°, ∠C=50°, calculate the angles of △DEF.

8 ABCD is a quadrilateral in which AC=8 cm and BD=10 cm. P is the mid-point of AB, Q that of BC, R that of CD, S that of DA. Applying the Mid-point Theorem to △ABC, find the length of PQ. Find, similarly, the lengths of QR, RS, SP. What sort of figure is PQRS, and why?

9 Draw a line AB 8 cm long, and by a geometrical construction divide it into three equal parts.

10 Draw a line AB 5 cm long, and find by construction a point X on it such that AX=2XB.

11 Draw a line 9 cm long, and divide it into seven equal parts by geometrical construction.

29. THE THEOREM OF PYTHAGORAS

Pythagoras was a famous Greek mathematician, and was born about the year 570 B.C. He travelled a good deal in Egypt before finally settling down in a Greek colony in the south of Italy. No doubt he learned many facts about mathematics from the Egyptians, and one fact in particular which would impress him was that a triangle with sides three, four and five units is right-angled. This was known long before Pythagoras' time, but the truth about *any* right-angled triangle was not understood.

Pythagoras may have obtained a hint of his theorem from a floor tiled as in Fig. 192, where the large shaded square consists of four tiles, while the two smaller shaded squares consist of two tiles each.

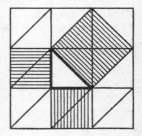

Now the shaded squares in Fig. 192 are the squares drawn on the sides of an isosceles right-angled triangle, and evidently the square on the side opposite the right angle is equal to the sum of the squares on the other two sides.

FIG. 192

A verification is given by the jig-saw puzzle known as **Perigal's dissection,** shown in Fig. 193.

Draw a triangle ABC, right-angled at A, on thin cardboard, and construct the three squares on its sides. Draw the diagonals of the square on AB, and thus find its centre. Through the centre of the square draw lines parallel and perpendicular to the hypotenuse BC. Cut out the squares on AB and AC, and cut up the square on AB into four pieces, as shown in the diagram. You will find that the five pieces can be

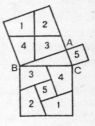

FIG. 193

fitted together so as to cover the square on BC exactly, and that the five pieces can be moved into their new positions without rotating any of them or turning them over.

It would not do to rely only on appearances, and a formal proof will be given later in Part II of this book. In the meantime we have *verified* that

In a right-angled triangle the area of the square on the hypotenuse is equal to the sum of the areas of the squares on the other two sides.

This is **Pythagoras' Theorem.**

The theorem has here been considered as a result connecting the areas of actual squares. But the theorem enables us to calculate lengths without having any squares drawn. For if *a* cm is the length of the hypotenuse and *b*, *c* cm are the lengths of the other two sides, as in Fig. 194 on the next page,

$$a^2 = b^2 + c^2.$$

This is the form in which the theorem is generally used in calculations.

The theorem also provides us with a test for a right-angled triangle; namely, a triangle is right-angled whenever the square on the longest side equals the sum of the squares on the other two sides. The reason why the triangle with sides three, four and five units is right-angled is that

$$5^2 = 25,$$

and also
$$3^2 + 4^2 = 25.$$

Pythagoras found other sets of numbers which can also be the sides of a right-angled triangle. A few are given below, and you should test that the sum of the squares of the first two numbers equals the square of the third number.

Shorter sides	Hypotenuse
3, 4	5
5, 12	13
7, 24	25
8, 15	17

EXERCISE 76

Nos. 1–6 refer to Fig. 194.   The lengths are in centimetres.

1 If $b = 6$, $c = 8$, find a.

2 If $b = 8$, $c = 15$, find a.

3 If $b = 5$, $c = 12$, find a.

4 If $b = 9$, $a = 15$, find c.

5 If $a = 25$, $b = 15$, find c.

6 If $a = 50$, $c = 48$, find b.

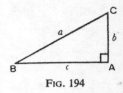

Fig. 194

7 A rectangle is 12 cm long and 5 cm wide.   Calculate the length of a diagonal.

8 The diagonals of a rhombus are 6 cm and 8 cm.   Calculate the length of a side of the rhombus.   (Hint: at what angle do the diagonals cut?)

9 The side of a rhombus is 20 cm long, and one diagonal is of length 24 cm.   Find the length of the other diagonal.

10 Find out whether a triangle with sides 11, 15, 18 cm is right-angled.

11 In Fig. 195, AB = 54 m, CD = 30 m and BD = 32 m. Calculate the length of AC.

Fig. 195

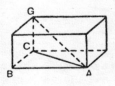

Fig. 196

12 A room is 16 m long, 12 m wide and 15 m high (see Fig. 196).   (i) Find AC from △ABC (notice that ∠ABC is a right angle).   (ii) Find AG from △ACG.   (Remember that GC is vertical and CA horizontal.)

30. FRACTIONS (II)

Straightforward operations with fractions were explained in § 3. In this section we shall extend our knowledge of fractions, and deal with some expressions which are a little more complicated.

One quantity as a fraction of another To express one quantity as a fraction of another, put the two quantities in the same units, and make a fraction with the first quantity on the top line and the second quantity on the bottom line. Then reduce the resulting fraction to its lowest terms.

More shortly, to express a as a fraction of b, write $\dfrac{a}{b}$.

Example 1 *What fraction of 5·25 m is 70 cm?*

$$\frac{70 \text{ cm}}{5·25 \text{ m}} = \frac{70 \text{ cm}}{525 \text{ cm}} = \frac{70}{525}$$

$$= \frac{14}{105} = \frac{2}{15}.$$

Brackets The examples so far have contained only one process at a time. We shall now consider some in which more than one operation is necessary. Where there is any doubt in which order the operations should be performed, brackets will be used to make it clear.

Thus $1\frac{1}{2} + (\frac{5}{6} \times 2\frac{1}{12})$ means that $\frac{5}{6}$ is to be multiplied by $2\frac{1}{12}$ first, and the result added to $1\frac{1}{2}$.

But $(1\frac{1}{2} + \frac{5}{6}) \times 2\frac{1}{12}$ means that $\frac{5}{6}$ is to be added to $1\frac{1}{2}$, and the result multiplied by $2\frac{1}{12}$.

Example 2 *Simplify* $6\frac{1}{3}-4\frac{7}{16}+3\frac{1}{9}-1\frac{1}{2}$.

The expression $= (6+3-4-1) + (\frac{1}{3}+\frac{1}{9}-\frac{7}{16}-\frac{1}{2})$

$= 4 + \frac{48+16-63-72}{144}$

$= 4\frac{64-135}{144}$

$= 3\frac{208-135}{144} = 3\frac{73}{144}.$

Example 3 *Simplify* $(7\frac{3}{8}-\frac{1}{3}) \div 3\frac{1}{4}$.

The expression $= 7\frac{9-8}{24} \div \frac{13}{4}$

$= 7\frac{1}{24} \div \frac{13}{4}$

$= \frac{\overset{13}{\cancel{169}}}{\underset{6}{\cancel{24}}} \times \frac{\cancel{4}}{\cancel{13}}$

$= \frac{13}{6} = 2\frac{1}{6}.$

EXERCISE 77

Simplify:

1 $13\frac{3}{4} - (4\frac{2}{3} \times 1\frac{5}{6})$

2 $2\frac{2}{9} - 1\frac{2}{3} + 3\frac{1}{5}$

3 $(\frac{1}{2}+\frac{1}{4}) \times \frac{1}{6}$

4 $\frac{1}{2} + (\frac{1}{4} \times \frac{1}{6})$

5 $1\frac{3}{5} \times (2\frac{1}{3} - \frac{5}{6})$

6 $5\frac{3}{4} \div (2\frac{2}{3} - \frac{3}{4})$

7 $2\frac{1}{3} + 3\frac{1}{2} - 1\frac{1}{5} - 4\frac{2}{3} + 5\frac{5}{6}$

8 $3\frac{4}{5} - 1\frac{3}{8} + 9\frac{27}{40} - 5$

9 $4\frac{1}{4} + (\frac{2}{3} \times 5\frac{1}{4}) - 2\frac{3}{8}$

10 $(3\frac{1}{6} - 1\frac{1}{4}) \div 1\frac{1}{3}$

11 $(\frac{1}{2} + \frac{1}{4}) \div (\frac{1}{3} - \frac{2}{7})$

12 $2\frac{2}{5} \times 1\frac{1}{6} \div (1\frac{1}{2} + 1\frac{3}{10})$

13 $(1\frac{1}{7} \times 1\frac{3}{4}) + 1\frac{1}{12}$

14 $3\frac{1}{6} + (\frac{1}{3} \times 6\frac{1}{4})$

15 $\frac{x}{2} + \left(\frac{7}{x} \times \frac{x^2}{21}\right)$

16 $\left(\frac{1}{a} + \frac{1}{2a}\right) \times \frac{a}{6}$

17 $2\frac{1}{9} \times 6\frac{3}{7} \div \frac{5}{14}$

18 $(\frac{5}{8} + \frac{5}{12}) \div (\frac{7}{15} + \frac{11}{30})$

19 $(1\frac{2}{3} + 3\frac{3}{8}) \times (2\frac{1}{3} + 1\frac{6}{11})$

20 $8\frac{1}{4} - (2\frac{3}{4} + 4\frac{2}{3})$

21 What fraction of £1·40 is 42p?

22 What fraction of 4·5 is 0·75?

23 What fraction of $5\frac{5}{6}$ is $5\frac{1}{4}$?

24 What fraction of 4·25 m is 1·75 m?

25 What fraction of 14·4 g is 9·6 g?

26 What fraction of $3\frac{1}{2}$ m is 21 cm?

27 What fraction of 4 litres is 600 cm³?

Complex fractions These are fractions in which the numerator, or the denominator, or both, are fractions; for example, $\dfrac{\frac{3}{4}}{\frac{5}{7}}$ and $\dfrac{2\frac{1}{2}}{3 \times 3\frac{3}{4}}$.

We have already considered an expression such as $\dfrac{\frac{3}{4}}{\frac{5}{7}}$; the rule is to turn $\frac{5}{7}$ the other way up and multiply:

Thus $\qquad\qquad \dfrac{\frac{3}{4}}{\frac{5}{7}} = \frac{3}{4} \times \frac{7}{5} = \frac{21}{20}.$

If the denominator of the complex fraction contains the product of several fractions, these should all be turned the other way up, as the next example illustrates.

Example 4   *Simplify* $\dfrac{3\frac{1}{9} \times 3\frac{1}{2}}{4\frac{2}{3} \times \frac{2}{5}}.$

The expression $= \dfrac{\frac{28}{9} \times \frac{7}{2}}{\frac{14}{3} \times \frac{2}{5}}$

$\qquad\qquad = \dfrac{\overset{}{28}}{9} \times \frac{7}{2} \times \frac{3}{\underset{}{14}} \times \frac{5}{2}$
$\qquad\qquad\quad\; 3$

$\qquad\qquad = \frac{35}{6} = 5\frac{5}{6}.$

Example 5 *Simplify* $\dfrac{12\frac{1}{3}+4\frac{1}{6}}{\frac{11}{16}\times 2\frac{1}{4}}$.

$$\text{The expression}=\dfrac{16\frac{2+1}{6}}{\frac{11}{16}\times\frac{9}{4}}$$

$$=\dfrac{16\frac{1}{2}}{\frac{11}{16}\times\frac{9}{4}}$$

$$=\dfrac{\frac{33}{2}}{\frac{11}{16}\times\frac{9}{4}}$$

$$=\dfrac{\overset{3}{\cancel{33}}\times 16\times\overset{2}{\cancel{4}}}{\underset{}{\cancel{2}}\times\cancel{11}\times\underset{3}{\cancel{9}}}$$

$$=\tfrac{32}{3}=10\tfrac{2}{3}.$$

Example 6 *Simplify* $2\frac{2}{3}+(3\frac{1}{7}\times 2\frac{4}{5})$.

The bracket, as we have seen, indicates that $3\frac{1}{7}\times 2\frac{4}{5}$ must be done first, and the result added to $2\frac{2}{3}$. However, do not take the bracket separately by itself, but keep the whole expression together and set the work out as follows:

$$\text{The expression}=2\tfrac{2}{3}+\left(\dfrac{22}{\cancel{7}}\times\dfrac{\overset{2}{\cancel{14}}}{5}\right)$$

$$=2\tfrac{2}{3}+\tfrac{44}{5}$$

$$=2\tfrac{2}{3}+8\tfrac{4}{5}$$

$$=10\tfrac{10+12}{15}$$

$$=10\tfrac{22}{15}=11\tfrac{7}{15}.$$

If the fractions contain letters, they are dealt with in the same way as if they contain only numbers.

Example 7 *Simplify* $\dfrac{1}{2a}+\dfrac{2}{3a}+\dfrac{1}{6a}$.

$$\text{The expression}=\dfrac{3+4+1}{6a}$$

$$=\dfrac{8}{6a}$$

$$=\dfrac{4}{3a}.$$

EXERCISE 78

Find the values of:

1 $7\frac{7}{12} - 2\frac{2}{15} + 3\frac{1}{6}$

2 $\dfrac{\frac{3}{5} \times 2\frac{1}{2}}{1\frac{1}{2} \times \frac{9}{10}}$

3 $\frac{2}{3} + (\frac{1}{4} \times \frac{8}{9} \times \frac{3}{7})$

4 $\dfrac{\frac{1}{4} + \frac{1}{9}}{\frac{2}{3} - \frac{1}{8}}$

5 $\dfrac{1\frac{1}{4}}{1\frac{1}{2} \times \frac{1}{6}}$

6 $\dfrac{3\frac{7}{8} - 2\frac{3}{4}}{5\frac{5}{8} + 3\frac{3}{4}}$

7 $2\frac{1}{4} + 3\frac{1}{7} - 1\frac{1}{2}$

8 $\dfrac{0.03 \times 0.05}{0.15}$

9 $\dfrac{1\frac{3}{4} - \frac{2}{3} - \frac{1}{5} + \frac{1}{15}}{\frac{1}{3} + \frac{1}{5}}$

10 $\dfrac{2\frac{1}{2} + 1\frac{2}{3}}{2\frac{1}{2} - 1\frac{2}{3}}$

11 $\dfrac{\frac{3}{5} \times 7\frac{1}{2}}{4\frac{1}{2} \times \frac{5}{12}}$

12 $4(\frac{2}{3} + \frac{1}{4} + \frac{3}{5})$

13 $3a + \frac{a}{5} - \frac{a}{3}$

14 $\frac{5a}{2} - \frac{3a}{2} + 4\frac{1}{3}a$

15 $\frac{x}{2} + \frac{x}{3} + \frac{x}{4} + \frac{x}{6}$

16 $\frac{2a^2}{b} \times \frac{b}{4a}$

17 $2\frac{5}{8} \times (2\frac{9}{14} - 1\frac{3}{7})$

18 $\frac{4}{5} \times (3\frac{1}{2} - 1\frac{5}{8})$

19 $\frac{2}{3} + 2(\frac{1}{4} \text{ of } 1\frac{7}{9})$

20 $\dfrac{1\frac{5}{8} + \frac{1}{8}}{\frac{7}{10} - \frac{1}{4}}$

21 $\frac{3a}{7b} \times \frac{35b}{6}$

22 $\frac{2}{3x} + \frac{1}{x} - \frac{1}{4x}$

23 $\dfrac{100 \times 121\frac{1}{2}}{4\frac{1}{2} \times 2\frac{1}{2}}$

24 $\dfrac{4\frac{1}{5} - \frac{5}{9}}{2\frac{2}{3} + 1\frac{3}{7} - \frac{2}{5}}$

25 $\frac{1}{xy} + \frac{1}{x^2}$

26 $\dfrac{3\frac{5}{8} + 2\frac{3}{4} - 4\frac{1}{16}}{3\frac{1}{12} \times 2\frac{2}{5} \times \frac{2}{5}}$

27 $\dfrac{\frac{3}{4} \times (2\frac{1}{2} + \frac{2}{3})}{\frac{3}{4} + \frac{1}{12}}$

28 $\dfrac{3\frac{1}{7} - 2\frac{1}{3}}{3\frac{1}{7} \times 9\frac{11}{12}}$

29 $\dfrac{2\frac{1}{14} + 3\frac{1}{2} - \frac{1}{7}}{3\frac{1}{7} - 2\frac{3}{5}}$

30 $2\frac{7}{12} + \dfrac{6\frac{1}{6} - 3\frac{2}{3}}{1\frac{1}{3}}$

31 $\dfrac{1 - \frac{1}{2} + \frac{1}{3} - \frac{1}{4}}{\frac{1}{5} - \frac{1}{6}}$

32 $\dfrac{5\frac{2}{3} - 4\frac{1}{4}}{1\frac{3}{5} + 3\frac{1}{2} - 1\frac{7}{10}}$

33 $\dfrac{1\frac{2}{7} \times (6\frac{4}{7} - 3\frac{11}{14})}{4\frac{1}{3}}$

34 $\frac{4}{3} \times 2\frac{2}{7} \times (\frac{7}{8})^2$

35 $\dfrac{(\frac{1}{2} + \frac{3}{26}) \times \frac{13}{36}}{(\frac{1}{5} + \frac{1}{3}) \times \frac{2}{9}}$

36 $\dfrac{3\frac{2}{3} - 2\frac{5}{6}}{3\frac{2}{3} + 3\frac{5}{6}}$

37 $\dfrac{2\frac{2}{9} + 2\frac{2}{3}}{(\frac{2}{9} + \frac{7}{18}) \times 1\frac{1}{3}}$

31. RATIO

In order to understand a model aeroplane or ship, you always need to know what scale is used. If the scale is described as $\frac{1}{50}$, it means that 1 cm length in the model represents 50 cm length in the actual object; or, in other words, any length in the model is $\frac{1}{50}$ of the corresponding length in the aeroplane or ship.

Another example of a scale is the Representative Fraction of a map (see page 134). We said that this is $\frac{1}{100\,000}$ for a map which is 1 cm to 1 km, meaning that every length on the map is $\frac{1}{100\,000}$ of the corresponding length on the ground.

The sizes of two quantities are often compared by saying what fraction the first is of the second. This fraction is called the **ratio** of the two quantities. The ratio of a to b is written $a:b$.

Thus the ratio $a:b$ is expressed by the fraction $\dfrac{a}{b}$.

This fraction should be reduced to its lowest terms, but it is sometimes convenient to express it in the form $\dfrac{n}{1}$ or $\dfrac{1}{n}$. In the case of maps, the R.F. is always in the form $1:n$ or $\dfrac{1}{n}$.

Notice that the two quantities must be of the same kind, and when we form the ratio of one to the other they must be expressed in the same units.

Example 1 *Express the ratio of 90 g to $1\frac{1}{2}$ kg in its simplest form.*

$$\frac{90\text{ g}}{1\frac{1}{2}\text{ kg}} = \frac{90}{1500} = \frac{3}{50}.$$

Hence 90 g is $\dfrac{3}{50}$ of $1\frac{1}{2}$ kg and $1\frac{1}{2}$ kg is $\dfrac{50}{3}$ of 90 g.

Example 2 *Express the ratio of 27p to 90p in the form $n:1$.*

$$\frac{27\text{p}}{90\text{p}} = \frac{27}{90} = \frac{3}{10} = 0\cdot3:1.$$

EXERCISE 79 (Oral)

Express the following ratios as fractions in their lowest terms:

1 9 cm : 12 cm   **2** 12p : 30p   **3** 1 m : 1 km

4 30 : 40   **5** 10 : 5   **6** $1\frac{1}{2} : 2\frac{1}{2}$

7 3 mg : 3 g   **8** 84p : £1   **9** 400 g : 4 kg

10 0·4 : 1   **11** 1 cm : 1 m   **12** 300 cm³ : 1 litre

13 If $a : b = \frac{3}{4}$, what fraction is a of b? By what number must a be multiplied to give b?

14 If $x : y = \frac{2}{3}$, x is how many times y? y is how many times x?

15 If $a = \frac{3}{5}b$, what is the ratio $a : b$? What is the ratio $b : a$?

16 What fraction of 15 is 12? What is the ratio 12 : 15?

17 If $P : Q = \frac{7}{10}$, by what number must Q be multiplied to give P? What multiplier makes P into Q?

EXERCISE 80

Simplify the following ratios, expressing them as fractions in their simplest forms:

1 £1 : £1·12$\frac{1}{2}$ **2** 1 m² : 600 cm²

3 10 : 1·2   **4** 0·25 : 1·5

5 28p : £2·10   **6** 32 mm : 80 cm

7 50 m per sec : 30 km per min   **8** 240 g : 2 kg

9 £3·63 : £4·62   **10** 2 tonnes : 450 kg

11 $\frac{3}{4} : \frac{5}{6}$ **12** $\frac{2}{3} : \frac{3}{4}$

13 A school contains 280 boys and 175 girls. Find the ratio of the number of girls to the number of boys. Find also the ratio of the number of girls to the total number of pupils.

14 The sides of two squares are 6 cm, 10 cm long. Find (i) the ratio of their sides, (ii) the ratio of their perimeters, (iii) the ratio of their areas.

15 The edges of two cubes are 4 cm, 6 cm. Find (i) the ratio of their edges, (ii) the ratio of the area of a face of the first to that of a face of the second, (iii) the ratio of their volumes.

16 A rectangle is 3 cm long and 2 cm wide. A second rectangle is 9 cm long and 6 cm wide. Find the ratio of the area of the first to that of the second.

17 If a map is drawn to the scale of 10 cm to a kilometre, find the Representative Fraction (i.e. the ratio of a length on the map to the corresponding length on the ground).

18 The R.F. of a map of England and Wales is $1:2\,000\,000$. How many kilometres does 1 cm on the map represent?

19 A map of Lancashire and Yorkshire has a R.F. of $1:500\,000$. What is the distance on the map between two towns 26·5 km apart?

Express the following ratios in the form $n:1$, giving n correct to two decimal places:

20 2·2 : 0·5   **21** 1 : 0·0625   **22** 12 : 15
23 450 m : 1½ km   **24** 7 : 9   **25** 1·75 : 4·25

Express the following ratios in the form $1:n$:

26 2 : 8·3   **27** 1 cm : 1 km   **28** 40 cm : 1 km

29 A map is drawn on a scale of $1:200\,000$. How many km^2 is the area represented on the map by 1 cm^2?

30 It is 320 km from London to Bolton. What will be the length of the line joining these two places on a map of England which has a R.F. of $1:2\,000\,000$?

31 Two towns are known to be 57 km apart. On a map the line joining them is 5·7 cm long. Find the scale of the map, (i) in km to the cm, (ii) as a R.F.

32 A map is drawn on the scale of 1 cm to 2 km. What is its R.F.?

33 On a map drawn to the scale of 1 cm to 10 km, a certain county has an area of 3·75 cm^2. What is the true area of the county? (First think how many square km on the ground are represented by 1 cm^2 on the map.)

34 The R.F. of a map is 1 : 50 000. What is the distance in kilometres between two places which are 4·8 cm apart on the map?

35 The scale of a map is 10 cm to 1 km. What is its R.F., and what length on the map will represent 3·8 km?

36 The R.F. of a map is $\frac{1}{n}$. Find the distance apart in kilometres of two places which are x cm apart on the map.

Ratio of two lengths If AB and CD are two lines, and AB = 6 cm, CD = 8 cm, the ratio AB : CD = 6 : 8 = 3 : 4 or $\frac{3}{4}$.

You might think at first that the ratio of the lengths of two lines could always be expressed as the ratio of two whole numbers; e.g. if AB = 1·67 cm and CD = 1·96 cm, then

$$AB : CD = \frac{1\cdot67}{1\cdot96} = \frac{167}{196}.$$

But we cannot always do this. For example, the ratio of the length of the side of a square to the length of the diagonal cannot be expressed in this simple way. However, we shall assume in what follows that the ratio of two lengths can be expressed in the form $\frac{p}{q}$, where p and q are whole numbers.

If AB : CD = 5 : 3, we can represent the lines as in Fig. 197, and the statement means that if AB is divided into five equal parts, CD will contain three of the same equal parts.

Division of a straight line in a given ratio Suppose AB is a straight line. The pieces into which P divides AB are AP and PB.

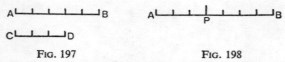

FIG. 197   FIG. 198

P will divide AB in the ratio 3 : 4, i.e. AP : PB = 3 : 4, provided AP = 3 parts and PB = 4 equal parts, as in Fig. 198. There are thus 7 equal parts in the whole line AB.

Thus to *calculate* the lengths AP and PB, we should have to divide the whole line AB by 7, and give 3 of these parts to AP and 4 of these parts to PB.

The intercept theorem provides us with a method of finding AP and PB by *construction*, without any calculation. This would often be preferable, especially if 7 did not happen to divide exactly into the length of AB.

Example 3   *Draw a straight line* AB 8 *cm long, and divide it in the ratio* 3 : 4.

Draw the line AB, 8 cm long.

Draw through A a straight line AX.

Along AX mark off 7 equal intervals, as in Fig. 199.

Join the last point of division to B, and through the third

FIG. 199

point of division draw a parallel to this line.

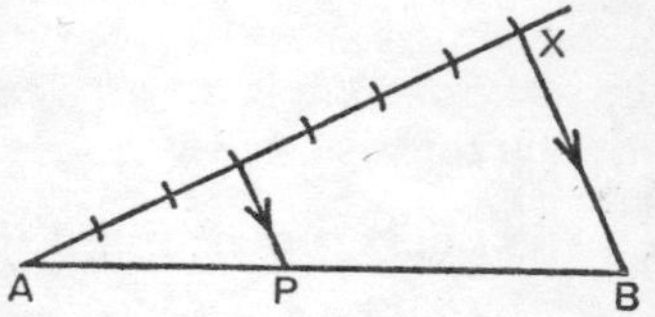

Let the parallel meet AB at P.

Then AP : PB = 3 : 4.

Division in a certain ratio.   To divide any quantity in a certain ratio, the method is the same as the calculation of AP and PB above.

Example 4   *Divide £35 between two people in the ratio* 3 : 4.

Since 3 + 4 = 7, we divide £35 into 7 equal parts.

Each part = £5.

∴ the first person receives $3 \times £5 = £15.$⎤
The second receives $4 \times £5 = £20.$⎦

Proportional parts   When we say that a, b, c are proportional to 2, 3, 4, we mean that

$$a : b = 2 : 3,$$
$$b : c = 3 : 4,$$

and $a : c = 2 : 4.$

This fact is written more shortly

$$a : b : c = 2 : 3 : 4.$$

As in the case of the ratio of two quantities, we can simplify ratios like $a:b:c$ by multiplying or dividing each term by the same number;

e.g. $8:12:16=2:3:4$ (dividing each term by 4),
and $\frac{3}{8}:\frac{1}{2}:\frac{1}{4}=3:4:2$ (multiplying each term by 8).

Example 5 *Divide £144 into 3 shares in the ratios* $4:7:5$.

$$4+7+5=16.$$
$$£144 \div 16 = £9.$$

$\therefore$ the first share is $4 \times £9 = £36,$
the second share is $7 \times £9 = £63,$
and the third share is $5 \times £9 = £45.$

(As a check, notice that $£36 + £63 + £45 = £144$.)

Example 6 *If* $x:y=5:7$ *and* $y:z=9:11$, *find three whole numbers proportional to* x, y, z.

The quantity which occurs in both the given ratios is y.

$\therefore$ the same number must represent y in both statements, and this number must be the L.C.M. of 7 and 9, i.e. 63.

Hence $x:y=5:7=45:63,$
and $y:z=9:11=63:77;$
$\therefore \; x:y:z=45:63:77.$

EXERCISE 81

1 Divide 60 cm in the ratio: (i) $5:1$, (ii) $3:2$, (iii) $7:8$.

2 Divide £48 in the ratio: (i) $7:9$, (ii) $19:5$, (iii) $5:7$.

3 Divide £18 into three shares in the ratios: (i) $1:2:3$, (ii) $2:3:4$.

4 Divide £70 into three shares in the ratios: (i) $3:5:2$, (ii) $6:3:5$.

5 The perimeter of a triangle is 45 cm, and the lengths of the sides are in the ratios $2:3:4$. Find the lengths of the sides.

6 Express $\frac{1}{90}:\frac{1}{20}:\frac{1}{45}$ as a ratio of whole numbers.

7 Find three whole numbers proportional to 1·65 m, 99 cm and 2·31 m.

8 AB is a straight line 8·4 cm long, and the point P divides it so that $AP : PB = 2 : 3$. Find the length of AP by drawing and measurement, and check your answer by calculation.

9 AB is a straight line 6·2 cm long. Find by construction and measurement the distance from A of the point P which divides AB so that $AP : PB = 2 : 1$.

10 Draw a straight line AB 5·8 cm long, and find by construction the point X which divides AB in the ratio $5 : 3$. Measure AX.

11 If $a : b = 3 : 8$ and $b : c = 12 : 17$, find three whole numbers proportional to a, b and c.

12 If $x : y = 5 : 4$ and $y : z = 14 : 15$, calculate the ratio $x : z$.

13 If $A : B = 3 : 2$ and $B : C = 4 : 1$, and $A + B + C = 220$, find A.

14 Divide £26 into three shares in the ratios $\frac{1}{2} : \frac{1}{3} : \frac{1}{4}$.

15 The profits of a business amount to £950. If they are to be divided among three men in the ratios $1 : 2 : 2$, how much does each man receive?

16 If $a : b = 5 : 1$ and $b = 3c$, find the ratios $a : b : c$.

Increase and Decrease in a given ratio If the number of pupils in a school has increased from 400 to 500, the ratio of the present number to the old number $= 500 : 400 = 5 : 4$. We say that the number has been **increased in the ratio 5 : 4**; in other words, the present number is $\frac{5}{4}$ of the old number.

On the other hand, if the number in the school has fallen from 400 to 300, the ratio of the present number to the old $= 300 : 400 = 3 : 4$. We say that the number has been **decreased in the ratio 3 : 4**; in other words, the present number is $\frac{3}{4}$ of the old number.

The fraction by which the old number has to be multiplied to make the present number is called the **multiplying factor.**

New Quantity = Multiplying Factor × Old Quantity.

Example 7   *Increase* 27p *in the ratio* 4 : 3.

Increased value $= \frac{4}{3} \times 27p$
$= 36p.$

Example 8   *Decrease* 20 *cm in the ratio* 4 : 5.

Decreased length $= \frac{4}{5} \times 20$ cm
$= 16$ cm.

Example 9   *If the cost of an article is reduced from* 35p *to* 15p, *in what ratio is the cost reduced?*

New cost : old cost $= 15p : 35p$
$= 15 : 35$
$= 3 : 7.$

∴ the cost is reduced in the ratio 3 : 7.

Example 10   *The price of electricity is reduced from* 4p *per unit to* 3p *per unit in a certain area.   At the same time a man increases his consumption in the ratio* 5 : 4.   *In what ratio does the amount of his electricity bill alter?*

The cost per unit is reduced in the ratio 3 : 4.
This causes the amount of the bill to be multiplied by the factor $\frac{3}{4}$.
The number of units consumed is increased in the ratio 5 : 4.
This causes the amount of the bill to be multiplied by the factor $\frac{5}{4}$.

∴ the effect of both changes is to multiply the amount of the bill by $\frac{3}{4} \times \frac{5}{4}$, or $\frac{15}{16}$.
∴ the bill is reduced in the ratio 15 : 16.

EXERCISE 82

1 Increase 20 in the ratio 8 : 5.
2 Increase 24 cm in the ratio 4 : 3.
3 Increase 24p in the ratio 7 : 6.
4 Decrease 60p in the ratio 11 : 12.
5 Decrease 9 m in the ratio 9 : 10.

6 Increase £1·50 in the ratio 6 : 5.

7 What multiplying factor changes 48 into 60? In what ratio must 48 be increased to become 60?

8 What multiplying factor reduces 42p to 30p? In what ratio must 42p be reduced to become 30p?

9 In what ratio must 120 be reduced to become 100? In what ratio must 100 be increased to become 120?

10 The price of petrol rises from $7\frac{1}{2}$p to 9p per litre. In what ratio is the price increased?

11 The price of an article falls from 54p to 45p. In what ratio is the price reduced?

12 A number is made half as large again. In what ratio is it increased?

13 A shopkeeper reduced the price of every article in the shop by 20p in the £. In what ratio are the prices reduced? What would be the new prices of articles previously costing £1·65 and £2·80?

14 A man reduces the quantity of tobacco he smokes by $\frac{3}{10}$ of the amount. In what ratio does he reduce it?

15 The price of tobacco is increased in the ratio 7 : 5, and so a man reduces the quantity he smokes in the ratio 5 : 6. In what ratio is his expenditure on tobacco increased or decreased?

16 A shop raises its prices by one quarter. In what ratio are the prices increased? In what ratio must the prices then be decreased in order to bring them back to their original level?

What fraction of the increased prices should be taken off in order to bring them back to their original level?

17 A family are in the habit of spending 72p a week on a certain commodity. The price goes up in the ratio 5 : 4, but at the same time the family reduce their consumption in the ratio 5 : 6. How much will they spend on that commodity in a week in future?

18 A man's salary goes up from £1280 to £1400. In what ratio is his salary increased? If he subsequently receives a reduction in salary of £100, in what ratio is his salary reduced?

Equal Ratios   In Fig. 200, AB is divided at P in the ratio
3 : 4, and PQ is drawn parallel to BC
to meet AC at Q.

Now AP contains three equal parts
and PB contains four of the same
parts.

Through the points of division,
draw parallels to BC. These

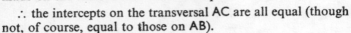

FIG. 200

parallels will all be the same distance apart, for the intercepts
made on the transversal AB are all equal.

∴ the intercepts on the transversal AC are all equal (though
not, of course, equal to those on AB).

∴ AQ contains three equal parts and QC contains four of
the same parts;

$$\therefore AQ : QC = 3 : 4.$$

The same argument could be used whatever the ratio in
which P divides AB.   Hence we can say that

**A straight line parallel to one side of a triangle divides the
other sides in the same ratio.**

In Fig. 200, what are the values of the ratios: (i) AP : AB,
(ii) PB : AB, (iii) BP : PA?   Compare these ratios with the
ratios: (i) AQ : AC, (ii) QC : AC, (iii) CQ : QA.

Notice that the Mid-point Theorem (see p. 180) is a special
case of the property shown above.   For if P and Q are the
mid-points of AB and AC, then

$$AP : PC = 1 : 1 \quad \text{and} \quad AQ : QC = 1 : 1.$$

PQ divides AB and AC in the same ratios, and so PQ must
be parallel to BC.

EXERCISE 83

1 In Fig. 201, if AB = 3 cm, AC = 2·5 cm, AP = 1·8 cm, find
the ratio AQ : QC, and hence calculate AQ.

2 In Fig. 201, if AB = 1·8 cm, AC = 1·2 cm, AQ = 0·7 cm, find
the ratio AP : PB, and hence calculate AP.

3 In Fig. 201, if AP=1·8 cm, PB=2·4 cm, AC=3·5 cm, find AQ.

4 In Fig. 201, if AP=4·2 cm, AB=6·3 cm, AC=7·2 cm, find AQ.

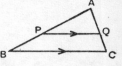

FIG. 201

5 P, Q are points on the sides AB, AC of △ABC; AP=7·5 cm, PB=4·5 cm, AQ=3 cm, QC=1·8 cm. Show that PQ is parallel to BC.

6 In the triangle PQR, QR : RP : PQ=5 : 6 : 7. If PQ=1·4 cm, find QR and RP.

7 In Fig. 202, OP : PA=3 : 2. If OC=4·5 cm, find OR.

8 In Fig. 202, OP=1·4 cm, PA=0·6 cm and OC=1·2 cm. Find OR.

9 In Fig. 202, OR=4 cm, OC=6 cm, OB=9 cm, OA=12 cm. Find OQ and OP.

10 In Fig. 202, OP=3 cm, OA=4 cm, OB=3·6 cm, OC=2·8 cm. Find OQ and OR.

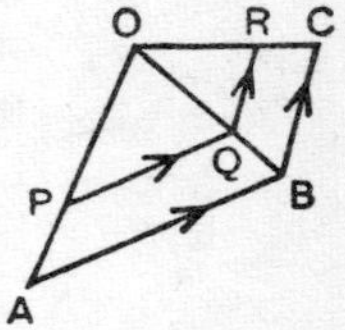

11 Draw △ABC in which AB=6 cm, BC=7 cm and CA=8 cm. Mark any point O inside the triangle, and join O to A, B and C. Find by construction the mid-points X, Y, Z of OA, OB, OC respectively. What do you notice about the triangle XYZ?

FIG. 202

12 Repeat No. 11, but take the point O *outside* the triangle ABC.

13 Draw a triangle ABC in which AB=7·5 cm, ∠A=48° and ∠B=56°. Mark any point O inside the triangle, and join it to A, B, C. Find by construction: (i) the point X in OA such that OX : XA=1 : 2; (ii) the point Y in OB such that OY : YB=1 : 2; (iii) the point Z in OC such that OZ : ZC=1 : 2. Draw the triangle XYZ, and measure ∠YXZ, ∠XYZ and XY. What do you notice about the triangle XYZ?

14 Repeat No. 13, but take the point O *outside* the triangle ABC.

32. DIRECT AND INVERSE PROPORTION

Refer again to the worked examples on Unitary Method, p. 54. Example 1 deals with the cost of a number of metres of cloth. Now if we double the number of metres, we double the cost; if we halve the number of metres we halve the cost. This is called **direct proportion.** The next worked example deals with the number of eggs which could be purchased, at a fixed price, for a sum of money. This, too, is an example of direct proportion, for double the money would buy double the number of eggs.

We will now set out the same examples, worked by the ratio method instead of by unitary method.

Example 1   *If 4 m of cloth cost* 180p, *what is the cost of* 11 *m*?

The number of metres is increased in the ratio $\frac{11}{4}$.

∴ the cost is increased in the ratio $\frac{11}{4}$.

∴ the cost $= \frac{11}{4} \times 180p = 11 \times 45p = 495p$.

Example 2   *If 10 eggs cost* 25p, *how many eggs can be bought for* 65p?

The sum of money is increased in the ratio $\frac{65p}{25p} = \frac{13}{5}$.

∴ the number of eggs is increased in the ratio $\frac{13}{5}$.

∴ the number of eggs $= \frac{13}{5} \times 10 = 26$.

A direct proportion graph is always a straight line. Examples of these have already been given on p. 167. Fig. 158 is a graph showing the distances a man walks in different times at the same rate. In twice the time, he walks twice as far; in three times the time, he walks three times as far, and so on. Fig. 160 is a graph showing how the length of the spring depends upon the load; twice as big a load produces twice the extension of the spring beyond 10 cm, three times as big a load produces three times the extension beyond 10 cm, and so on.

Now look at the worked examples on p. 56. Example 3

deals with the number of men working on a certain job and the number of days they take. If we double the number of men, we should halve the number of days taken; if we halve the number of men, we should double the number of days taken. This is called **inverse proportion.** The next worked example deals with the number of men in a camp and the number of days the stock of food will last. This, too, is an example of inverse proportion, for twice as many men would eat up the food in half as many days, whereas half as many men would eat it in twice as many days.

Here are the same examples worked by the ratio method instead of by unitary method.

Example 3 *If* 8 *men can do a piece of work in* 5 *days, in how many days will* 10 *men do the work?*

The number of men is increased in the ratio $\frac{10}{8}$.

∴ the number of days is decreased in the ratio $\frac{8}{10}$.

∴ the number of days $= \frac{8}{10} \times 5 = 4$ days.

Example 4 *The stock of food in a camp would last* 12 *men for* 10 *days. How many men could live for* 8 *days on the same stock?*

The number of days is decreased in the ratio $\frac{8}{10}$.

∴ the number of men is increased in the ratio $\frac{10}{8}$.

∴ the number of men $= \frac{10}{8} \times 12 = 15$ men.

The ratio in which one of the two quantities involved is increased or decreased may not be so simple as in the foregoing worked examples, but the method is the same.

Example 5 *If* $6\frac{1}{4}$ *tons of coal cost* £58, *find the cost of* $7\frac{1}{2}$ *tons at the same rate.*

The number of tons is increased in the ratio $\dfrac{7\frac{1}{2}}{6\frac{1}{4}}$.

∴ the cost is increased in the ratio $\dfrac{7\frac{1}{2}}{6\frac{1}{4}}$.

∴ the cost $= \dfrac{7\frac{1}{2}}{6\frac{1}{4}} \times £58$

$$= £\frac{\overset{3}{15} \times \overset{2}{4} \times 58}{\underset{5}{\cancel{2} \times \cancel{25}}} = £\frac{348}{5} = £69 \cdot 60.$$

EXERCISE 84

1 If 200 g of a substance costs £6·50, what will 280 g cost?

2 If 1·6 cm³ of a substance weigh 3·64 g, find the weight of 10 cm³.

3 If a kg of a substance costs £b, how many kg can be bought for x pence?

4 A field holds 81 sheep, allowing $2\frac{3}{4}$ m² for each sheep. How many sheep will it hold if only $2\frac{1}{4}$ m² are allowed for each sheep?

5 A cycle wheel turns 27 times in $67\frac{1}{2}$ m. How many times will it turn in 1000 m?

6 If 22 men can do a piece of work in $13\frac{1}{2}$ hours, how many men would be required to do the same work in $8\frac{1}{4}$ hours?

7 If p men take a hours for a certain job, how long should q men take?

8 A piece of road 928 m long costs £1155 to repair. Find the cost of repairing a piece of the same road 836 m long.

9 A metal bar 42 cm long weighs 1·5 kg. Find to the nearest gramme the weight of a bar 72 cm long and of the same metal.

10 A factory has enough coal in stock to last for 10 weeks if it uses $2\frac{1}{4}$ tons per week. How many weeks would the coal last if the factory used only $1\frac{1}{2}$ tons per week.

11 If 32 cm of ribbon cost 24p, find the cost of 44 cm.

12 A train travelling at an average speed of 64 km per hour can do a certain journey in 4 hours. How long would the same journey take at an average speed of 80 km per hour?

13 If 134·4 kg of a substance cost £3·15, find the cost of 96 kg.

14 If 20 m of cloth cost £4·80, find the cost of $32\frac{1}{2}$ m.

15 If x metres of cloth cost y pence, find the cost (i) in pence, (ii) in pounds, of p metres.

16 A car travels d km in x hours. How far does it travel in y hours at the same speed?

17 A train takes x hours for a certain journey when travelling at an average speed of a km per hour. How long would it take for the same journey at an average speed of b km per hour?

Hitherto we have had questions where one variable depended on another, sometimes in direct proportion and sometimes in inverse proportion. We shall now consider some cases where one variable depends on two or more variables. This is called **compound proportion.**

Example 6 *If 13 men earn £546 in 3 weeks, in what time will 18 men earn £630 if paid at the same rate?*

The number of men is increased in the ratio $\frac{18}{13}$.

∴ the time to earn a given sum is decreased in the ratio $\frac{13}{18}$.

Also the total wages are increased in the ratio $\frac{630}{546}$.

∴ the time to earn those wages is increased in the ratio $\frac{630}{546}$.

Now 13 men earn £546 in 3 weeks.

∴ 18 men earn £630 in $3 \times \frac{13}{18} \times \frac{630}{546}$ weeks

$$= 3 \times \frac{13}{18} \times \frac{630}{546} \text{ weeks} = 2\tfrac{1}{2} \text{ weeks}.$$

Example 7 *If 32 tons can be carried 28 km for £12, what should be the charge for carrying 40 tons a distance of 42 km at the same rate?*

The number of tons is increased in the ratio $\frac{40}{32}$.

∴ the charge is increased in the ratio $\frac{40}{32}$.

The distance is increased in the ratio $\frac{42}{28}$.

∴ the charge is increased in the ratio $\frac{42}{28}$.

Now the charge for carrying 32 tons for 28 km = £12.

∴ the charge for carrying 40 tons for 42 km

$$= £12 \times \frac{40}{32} \times \frac{42}{28}$$

$$= £12 \times \frac{40}{32} \times \frac{42}{28} = £22\tfrac{1}{2} = £22 \cdot 50.$$

EXERCISE 85

1 A carpet 12 m long, 9 m wide costs £180.   Find the cost of a carpet of the same quality 15 m long and 7 m wide.

2 If 1000 kg of potatoes last 70 people for 30 days, how long would 700 kg last 50 people?

3 If 13 men earn £400 in 2 weeks, in what time will 9 men earn £1500?

4 If 15 horses eat 9 sacks of corn in 14 days, for how many days will 33 sacks feed 21 horses?

5 If 9 men can dig a trench 8 m long in 24 h, how many men should dig a trench 28 m long in 36 h?

6 If 3 fires burn $3\frac{1}{2}$ tonnes of coal in 28 days, in how many days will 12 fires burn 4 tonnes at the same rate?

7 If 20 men can do a piece of work in 9 days, how long will it take 15 men to do half as much again?

8 If 12 men working 8 h a day can do a piece of work in 15 days, how many hours a day must 20 men work in order to do it in 8 days?

9 If 13 men can dig a trench 30 m long in 24 days, how many men will be required to dig a trench 45 m long at the same rate in 39 days?

10 5 men dig 130 m of a trench in 12 days.   How long would it take 2 men to dig 39 m at the same rate?

11 If the wages of 7 men in 16 days, working 10 h a day, amount to £340, find the wages of 6 men in 14 days, working 8 h a day, if a man's wages are proportional to the number of hours worked.

12 The weight of a piece of wood 2 m long and $1\frac{1}{2}$ m wide is 40 kg.   Find the weight of a piece of the same kind of wood 3 m long, $1\frac{3}{4}$ m wide and three times as thick.

13 If p kg can be carried a km for £x, find the cost of carrying q kg a distance of b km.

14 If x men earn £P in t weeks, in how many weeks will y men earn £Q if they are paid at the same rate?

33. POWERS AND EASY FRACTIONS

Multiplication of powers

You have already learned that

$$x^2 = x \times x,$$
$$x^3 = x \times x \times x,$$
$$x^4 = x \times x \times x \times x,$$

and so on.

We call x^2, x^3, x^4, etc., **powers** of x, and the numbers 2, 3, 4, etc. are the **indices**.

To see how to multiply powers of x, notice that

$$x^2 \times x^3 = x \times x \times x \times x \times x = x^5,$$
and $\qquad x^3 \times x^5 = x \times x \times x \times x \times x \times x \times x \times x = x^8.$

The rule is evidently

To multiply two different powers of x, add the indices.

Division of powers

Again, $\quad x^5 \div x^3 = \dfrac{x^5}{x^3} = \dfrac{x \times x \times x \times x \times x}{x \times x \times x} = x^2,$

and $\qquad x^6 \div x^3 = \dfrac{x^6}{x^3} = \dfrac{x \times x \times x \times x \times x \times x}{x \times x \times x} = x^3.$

The rule is

To divide two powers of x, subtract the indices.

Example 1 *Simplify:* (i) $6x^5 \times 2x^4$, (ii) $10x^8 \div 5x^4$.

(i) $6x^5 \times 2x^4 = 6 \times 2 \times x^5 \times x^4$
$$= 12 \times x^9 = 12x^9.$$

(ii) $10x^8 \div 5x^4 = \dfrac{10x^8}{5x^4} = 2x^4.$

Example 2 *Reduce the fraction* $\dfrac{16x^2}{24x^6}$ *to its lowest terms.*

Divide numerator and denominator by $8x^2$.

$$\frac{16x^2}{24x^6} = \frac{2}{3x^4}.$$

EXERCISE 86

Simplify:

1 $x^3 \times x^4$	**2** $a^2 \times a^5$	**3** $y^4 \times y$	**4** $b^3 \times b^3$
5 $(x^4)^2$	**6** $(x^2)^4$	**7** $t^6 \div t^2$	**8** $x^{12} \div x^4$
9 $2x^2 \times 3x^3$	**10** $2a^3 \times 4a^5$	**11** $3x \times 3x^4$	**12** $2a^2 \times 5a^4$
13 $3b^4 \times 4b^3$	**14** $9x^3 \div 3x$	**15** $25a^4 \div 5a^2$	**16** $21x^3 \div 7x$
17 $15x^{15} \div 5x^5$	**18** $8y^5 \div 4y^4$	**19** $63x^7 \div 9x^4$	**20** $3x^5 \times 8x^4$
21 $(4a^2)^2$	**22** $(3y)^3$	**23** $5x^3 \times 8x$	**24** $3z^2 \times 5z^5$
25 $6x^4 \div 6x^2$	**26** $7p \times 3p^3$	**27** $\sqrt{36x^2}$	**28** $\sqrt{9x^6}$
29 $8a^3 \times 4a^3$	**30** $2x \times 3x^2 \times 4x^3$		**31** $5a \times 3a^4 \times 2a^2$
32 $\dfrac{24x^3}{12x}$	**33** $\dfrac{(4a^2)^2}{4a}$	**34** $\dfrac{6a^2 \times 2a^3}{12a}$	**35** $\sqrt{25x^4}$
36 $4x^3 \times 3x^2$	**37** $(2x)^3 \div 4x$	**38** $16x^6 \div 2x^3$	**39** $6y^4 \div 2y^3$
40 $\dfrac{10b^6}{15b^2}$	**41** $\dfrac{8a^3}{16a}$	**42** $\dfrac{9x^4}{12x^5}$	**43** $\dfrac{12y^2}{16y^4}$

H.C.F. and L.C.M.

The method for finding H.C.F. and L.C.M. when the expressions contain letters as well as numbers is the same as we used in § 1.   Consider the two expressions $12a^2bc$, $15a^3b^2$.

$$12a^2bc = 2^2 \times 3 \times a \times a \times b \times c.$$
$$15a^3b^2 = 3 \times 5 \times a \times a \times a \times b \times b.$$

Both expressions have 3, a^2 and b as factors, so **$3a^2b$** is called **the H.C.F.**   It is made up of all the common factors of the two expressions.   It divides into the first expression $4c$ times, and into the second expression $5ab$ times.

Both expressions are contained an exact number of times in $2^2 \times 3 \times 5 \times a^3 \times b^2 \times c$, or $60a^3b^2c$.   We therefore call **$60a^3b^2c$ the L.C.M.**   This L.C.M. contains the first expression $5ab$ times and the second expression $4c$ times.

Reduction of fractions

Example 3 *Simplify* $\dfrac{42x^2y^3}{70x^3y}$.

We can cancel $\frac{42}{70}$ down to $\frac{3}{5}$.
The fraction then becomes

$$\frac{3x^2y^3}{5x^3y} = \frac{3y^2}{5x}.$$

EXERCISE 87

Find the H.C.F. of the following expressions, and state how many times each expression contains it.

1 $6x$, $3xy$ **2** $12x^2$, $16xy$ **3** $6x^3$, $8x^2y$ **4** $4x$, $8x^2$

5 $2xy$, xyz^2 **6** 24, $6xy$ **7** $10x^3$, $15x^2y^2$

8 $18p^2q$, $42pq$ **9** $20abc$, $10a^2b$ **10** $2xy$, $3z$

Find the L.C.M. of the following expressions, and state how many times each expression is contained in the L.C.M.

11 $4xy$, $12x^2y$ **12** $4xyz$, $14y^2z$ **13** $3ab$, $3abc$

14 $10x^3$, $15x^2y$ **15** $9a^3b$, $12a^2c^2$ **16** $2x^2$, $3x^3$, $4x^4$

17 4, $9x^2$, $2x^2y$ **18** $4xyz$, $6x^2z$ **19** $4a$, $20a^2b$

20 $3x^3$, $27x^4$ **21** $14x^2y^2$, $35x^3y$ **22** $10a^4$, $6a^3b$

Find the H.C.F. and the L.C.M. of:

23 $6x^2y^2$, $9xyz$, $12x^4y^2z^2$ **24** $12pq$, $10p^2$, $60pq^2$

25 $8xy$, $16yx$, $4y^2$ **26** $2a^6b^2$, $3a^3b$, $4a^2b^3$ **27** $4a^3$, $12b^3$

Simplify the following fractions:

28 $\dfrac{5a^3}{2a}$ **29** $\dfrac{15x^5}{5x}$ **30** $\dfrac{20x^5}{4x^4}$ **31** $\dfrac{20x^3}{24x^4}$ **32** $\dfrac{a^4b^3}{a^3b^4}$

33 $\dfrac{4x^2y}{8xy^2}$ **34** $\dfrac{2x^7}{4x^2}$ **35** $\dfrac{9x^4}{18x^2}$ **36** $\dfrac{3xy}{3x^2y}$ **37** $\dfrac{2x}{2x^2}$

38 $\dfrac{a^2xy}{ayz}$ **39** $\dfrac{2x^2y^2}{xy}$ **40** $\dfrac{4x^6y}{2x^3z}$ **41** $\dfrac{3ab}{a^3}$ **42** $\dfrac{6x^2y}{15xy^3}$

43 $\dfrac{8a^4b^3c^2}{12a^2b^4c}$ **44** $\dfrac{2x^3yz^2}{8xyz}$ **45** $\dfrac{x^5}{4x^4}$ **46** $\dfrac{21ab^3c}{56a^2c^2}$

47 $\dfrac{15p^4qr}{12pq^2r}$ **48** $\dfrac{3a^2bc}{6a}$ **49** $\dfrac{6x^2}{15x^3y}$ **50** $\dfrac{2x^2}{4xz}$

51 $\dfrac{21ab}{27a^4b^2}$ **52** $\dfrac{10x^{10}y^3}{25x^5y^6}$ **53** $\dfrac{6a^5b^6}{9a^3b^2}$ **54** $\dfrac{18pq^2}{45pq^3}$

Addition and subtraction of fractions

Example 4   *Simplify:*   (i) $\dfrac{3x}{2y}+\dfrac{4x}{5y}$, (ii) $\dfrac{15x}{7}-\dfrac{3x}{2}$.

$$\text{(i)} \quad \frac{3x}{2y}+\frac{4x}{5y}=\frac{15x}{10y}+\frac{8x}{10y}$$
$$=\frac{23x}{10y}.$$

(The L.C.M. of $2y$ and $5y$ is $10y$, so we put both fractions over $10y$. Now $2y$ into $10y$ is 5, so we have to multiply $3x$ by 5 in order to make the denominator $10y$. Again, $5y$ into $10y$ is 2, so we have to multiply $4x$ by 2.)

$$\text{(ii)} \quad \frac{15x}{7}-\frac{3x}{2}=\frac{30x}{14}-\frac{21x}{14}=\frac{9x}{14}.$$

(7 into 14 is 2, so we multiply $15x$ by 2. 2 into 14 is 7, so we multiply $3x$ by 7.)

EXERCISE 88

Simplify:

1 $\dfrac{x}{2}+\dfrac{x}{3}$ **2** $\dfrac{x}{2}+\dfrac{2x}{5}$ **3** $\dfrac{4x}{5}+\dfrac{3x}{10}$ **4** $\dfrac{2a}{3}+\dfrac{a}{6}$

5 $\dfrac{3x}{14}+\dfrac{5x}{7}$ **6** $\dfrac{x}{5}+\dfrac{x}{10}$ **7** $\dfrac{1}{x}+\dfrac{1}{2x}$ **8** $\dfrac{5}{x}+\dfrac{4}{3x}$

9 $\dfrac{1}{6x}+\dfrac{1}{2x}$ **10** $\dfrac{3a}{4}-\dfrac{2a}{3}$ **11** $\dfrac{7}{x}-\dfrac{3}{2x}$ **12** $\dfrac{4}{3x}-\dfrac{2}{5x}$

13 $\dfrac{3y}{7}-\dfrac{2y}{35}$ **14** $\dfrac{3x}{2}-\dfrac{x}{3}$ **15** $\dfrac{5}{2x^2}-\dfrac{1}{x^2}$ **16** $\dfrac{2x}{3}+\dfrac{5x}{6}$

17 $\dfrac{3}{x}+\dfrac{7}{3x}$ **18** $\dfrac{4}{x}+\dfrac{3}{5x}$ **19** $\dfrac{5}{x}+\dfrac{16}{3x}$ **20** $\dfrac{4a}{5}-\dfrac{2a}{3}$

21 $\dfrac{x}{3} + \dfrac{x}{7}$ **22** $\dfrac{1}{x} + \dfrac{2}{5x}$ **23** $\dfrac{3}{5a} - \dfrac{1}{10a}$ **24** $\dfrac{2}{3y} - \dfrac{1}{6y}$

25 $\dfrac{6}{2a} - \dfrac{10}{5a}$ **26** $\dfrac{5}{x} - \dfrac{3}{2x}$ **27** $\dfrac{1}{a} + \dfrac{2}{5a}$ **28** $\dfrac{1}{3y} + \dfrac{1}{6y}$

29 $\dfrac{7x}{10} + \dfrac{2x}{15}$ **30** $\dfrac{x}{4y} - \dfrac{x}{6y}$ **31** $\dfrac{a}{2} + \dfrac{a}{3} + \dfrac{a}{6}$ **32** $\dfrac{3x}{4} - \dfrac{x}{2}$

Multiplication and division of fractions

The method is the same as when we are dealing with numbers.

Example 5 *Multiply* $\dfrac{2x}{3y^3}$ *by* $\dfrac{6y^2}{x^3}$.

$$\frac{2x}{3y^3} \times \frac{6y^2}{x^3} = \frac{2 \times \cancel{x} \times \overset{2}{\cancel{6}} \times \cancel{y^2}}{\cancel{3} \times \underset{y}{\cancel{y^3}} \times \underset{x^2}{\cancel{x^3}}}$$

$$= \frac{4}{x^2 y}.$$

Example 6 *Divide* $\dfrac{21a^2}{16b^3}$ *by* $\dfrac{3a}{4b^2}$.

$$\frac{21a^2}{16b^3} \div \frac{3a}{4b^2} = \frac{21a^2}{16b^3} \times \frac{4b^2}{3a}$$

$$= \frac{\overset{7}{\cancel{21}} \times \overset{a}{\cancel{a^2}} \times \cancel{4} \times \overset{}{\cancel{b^2}}}{\underset{4}{\cancel{16}} \times \underset{b}{\cancel{b^3}} \times \cancel{3} \times \cancel{a}}$$

$$= \frac{7a}{4b}.$$

EXERCISE 89

Simplify:

1 $\dfrac{4x^2}{9} \times \dfrac{3}{2x}$ **2** $\dfrac{2x}{5} \times \dfrac{10}{x^2}$ **3** $\dfrac{5}{3x} \times \dfrac{9x^2}{10}$ **4** $\dfrac{3a^3}{4} \div \dfrac{2a}{3}$

5 $9x^2 \times \dfrac{5}{3x}$ **6** $\dfrac{a}{4} \times 4$ **7** $\dfrac{a}{4} \div 4$ **8** $\dfrac{1}{6x^2} \times 4xy$

9 $\dfrac{3x}{2y} \div 3$ **10** $\dfrac{4}{3x^2} \div \dfrac{8}{9x}$ **11** $\dfrac{2a}{5} \times \dfrac{10}{a^2} \times \dfrac{5a}{3}$

12 $\dfrac{5x}{3} \div \dfrac{x^2}{6}$ **13** $\dfrac{12a^2}{7} \div \dfrac{3a}{14}$ **14** $\dfrac{5}{3x} \times \dfrac{9x}{8} \times 2$

15 $\dfrac{5a}{3a^2} \times \dfrac{7a^3}{5a^2} \times \dfrac{9a}{7}$ **16** $\dfrac{x}{2y^2} \times \dfrac{3y}{x^2} \times \dfrac{1}{6y}$ **17** $\dfrac{24x^6}{5y^2} \times \dfrac{10y}{3x^2}$

18 $\dfrac{15ab^2}{7} \div \dfrac{5a^2b^2}{21}$ **19** $\dfrac{2x}{7y} \times \dfrac{3x}{8y} \times \dfrac{4x}{9y}$ **20** $\dfrac{2ab}{3b^2} \times \dfrac{3bc}{4c^2}$

21 $\dfrac{2a}{3b} \div \dfrac{a}{12b^2}$ **22** $\dfrac{3y^2}{2} \div \dfrac{9}{8y}$ **23** $\dfrac{a}{2b} \times \dfrac{2b}{3c} \times \dfrac{3c^2}{4a}$

24 $\dfrac{6a}{b^2} \times \dfrac{b}{4a^2} \times \dfrac{c}{3a}$ **25** $3 \times \dfrac{y}{2x^2} \times \dfrac{2x}{y}$ **26** $\dfrac{2}{3ac} \times \dfrac{6a^3}{b} \div \dfrac{c}{2b}$

27 A rectangle is $\dfrac{3x}{4}$ m long and $\dfrac{x}{3}$ m wide. Find (i) its perimeter in metres, (ii) its area in m².

28 A rectangle is $\dfrac{2x}{3}$ cm wide, and its area is $8x^2$ cm². Find its length.

29 A rectangular block is x cm long, $\dfrac{3x}{4}$ cm wide and $\dfrac{x}{3}$ cm high. Find its volume in cubic centimetres.

30 A rectangular block is $2x$ m long, $\dfrac{2x}{3}$ m wide and $\dfrac{x}{4}$ m high. Find (i) the total surface area in square metres, (ii) the volume in cubic metres.

31 A tank is $\dfrac{4x}{3}$ m long and $\dfrac{9x}{8}$ m wide, and it contains $\dfrac{3x^3}{4}$ m³ of water. Find the depth of the water.

34. LOCI

Suppose there are two trees in a field, 20 m apart. Mark two points A and B on your paper 4 cm apart, to represent the positions of the trees on a scale of 1 cm to 5 m.

Indicate by a series of dots the path of a boy who walks:

    (i) so that he is always 5 m from A;
    (ii) so that he is always in line with A and B;

(iii) so that he is always 10 m from the line joining A and B;

(iv) so that his distance from A is always the same as his distance from B.

Observe that in each of these cases the boy cannot walk anywhere he likes; he is told to obey certain conditions. His path, when he moves so as always to obey certain conditions, is called his **locus.** (The plural is '*loci*'.)

Your sketches of the boy's path in the four cases given above will have shown you what is the locus of a point which moves so as always to be

  (i) 5 m from A;
 (ii) in line with A and B;
(iii) 10 m from the line AB;
(iv) the same distance from A as from B.

Suppose we want to find the locus of a point which moves so as always to fulfil certain conditions; for example, always to be 1 cm from a fixed straight line AB drawn on the paper. One point after another is marked until the pattern of all such points begins to be clear, as in Fig. 203, and the more points we add, the more complete does the pattern become. This is called **plotting the locus.** Sometimes it is possible to visualize the path along which the point moves. For example, the locus of a marked point on the handle of a door as the door is opened is a portion of the circumference of a circle, or an arc, as it is called. Again, the locus of the end of the minutes hand of a clock is a circle.

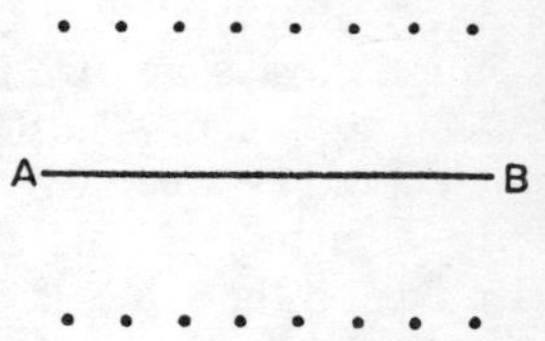

FIG. 203

In the following exercise you should guess what the locus is, either by visualizing the path of the point or by marking a series of possible positions.

EXERCISE 90 (Oral)

State the loci in the following cases:

1 The centre of a bicycle wheel when the bicycle moves along a straight level road.

2 The tip of the seconds-hand of a watch.

3 A mark on the seat of a swing.

4 A mark on a see-saw.

5 The top of the head of a boy as he slides down the banisters.

6 The centre of a billiard ball which rolls about on a horizontal table.

7 A boy who walks in such a way as to be always 2 m away from a straight wall.

8 The centre of one end of a round ruler as it rolls down a sloping desk.

9 The centre of a marble which rolls about inside a hollow sphere (or globe).

10 The right-angled corner of a set square if the hypotenuse is held firm and the set square made to rotate round it.

11 A man who walks round a circular lawn of radius 4 m, keeping always 1 m from the edge.

12 The mid-point of the portion of a variable straight line intercepted between two fixed parallel lines.

13 A penny is held flat on the table, and another penny also flat on the table, is rolled round it. Find the locus of the centre of the moving penny.

The **distance of a point from a line** must always be taken to mean the length of the perpendicular drawn from the point to the line. It may be necessary to produce the line before this perpendicular can be drawn. In Fig. 204, PM is the distance of P from AB, and QN is the distance of Q from AB.

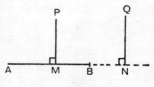

FIG. 204

EXERCISE 91

Plot the loci in the following cases:

1 AB is a fixed line and O is a fixed point not on the line. P is a point which moves along AB. Plot the locus of the mid-point of the line OP.

2 ABC is a triangle. A variable line moves so as to be always parallel to BC. If this line cuts AB at P and AC at Q, plot the locus of the mid-point of PQ.

3 Draw two lines crossing near the middle of your paper, making an angle of 60° with each other. Mark a number of points in each of the four angles formed by the lines, each point being such that its distance from both lines is the same.

4 Draw a circle with radius 6 cm and mark a point O which is 4 cm from the centre of the circle. A point P moves round the circumference of the circle. Plot the locus of the mid-point of OP.

5 Mark a point O near the centre of a sheet of squared paper, and draw two perpendicular lines XOX′, YOY′ through it, as in Fig. 205. P is any point on the paper, and perpendiculars PM, PN are drawn to the lines XOX′, YOY′. Plot the locus of P if (i) PM = 2PN, (ii) PM = 3PN, (iii) PM + PN = 3 cm.

6 Draw two lines XOX′ and YOY′, as in Fig. 205. Place the ruler so that the zero mark is on YOY′ and the 8 cm mark on XOX′. Plot the locus of the 4 cm mark as the ruler slides about.

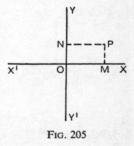

Fig. 205

In Nos. 7–10 you can use cardboard strips to represent the moving lines. Drawing pins will do for the hinges. To mark the various positions of a point on one of the strips, make a small hole in the strip with the compass point.

7 AB is pivoted at A, and BC is hinged to AB at B. A ruler is held on the paper so that its edge passes through A, and the point C moves along the edge of this ruler. P is the mid-point of BC. If AB = 2 cm and BC = 3 cm, plot the locus of P. (See Fig. 206.)

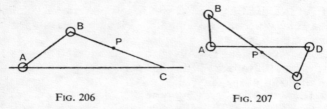

FIG. 206   FIG. 207

8 Repeat No. 7 with AB 2½ cm and BC 2 cm.

9 A and D are fixed points 6 cm apart. AB and DC are each 2 cm long, and are pivoted at A and D. The strip BC is 7 cm long, hinged at B and C, and P is the mid-point of BC. Plot the locus of P. (See Fig. 207.)

10 Repeat No. 9 with AD 6 cm, AB 2 cm, DC 3 cm, BC 7 cm.

11 Stick two pins in the paper at A and B, at a convenient distance apart, and slide the set square so that two edges touch the pins, as shown in Fig. 208. Plot the locus of the

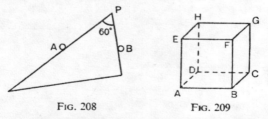

FIG. 208   FIG. 209

vertex of the 60° angle, i.e. the locus of a point P such that ∠APB = 60°.

12 The cube shown in Fig. 209 stands with ABCD on a table. It is rolled over, without slipping, rotating about the edge BC, until the face BCGF is on the table. The cube is then rolled over again so that FGHE and ADHE in turn are on the table. Sketch the locus of the point A during the motion.

Four important loci For the time being we shall think only of points which are all in the same plane, for example in the plane of the paper. Later we can consider what the loci become if the points can be anywhere in space.

There are four loci which are particularly important:

(i) **The locus of points at a given distance from a given point O is a circle.**

This is really the definition of a circle. The centre of the circle is O and the radius is the given distance. See Fig. 210.

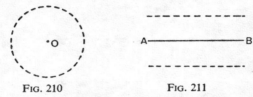

FIG. 210   FIG. 211

(ii) **The locus of points at a given distance from a given straight line AB is the pair of lines, one on each side of AB, parallel to AB and the given distance away.** See Fig. 211.

(iii) **The locus of points equidistant from two given points X and Y is the perpendicular bisector of XY.** See Fig. 212.

(iv) **The locus of points which are equidistant from two given intersecting straight lines is the pair of lines which bisect the angles between the given lines.** See Fig. 213, where the dotted lines which form the locus are perpendicular to each other.

A formal proof of statements (iii) and (iv) will be given later. For the present it will be sufficient if the pupil satisfies himself of their truth by drawing.

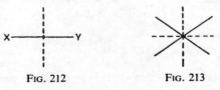

FIG. 212   FIG. 213

Intersection of loci If the position of a point is given by two distinct conditions, the point or points can be found by constructing the two corresponding loci, and taking the intersection of these loci, as in the next example.

Example *Draw a triangle* ABC *in which* AB = 6·4 *cm,* BC = 6 *cm,* CA = 3·6 *cm. Find a point* P *which is equidistant from* CA, CB *and which is* 5·2 *cm from* A.

All points which are equidistant from CA and CB lie on the two perpendicular lines which bisect the angles between these lines, both produced.

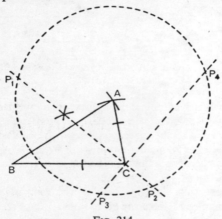

Fig. 214

All points which are 5·2 cm from A lie on a circle, centre A and radius 5·2 cm.

The point P must therefore lie on both loci.

The two loci are shown in the figure by dotted lines. P_1, P_2, P_3 and P_4 are the four possible positions for P.

EXERCISE 92

In the following questions the given straight lines must be produced in both directions as far as necessary. Find all the possible solutions when there is more than one.

1 Draw two straight lines AOB, COD intersecting at an angle of 70° at the point O. Find a point (or points) distant 3 cm from AB and 4 cm from CD. Measure their distances from O.

2 Draw a straight line AB and mark a point O which is 2 cm from it. Construct the locus of (i) points distant 1 cm from AB, (ii) points distant 4 cm from O. Mark the points which satisfy both conditions.

3 A and B are two points 5 cm apart. Find a point (or points) distant 4 cm from A and 3 cm from B.

4 ABC is an equilateral triangle of side 5 cm. Construct the locus of (i) points distant 3 cm from B, (ii) points distant 2 cm from AC. Mark the points which satisfy both conditions, and measure their distances from A.

5 Draw a triangle ABC in which AB=4 cm, BC=4 cm, AC=6·5 cm. Construct the locus of (i) points distant 1 cm from AC, (ii) points equidistant from AB and AC. Mark the points which satisfy both conditions, and measure their distances from C.

6 Draw a triangle ABC in which AC=6 cm, AB=4·2 cm, BC=3·4 cm. Find by construction a point P which is equidistant from A and C, and which is 1 cm from B. Measure PC.

7 A and B are two points 3 km apart on a straight road, B being due east of A. A church is 4 km from the road AB, and is observed to bear N. 65° E. from A. Make a scale drawing to the scale of 1 cm to a kilometre, and find the distance of the church from B.

8 Draw an equilateral triangle ABC of side 4 cm. Find by construction a point P, 2 cm from AC and equidistant from BA and BC. Measure PA.

9 Construct a triangle ABC in which BC=5 cm, AB=4 cm and the perpendicular distance of A from BC is 2·8 cm. Measure AC. (First draw BC; then construct two loci for A.)

10 Construct a triangle ABC in which AB=5·4 cm, ∠A=90° and BC=6·2 cm. (First draw AB, and make a right angle at A. What is the locus of C if BC=6·2 cm?) Measure AC.

11 Draw a triangle ABC in which AB = 3·6 cm, BC = 4·2 cm, CA = 3·2 cm. Construct the locus of (i) points equidistant from A and B, (ii) points equidistant from A and C. Mark the point O which satisfies both these conditions, measure its distance from A, and draw the circle with centre O and the length of OA as radius. This circle is called the **circumcircle** of the triangle.

12 Draw a triangle ABC in which AB = 7·2 cm, BC = 7·2 cm, CA = 5·4 cm. Construct the locus of (i) points inside the triangle which are equidistant from AB and AC, (ii) points inside the triangle which are equidistant from BA and BC. Mark the point I which satisfies both conditions, draw IX perpendicular to AB meeting AB at X, and draw the circle whose centre is I and radius IX. This circle is called the **incircle** of the triangle. Measure IX.

13 Draw a triangle ABC in which AB = 4 cm, ∠A = 105°, ∠B = 45°, and produce the sides in both directions. Find by construction the points which are equidistant from A and C, and also equidistant from BA and BC. Measure their distances from C.

14 Draw a triangle ABC such that BC = 8 cm, ∠B = 25° and the perpendicular distance from A to BC is 2·4 cm. Measure AC.

35. PERCENTAGE

Suppose that $\frac{3}{5}$ of the pupils in a school are boys, and $\frac{2}{5}$ are girls.

Since $\frac{3}{5}$, or $\frac{60}{100}$, of the pupils are boys, we say that **60 per cent** are boys. In the same way, $\frac{2}{5} = \frac{40}{100}$, so we say that 40 per cent are girls. 'Cent' is short for *centum*, which means 100. Thus the percentage tells us how many hundredths are taken; in other words:

Percentages are fractions with denominator 100.

60 per cent is written 60%.

Thus, $60\% = \frac{60}{100} = \frac{3}{5}$;

$50\% = \frac{50}{100} = \frac{1}{2}$;

$25\% = \frac{25}{100} = \frac{1}{4}$;

$33\frac{1}{3}\% = \frac{33\frac{1}{3}}{100} = \frac{100}{300} = \frac{1}{3}$, and so on.

Frequently a fraction can be expressed as a percentage by mentally making its denominator 100;

thus, $\frac{1}{5} = \frac{20}{100} = 20\%$; $\frac{3}{20} = \frac{15}{100} = 15\%$.

Learn by heart:

$\frac{1}{4} = 25\%$, $\frac{1}{2} = 50\%$, $\frac{3}{4} = 75\%$;

$\frac{1}{8} = 12\frac{1}{2}\%$, $\frac{3}{8} = 37\frac{1}{2}\%$, $\frac{5}{8} = 62\frac{1}{2}\%$, $\frac{7}{8} = 87\frac{1}{2}\%$;

$\frac{1}{3} = 33\frac{1}{3}\%$, $\frac{2}{3} = 66\frac{2}{3}\%$.

Example 1 *Express 0·435 as a percentage.*

$$0{\cdot}435 = \frac{435}{1000} = \frac{43{\cdot}5}{100} = 43\frac{1}{2}\%.$$

In order to express one quantity *a* as a percentage of another quantity *b*, we first express *a* as a fraction of *b*.

This is $\frac{a}{b}$.

To change this to a percentage, suppose that

$$\frac{a}{b} = \frac{x}{100}.$$

Then $\frac{x}{100} = \frac{a}{b}.$

Multiply both sides by 100;

$$x = \frac{a}{b} \times 100.$$

The rule is:

To express *a* as a percentage of *b*, put *a* over *b* and multiply by 100.

Example 2 *Express £4·50 as a percentage of £20.*

$$\frac{£4{\cdot}50}{£20} \times 100 = \frac{450}{20} = 22\frac{1}{2}.$$

∴ £4·50 is $22\frac{1}{2}\%$ of £20.

A useful fact to remember is that 1% of £1 is a penny. In other words, 1% of a sum of money is equivalent to a penny in the £. For example, 1% of £27 = 27p.

Example 3 *Find $7\frac{1}{2}\%$ of £36.*

$$7\frac{1}{2}\% \text{ of } £36 = 7\frac{1}{2} \times 36p$$
$$= 270p = £2 \cdot 70.$$

In the case of a more awkward percentage of a sum of money, either of the methods in the next example may be used.

Example 4 *Find, correct to the nearest penny, the value of $2\frac{3}{4}\%$ of £86·40.*

Method 1
$$\frac{2\frac{3}{4}}{100} = \frac{11}{400}.$$

$$£\frac{11}{400} \times 86 \cdot 40 = £\frac{950 \cdot 40}{400} = £2 \cdot 376. \qquad Ans. \text{ £2·38}$$

Method 2

$$
\begin{aligned}
& \qquad\qquad\qquad\qquad \text{£} \\
& 2\% \text{ of } £86 \cdot 40 = 1 \cdot 728 \\
& \tfrac{1}{2}\% = \tfrac{1}{4} \text{ of } 2\% = 0 \cdot 432 \\
& \tfrac{1}{4}\% = \tfrac{1}{2} \text{ of } \tfrac{1}{2}\% = \underline{0 \cdot 216} \\
& \qquad\qquad\qquad\qquad 2 \cdot 376 \qquad Ans. \text{ £2·38}
\end{aligned}
$$

EXERCISE 93 (Oral)

Express the following percentages (i) as fractions in their lowest terms, (ii) as decimals:

1 25%, 5%, 4%, $2\frac{1}{2}\%$ **2** 75%, 50%, 60%, $37\frac{1}{2}\%$

3 20%, 80%, 30%, $12\frac{1}{2}\%$ **4** 10%, 2%, 70%, $66\frac{2}{3}\%$

Express the following fractions as percentages:

5 $\frac{1}{5}$, $\frac{1}{2}$, $\frac{1}{10}$, $\frac{7}{5}$ **6** $\frac{2}{5}$, $\frac{1}{4}$, $\frac{1}{20}$, $\frac{7}{8}$

7 $\frac{1}{25}$, $\frac{3}{4}$, $\frac{1}{50}$, $\frac{23}{20}$ **8** $\frac{1}{2}$, $\frac{2}{3}$, $\frac{5}{8}$, $\frac{5}{6}$

9 If brass consists of 74% copper and the rest bronze, what is the percentage of bronze?

10 If 31% of the population are men, 34% women, and the rest children, what percentage are children?

11 A man spends 85% of his income. What percentage does he save?

12 In a school containing boys and girls, the percentage of boys is 40%. There are 220 boys. How many girls are there?

13 10% of $x = 12$. Find x.

14 75% of $y = 30$. Find y.

15 A shopkeeper allows 5% off the prices marked in the window. How much would you expect to pay for an article marked £1?

16 What percentage is 3 m of 1 km?

17 What is 1% of: (i) £a, (ii) b kg, (iii) c metres?

18 What is 5% of: (i) £2, (ii) £40, (iii) 3 m, (iv) 4 kg?

EXERCISE 94

Express the following as fractions in their lowest terms:

1 $33\frac{1}{3}$%, $102\frac{1}{2}$%, 150%, $37\frac{1}{2}$%

2 300%, $66\frac{2}{3}$%, $112\frac{1}{2}$%, $\frac{1}{2}$%

3 135%, $9\frac{1}{2}$%, $317\frac{1}{2}$%, $62\frac{1}{2}$%

4 Express as decimals 24%, $5\frac{1}{4}$%, $212\frac{1}{2}$%, $3\frac{1}{8}$%, $67\frac{3}{4}$%.

Find the values of:

5 40% of 60p   **6** $12\frac{1}{2}$% of £80   **7** $166\frac{2}{3}$% of 36p

8 What percentage is (i) 7 cm of 3·5 m, (ii) 50 g of 1 kg, (iii) 475 cm^3 of 1 litre, (iv) 1 mm of 1 m?

9 What percentage is (i) 125 cm of 1 m, (ii) 3p of £1·20, (iii) 13·2 cm of 2·64 m, (iv) 140 mg of 3·5 g?

10 35% of $x = 56$. Find x.

11 The value of a house is £2400, and the rent is fixed at 4% of the value. How much rent is paid?

12 There are 2480 candidates for an examination, and 55% pass. How many fail?

Find, correct to the nearest penny:

13 7% of £10·58   **14** 13% of £218
15 $3\frac{1}{2}$% of £46   **16** $4\frac{3}{4}$% of £6·18
17 $6\frac{1}{2}$% of £5·72   **18** 4·2% of £530

19 Out of 5000 kg of potatoes, 360 kg are bad. What percentage are bad?

20 The price of an article is 60p but the shopkeeper reduces the price in a sale by 15%. What is the sale price of the article?

21 If 8% of the pupils in a class are absent, and there are 46 present, how many are absent?

22 The population of a town increases from 10 000 to 11 500. By how much per cent has it increased?

23 What percentage of a is b?

Percentage changes An increase of 3% in a number means that the number has increased by $\frac{3}{100}$ of itself. If the original number is represented by 100, the increase is 3, and the new number is 103.

The ratio of the new number to the old = 103 : 100.

∴ the multiplying factor = $\frac{103}{100}$.

Similarly, a decrease of 7% means that if the original number is represented by 100, the decrease is 7, and the new number is 93.

The ratio of the new number to the old = 93 : 100.

∴ the multiplying factor = $\frac{93}{100}$.

EXERCISE 95 (Oral)

Say what multiplying factor increases a number by:

  1 15%   **2** 73%   **3** 40%   **4** 140%   **5** 100%

Say what multiplying factor decreases a number by:

  6 10%   **7** 30%   **8** 52%   **9** 8%   **10** 75%
11 Increase 200 by 16%   **12** Increase 80 by 5%
13 Decrease 500 by 40%   **14** Decrease 150 by $33\frac{1}{3}$%
15 Increase 400 by 3%   **16** Increase 50 by 60%
17 Increase $100x$ by 6%   **18** Decrease $8y$ by $12\frac{1}{2}$%

EXERCISE 96

1 Increase 40 by 35%   **2** Increase 75 by 124%

3 Decrease 208 by $12\frac{1}{2}$%   **4** Decrease 72 by $37\frac{1}{2}$%

Find x in the following cases:

5 38% of $x = 57$ **6** $37\frac{1}{2}$% of $x = 42$

7 $7\frac{1}{2}$% of $x = 150$ **8** $16\frac{2}{3}$% of $x = 8$

9 What amount, when increased by 20%, becomes £72?

10 What amount, when increased by 35%, becomes £216?

11 What amount, decreased by 35%, becomes £312?

12 What amount, decreased by 8%, becomes £69?

13 Goods are bought for £5·25. For what should they be sold to gain $33\frac{1}{3}$% of the cost price?

14 The price of an article in a shop was £8, but 5% was deducted during a sale. What was the sale price of the article?

15 After being decreased by 10%, the cost of an article was £36. What was the original cost?

16 If there are 287 boys in a mixed school, and these are 35% of the whole number, find the total number of pupils.

17 If 15% of a sum of money is £83·25, find the sum of money.

18 The duty on an article is 8% of its value. If the duty is £1·20, find the value of the article.

19 5% of a number is 96. Find $7\frac{1}{2}$% of the number.

20 A shopkeeper sold an article for £27, thus gaining $12\frac{1}{2}$% of the amount the article cost him. How much did it cost him?

21 At an election there were two candidates. One received 53% of the votes cast, and he had 96 votes more than his opponent. How many votes were cast?

22 When a sum of money is decreased by $7\frac{1}{2}$%, it becomes £7·40. What is the original sum?

23 A line 4 cm long was incorrectly measured as $3\frac{1}{2}$ cm. Find the error as a percentage of the true length.

24 A man sold a car for £340, thus losing 15% of what he had paid for the car.   How much had he paid for it?

25 If 23% of a number is 69, find 4% of it.

26 What does £2·46 become, to the nearest penny, if reduced by 15%?

27 How many kg are there in 6% of 1·75 tonnes?

Profit and loss per cent   In order to compare two transactions, when goods are bought and sold, it is useful to express the actual profit (or loss) as a **percentage of the cost price.**

Consider the following transactions:

Cost Price £20, Selling Price £25, Profit £5
   ,, £50, ,, £55, ,, £5

The profit is the same in both cases, namely £5.   But in the first case the profit is $\frac{1}{4}$, or 25%, of the cost price; while in the second case the profit is only $\frac{1}{10}$, or 10%, of the cost price.

We call the first a profit of 25%, and the second a profit of 10%.

If the cost price is £20 and the selling price is £15, there is a loss of $\frac{1}{4}$ of the cost price, or 25% of the cost price.   We call this a loss of 25%.

Profit (or loss) per cent tells us what per cent the profit (or loss) is of the cost price.

Notice that profit per cent is not the profit on 100 articles. Another point to note is that business people find it more convenient to reckon their profit as a percentage of the selling price, instead of the cost price.   But this should never be done in mathematics.   Profit per cent must be reckoned on the *cost price* in all cases.

We shall write C.P. for cost price and S.P. for selling price.

Example 5   *If the C.P. is £30 and the S.P. is £42, find the profit %.*

$$\frac{\text{Profit}}{\text{C.P.}} = \frac{12}{30} = \frac{4}{10} = \frac{40}{100}.$$
$$\therefore \text{ the profit} = 40\%.$$

Example 6 *If the C.P.* = 40p *and the profit is* $17\frac{1}{2}\%$, *find the S.P.*

$$\text{Profit} = \frac{17\frac{1}{2}}{100} \times 40\text{p} = \frac{35 \times 40}{200} \text{ pence}$$

$$= 7\text{p}.$$

$$\therefore \text{ the S.P.} = 40\text{p} + 7\text{p} = 47\text{p}.$$

Example 7 *If the S.P.* = £15 *and the loss* = £5, *find the loss* %.

$$\text{The C.P.} = £20.$$

$$\therefore \frac{\text{loss}}{\text{C.P.}} = \frac{5}{20} = \frac{25}{100}.$$

$$\therefore \text{ the loss} = 25\%.$$

Example 8 *If the S.P.* = £252 *and the profit* = 44%, *find the C.P.*

If the C.P. were £100, the profit would be £44 and so the S.P. would be £144.

$$\therefore \text{ the C.P.} = \frac{100}{144} \text{ of the S.P.}$$

$$= £\frac{\overset{7}{\cancel{63}}{\overset{}{\cancel{100 \times 252}}}}{\underset{4}{\underset{\cancel{36}}{\cancel{144}}}}$$

$$= £\frac{700}{4} = £175.$$

EXERCISE 97 (Oral)

State the S.P. in the following cases:

1 C.P. £20, profit 5%   2 C.P. £10, loss 20%
3 C.P. 8p, loss 25%   4 C.P. £60, profit $33\frac{1}{3}\%$
5 C.P. £40, profit 30%   6 C.P. £200, profit $12\frac{1}{2}\%$

State the factor by which the S.P. must be multiplied to give the C.P. in the following cases:

7 Profit 5%   8 Loss 5%
9 Profit 40%   10 Loss 12%

State the C.P. in the following cases:

11 S.P. £7, profit 40%	**12** S.P. £1·20, profit 20%
13 S.P. £30, profit 50%	**14** S.P. £7, loss 30%
15 S.P. £42, profit 5%	**16** S.P. £5, profit 25%
17 S.P. 6p, loss $33\frac{1}{3}$%	**18** S.P. £44, profit 10%

State the profit or loss per cent in the following cases:

19 C.P. £20, profit £4	**20** C.P. £12, loss £3
21 C.P. £50, loss £6	**22** S.P. £10, profit £2
23 S.P. £6, loss £2	**24** S.P. £24, loss £6
25 C.P. £25, S.P. £29	**26** C.P. £200, S.P. £230
27 C.P. 54p, S.P. 72p	**28** C.P. £2·50, S.P. £2
29 C.P. 30p, S.P. 36p	**30** C.P. £8, S.P. £10

EXERCISE 98

1 Find the S.P. when a car which cost £300 is sold at a loss of 40%.

2 Eggs are bought at 30p per dozen and sold at 3p each. Find the gain per cent.

3 A car is sold for £660 at a gain of 10%. Find the C.P.

4 If the C.P. = £85 and the profit is 30%, find the S.P.

5 A house was bought for £1800 and sold at a profit of 15%. Find the S.P.

6 A book is sold for £3 at a gain of 20%. Find the bookseller's profit.

7 A man sold an article for £60 at a loss of $16\frac{2}{3}$%. Find how much it cost him.

8 If the cost price is £17·50 and the profit is 10%, find the selling price.

9 If bananas are bought at 120p per 100 and sold for 3p each, find the profit per cent.

10 A grocer buys sugar at £75 per tonne, and sells it for $9\frac{1}{2}$p per kg. Find his profit per cent.

11 A man bought a car for £750 and sold it at a loss of 12%. Find how much he lost.

12 A merchant buys 1 tonne of tea for £420. Find the price per kg at which he must sell it so as to gain 25%.

13 A shopkeeper buys Christmas cards at £6·40 per 100, and sells them at 8p each. Find the profit per cent.

14 A dealer sells a picture for £36, thereby making 80% profit. Find how much the picture cost him.

15 An article costs £4 and is sold at a profit of $22\frac{1}{2}$%. Find the S.P.

16 A fruit-seller buys apples at 15 for 12p and sells them at 10p per dozen. Find his profit per cent.

17 A greengrocer gains 60% on his cost price by selling potatoes at 4p per kg. Find how much he paid per tonne.

18 A coal merchant sells coal at £1·14 for 100 kg. If the coal costs him £9·50 per tonne, find his profit per cent.

19 A shopkeeper marks the goods in his window so as to make a profit of 60%, but he allows 5% off the marked price for cash. Find his profit per cent on a cash purchase. (Consider the case of an article which cost the shopkeeper 100p.)

20 By selling an article for £30 a man would gain 20%. Find how much the article cost him, and for how much he must sell it in order to gain 30%.

21 A motor car is sold for £672 at a profit of 40%. What would be the profit per cent if the price were reduced to £600?

22 A bookseller sells 100 copies of a book at 54p per copy, thus making a total profit of £6. Find his profit per cent.

23 A greengrocer buys oranges in boxes, each holding 120, at £3·36 per box. Find his profit per cent if he sells the oranges at 3p each.

24 A man buys a horse for £46 and sells it at a profit of $22\frac{1}{2}$%. How much did he sell it for?

25 A shopkeeper buys eggs from a farm by the score, and sells them at 3p each, thus gaining 20%. How much does he have to pay for a score?

MISCELLANEOUS EXAMPLES ON PERCENTAGE

EXERCISE 99

1 Express the following percentages as fractions in their lowest terms: (i) 150%, (ii) 275%, (iii) 35%, (iv) $27\frac{1}{2}$%.

2 Express as percentages: (i) $\frac{2}{3}$, (ii) $\frac{7}{2}$, (iii) $\frac{x}{y}$, (iv) $\frac{3}{8}$.

3 What percentage is: (i) 8·5 cm of 3·4 m, (ii) 570 g of 24 kg, (iii) 50p of £1·20, (iv) 380 cm³ of 1·9 litres.

4 The price of an article in a shop is £2·80, but during a sale there is a reduction of $2\frac{1}{2}$% from the marked price. Find the actual cost of the article.

5 Two men both had a salary of £2500. One of them receives an increase of 12% and the other an increase of 13%. Find by how much the salary of one man now exceeds that of the other.

6 If x cm³ of a liquid A are mixed with $3x$ cm³ of another liquid B, what percentage of each liquid is there in the mixture?

7 A man sold an article for £38, thereby losing 5% on his cost price.   Find how much he gave for the article.

8 A coal merchant buys coal at £7·50 per tonne and sells it at 90p for 100 kg.   Find his gain per cent.

9 An article is bought for £28 and sold at a profit of $37\frac{1}{2}$%. Find the selling price.

10 Express $7\frac{1}{2}$% of £2x in pence.

11 A grass plot is 40 m by 30 m.   If the length and the breadth are each increased by 5%, by what percentage is the area increased?

12 If the sides of a square are each increased by 10%, by what percentage is the area increased?   (Take the original side to be 10 cm.)

13 If the edges of a cube are each increased by 10%, by what percentage is the volume increased?   (Take the original edge to be 10 cm.)

14 Express as percentages: (i) $\dfrac{x}{5}$, (ii) $\dfrac{3y}{20}$, (iii) $\dfrac{1}{x}$.

15 If the cost price of an article is £x, and the profit is 10%, find an expression for the selling price in pence.

36. CHORD PROPERTIES OF THE CIRCLE

Suppose AB is a chord of a circle, centre O (see Fig. 215). Then OA = OB (radii).

Now the perpendicular bisector of the line AB is the locus of points equidistant from A and B.

∴ O lies on the perpendicular bisector of AB.

Hence we see that

The centre of a circle lies on the perpendicular bisector of any chord.

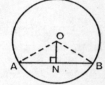

Fig. 215

Thus the foot of the perpendicular from O to AB will be the mid-point of AB.

ON, the length of the perpendicular from O to AB, is called the **distance** of the chord AB from the centre.

By Pythagoras' Theorem in the right-angled triangle ONA,

$$ON^2 + AN^2 = OA^2.$$

If we are told the radius of the circle, OA, and the distance, ON, of a chord from the centre, we know two sides of the right-angled triangle ONA, and so the other side AN can be found from Pythagoras' Theorem. The length of the chord AB can then be found by doubling AN.

Again, suppose we are told the radius of the circle and the length of the chord. We know OA and AN (which is half the length AB), and so ON can be found. This shows that

Equal chords are equidistant from the centre; and chords which are equidistant from the centre are equal.

Circumcircle of a triangle   Let ABC be a triangle. The circle which passes through the vertices A, B, C is called the

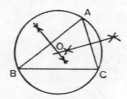

FIG. 216

circumcircle of the triangle, and its radius the **circumradius** of the triangle.   (See p. 220, No. 11.)

In order to draw this circle, we observe that the sides of the triangle will be chords of the circle.   Now we have already seen that the perpendicular bisector of a chord always passes through the centre of the circle.   We therefore draw the perpendicular bisectors of two sides of the triangle, AB and AC.   Let these meet at O.

With centre O, radius OA, draw a circle.

This is the circumcircle of the triangle.

Notice that it is not necessary to draw the perpendicular bisectors of all three sides, as they would all meet at the same point.

Example   *A chord* AB *of a circle of radius* 13 *cm is* 24 *cm long.   Calculate the distance of* AB *from the centre of the circle.*

Let O be the centre of the circle.

Join OA, and let N be the foot of the perpendicular from O to AB (see Fig. 217).

Then $AN = \frac{1}{2}AB = 12$ cm.

By Pythagoras' Theorem in the right-angled triangle ONA,

$$ON^2 + AN^2 = OA^2.$$
$$\therefore \ ON^2 + 144 = 169.$$
$$\therefore \ ON^2 \qquad = 25.$$
$$\therefore \ ON \qquad = 5 \text{ cm.}$$

EXERCISE 100

1 In Fig. 217, if AB = 6 cm and OA = 5 cm, calculate ON.

2 In Fig. 217, if OA = 13 cm and ON = 5 cm, calculate AB.

3 In Fig. 217, if OA = 25 cm and ON = 7 cm, calculate AB.

4 In Fig. 217, if OA = 17 cm and AB = 16 cm, calculate ON.

5 PQ is a variable chord of a fixed circle of radius 5 cm. If PQ is always 8 cm long, state the locus of the mid-point of PQ.

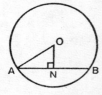

FIG. 217

6 Two parallel chords of a circle of radius 10 cm are 12 cm and 16 cm long. Calculate the distance between them when the chords are: (i) on the same side of the centre, (ii) on opposite sides of the centre.

7 State the locus of the mid-points of parallel chords of a fixed circle, and illustrate by a sketch.

8 State the locus of the centres of all circles which have a given line AB as a chord.

9 Draw a triangle ABC in which AB = 5 cm, BC = 6 cm, CA = 7 cm. Construct the circumcircle, and measure its radius.

10 Draw a straight line AB 4 cm long, and construct a circle of radius 3 cm to pass through A and B.

11 Draw any chord AB of length 2 cm in a circle of radius 3 cm. Construct a circle to pass through A and B, and to have its centre on the first circle.

12 Draw a circle of radius $2\frac{1}{2}$ cm and mark any point P inside it. Construct the chord which has P as its mid-point.

13 Draw a circle of radius 5 cm, and construct the locus of the mid-points of chords which are 6 cm long.

14 Draw a circle by means of a 10p coin, and find its centre by geometrical construction.

15 Draw a triangle ABC in which AB = 6·5 cm, $\angle A = 61°$ and $\angle B = 48°$. Construct its circumcircle and measure the radius.

16 Draw a triangle with sides 3 cm, 4 cm and 5 cm. Construct its circumcircle and measure the radius.

17 Draw a triangle ABC in which AB = 5 cm, BC = 7 cm and $\angle$BAC = 120°. Construct its circumcircle and measure the radius.

18 Draw a triangle with sides 4 cm, 5 cm and 6 cm. Without using a set square or protractor, construct equilateral triangles on its three sides, all the triangles pointing outwards. Construct the circumcircles of the three equilateral triangles. (They should all meet at a point inside the original triangle.)

37. SYMMETRY

Symmetry about a line Take a piece of paper, and fold it along a line AB. Cut out a figure like the shaded part in Fig. 218 and open out the paper. The shape of the hole will be as

FIG. 218

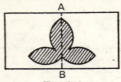

FIG. 219

shown in Fig. 219. Such a figure is said to be **symmetrical about the line** AB, and AB is called an **axis of symmetry**. To every point P on the right-hand side of AB (see Fig. 220) there corresponds a point P' on the left-hand side. If PP' meets AB at N, then PN = P'N and $\angle$ANP = $\angle$ANP' = 90°.

In the case of solid objects we often have a *plane* of symmetry; for example, a pair of gloves, or a pair of semi-detached houses. In the case of the reflection in a mirror of the interior of a room, the mirror forms the plane of symmetry.

FIG. 220

Many examples of symmetry about a line have been met already. Examples are to be found in the construction for bisecting an angle (p. 119); the construction for drawing a perpendicular from a point to a line (p. 121); the isosceles triangle (see Fig. 165 on p. 175), which is symmetrical about the bisector of the vertical angle; the figure formed by the perpendicular from the centre of a circle to a chord (Fig. 215 on p. 231), which is symmetrical about the perpendicular. A circle is obviously symmetrical about any diameter. The leaves of trees provide good natural illustrations of symmetry about a line.

As an example of symmetry, consider Fig. 221. P and Q are the centres of the circles. AB is called the 'common

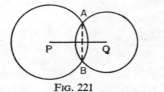

FIG. 221   FIG. 222

chord', i.e. it is a chord of both circles. The figure is symmetrical about PQ, and therefore, since A and B are corresponding points, the line AB must be perpendicular to PQ and must be bisected by that line.

Some figures have more than one axis of symmetry. For example, the square in Fig. 222 is symmetrical about *four* axes, shown by dotted lines.

Symmetry about a point   A parallelogram has no axis of symmetry. But if you draw a series of straight lines through O, the point where the diagonals cross, you will notice that if one of these lines meets the parallelogram at P and P', then PO = OP' (see Fig. 223). Every straight line drawn through O and bounded by the parallelogram is bisected at O.

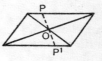

FIG. 223

The figure is said to be **symmetrical about the point** O, and O is called the **centre of symmetry.**

The capital letters of the alphabet illustrate both types of symmetry, that about a line and that about a point. The letter T is an example of the first, and S of the second.

EXERCISE 101

Draw free-hand sketches of the figures in Nos. 1–10, and show by dotted lines any axes of symmetry they possess.

1 Isosceles triangle.   **2** Equilateral triangle.
3 Rectangle.   **4** Square.
5 Parallelogram.   **6** Rhombus.
7 Regular hexagon.   **8** Semicircle.
9 Two unequal intersecting circles.
10 Two equal intersecting circles.
11 Which of the figures in Nos. 1–10 are symmetrical about a point?
12 Describe the symmetry of the following capital letters:

A E H L X Z M C

38. ANGLE PROPERTIES OF THE CIRCLE

Arcs and segments Look again at the definitions of arc and chord on p. 70. The part of the plane between an arc and the chord joining the ends of the arc is called a **segment** of the circle.

There are two kinds of segments; a **minor segment,** which is less than a semicircle, and a **major segment,** which is greater than a semicircle. These are shown in Fig. 224.

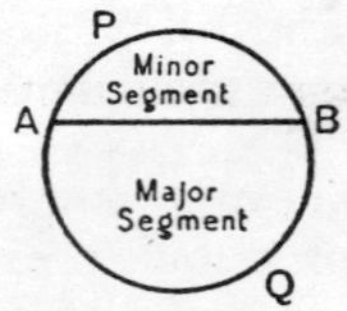

In the same figure, the arc APB is called a **minor arc,** as it is less than a semicircle; the arc AQB is called a **major arc,** as it is greater than a semicircle.

FIG. 224

Angles subtended by an arc at the centre The angle **subtended** at a point P by a line AB (straight or curved) is the angle APB.

If AB is an arc of a circle, and O is the centre of the circle, the angle which the arc AB **subtends at the centre** of the circle is ∠AOB.   When the arc AB is a minor arc, ∠AOB will be less than 180°;   when the arc AB is a major arc, ∠AOB will be greater than 180°.

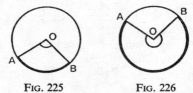

FIG. 225   FIG. 226

In Fig. 225 the angle AOB, which is marked, is subtended by the arc AB, which is shown thicker than the rest of the circle.   The angle AOB marked in Fig. 226 is called a **reflex** angle (see p. 79) to distinguish it from the other angle AOB.

Angles subtended by an arc at the circumference   In Fig. 227 the angles APB, AQB are subtended at points P and Q

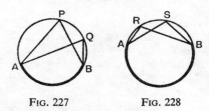

FIG. 227   FIG. 228

on the circumference of the circle by the same arc AB.   They are said to be **in the same segment** (namely, the major segment cut off by the chord AB).   They are also said to **stand on the same arc** (namely, the minor arc AB).

Similarly, in Fig. 228, the angles ARB, ASB are *in* the minor segment cut off by AB, but they stand *on* the major arc AB; or they may be said to be subtended *by* the major arc AB.

In both figures the angles are subtended by the arcs which are thickened.

EXERCISE 102 (Oral)

All the questions refer to Fig. 229:

1 What angles are subtended by the arcs ABC, AED, EABC, EDC at the circumference of the circle?

2 Find angles which are subtended at the circumference by the same arc as: (i) ∠EAD, (ii) ∠EBC, (iii) ∠DEB.

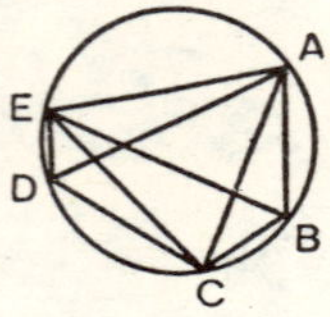

3 Name the angles subtended at the circumference by the chord AC.

4 What angles are in the segments ABCD, AEDC, BCDE?

FIG. 229

5 Name three angles subtended at points on the circumference by the chord BD. Are they all subtended by the same arc?

Angles at the circumference and centre of a circle Turn back to Exercise 51 on p. 79, and look at Nos. 11–14. If you did not do these drawing exercises when you were at this part of your work, you should do them now, before reading any farther.

In No. 11 you should have found that the angles APB, AQB both measured 35°. Now ∠AOB is 70°; and the angles APB, AQB (which we now call 'angles subtended by the arc AB at the circumference') are each one-half of ∠AOB (which we now call 'the angle subtended by the arc AB at the centre').

Is this always the case?   Let us take a numerical calculation.

Example 1   *In Fig. 230, O is the centre of the circle, and AB (thickened) is an arc. P is a point on the remaining part of the circumference.* ∠APB = 75°, ∠APO = 21° *and* ∠OPB = 54°. *Calculate* ∠AOB.

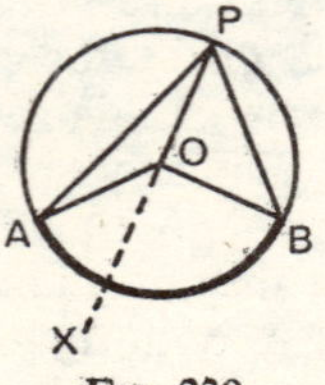

Produce PO to any point X.
Now OA = OP, being radii of the circle.
∴ ∠OAP = ∠OPA = 21°.

FIG. 230

But $\angle AOX$ is an exterior angle of $\triangle OAP$.

$$\therefore \ \angle AOX = \angle OAP + \angle OPA$$
$$= 21° + 21°$$
$$= 42°.$$

Similarly, $\angle OBP = \angle OPB = 54°$,

and $\angle XOB = \angle OPB + \angle OBP$
$$= 54° + 54° = 108°.$$

$$\therefore \ \angle AOB = \angle AOX + \angle XOB$$
$$= 42° + 108° = 150°.$$

Notice that $\angle AOB$ is equal to twice $\angle APB$. Let us see if this is always true.

Suppose that in the example above $\angle APO = x°$ and $\angle OPB = y°$.

By the same reasoning as above, $\angle OAP$ is also equal to $x°$.

$$\therefore \ \angle AOX = x° + x° = 2x°.$$

Similarly $\angle XOB = 2y°$.

$$\therefore \ \angle AOB = \angle AOX + \angle XOB$$
$$= 2x° + 2y°.$$

But $\qquad \angle APB = x° + y°.$

$$\therefore \ \angle AOB = 2\angle APB.$$

Before we can be sure that the angle which the arc AB subtends at the centre is always twice that which it subtends at any point on the remaining part of the circumference, it is necessary to consider two other possible figures. These are illustrated by the two examples which follow.

Example 2 *In Fig. 231, O is the centre of the circle and AB (thickened) is an arc. If $\angle APB = 126°$, $\angle APO = 56°$ and $\angle OPB = 70°$, prove that the reflex angle $AOB = 2\angle APB$.*

Produce PO to any point X.

By the same reasoning as in the last example, $\angle OAP = 56°$, $\angle AOX = 112°$, $\angle OBP = 70°$, $\angle XOB = 140°$.

$$\therefore \ \text{the reflex angle } AOB = 112° + 140° = 252°.$$

But $\angle APB = 126°$.

$$\therefore \ \text{reflex angle } AOB = 2\angle APB.$$

FIG. 231

Example 3 *In Fig.* 232, $\angle APB = 43°$, $\angle OPA = 32°$, $\angle OPB = 75°$. *Prove that* $\angle AOB = 2\angle APB$.

As before, $\angle OAP = 32°$, $\angle AOX = 64°$.

$$\angle OBP = 75°, \quad \angle XOB = 150°.$$

Now $\angle AOB = \angle XOB - \angle AOX$

$$= 150° - 64° = 86°.$$

$$\therefore \angle AOB = 2\angle APB.$$

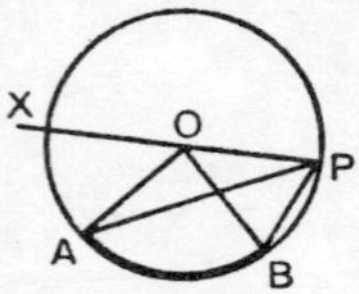

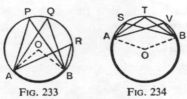

FIG. 232

These examples show that, whether the arc AB is a major or a minor arc, and wherever P may be on the remaining part of the circumference, the angle AOB is in all cases twice the angle APB. In words,

The angle which an arc of a circle subtends at the centre is double that which it subtends at any point on the remaining part of the circumference.

Angles in the same segment

In Fig. 233, O is the centre of the circle, and the arc AB which is thickened subtends a number of angles APB, AQB, ARB, ... at different points on the remaining part of the circumference.

FIG. 233   FIG. 234

These are angles in the same segment.

They must be equal, because they are each one half of $\angle AOB$.

In Fig. 234, the arc AB is a major arc, and the angles ASB, ATB, AVB, ... are the angles which the arc AB subtends at different points on the remaining part of the circumference. These, too, are angles in the same segment. They are equal because they are each one half of the reflex angle AOB.

It is therefore evident that

Angles in the same segment of a circle are equal.

This fact was verified by drawing in Exercise 51, No. 13 (p. 81).

The angle in a semicircle   A particularly important case of angles in the same segment occurs when the segment is a semicircle. Exercise 51, No. 12 (p. 80), should have helped you to guess how big the angle is in that special case; and Exercise 62, No. 19 (p. 115) shows you a way of proving it, using only the property of the isosceles triangle and the angle-sum of a triangle. We can apply what we have learned about the angle at the centre of a circle, and prove that the angle in a semicircle is always a right angle, as follows:

In Fig. 235, AB is a diameter of the circle, centre O, and P is any point on the circle. Join PA, PB.

Now $\angle AOB = 180°$, since AOB is a straight line.

But $\angle AOB = 2\angle APB$, for the angle subtended at the centre is double the angle subtended at the circumference.

$\therefore \angle APB = 90°$. Hence

FIG. 235

The angle in a semicircle is a right angle.

The cyclic quadrilateral   A polygon through whose vertices a circle can be described is said to be **cyclic**. Four or more points lying on a circle are said to be **concyclic**.

Exercise 51, No. 14 (p. 81) should have led you to discover a property of the opposite angles of a cyclic quadrilateral. We can now prove that the fact is always true.

Suppose, in Fig. 236, that ABCD is a cyclic quadrilateral, and O is the centre of the circle through the vertices. Join BO, DO, and suppose that $\angle A = x°$, $\angle C = y°$.

Then $\angle BOD = 2y°$,
and reflex $\angle BOD = 2x°$ (angle at centre twice the angle at the circumference).

But $\angle BOD + \text{reflex } \angle BOD = 360°$.

$\therefore 2x + 2y = 360.$

$\therefore x + y = 180.$

FIG. 236

Hence the opposite angles DAB, DCB together make 180°.

Similarly it may be shown that the opposite angles ABC, ADC together make 180°.

Thus

A pair of opposite angles of a cyclic quadrilateral together make two right angles.

Produce the side DC of the cyclic quadrilateral ABCD to X, as in Fig. 237. We call $\angle$BCX an exterior angle of the quadrilateral, and $\angle$BAD is the interior opposite angle.

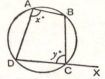

Since DCX is a straight line,

$\angle$BCX $+ y° = 180°$.

But $x° + y° = 180°$ (opposite angles of a cyclic quadrilateral).

$\therefore \angle$BCX $= x°$.

Hence $\angle$BCX $= \angle$BAD; or, in words,

FIG. 237

If a side of a cyclic quadrilateral is produced, the exterior angle is equal to the interior opposite angle.

EXERCISE 103

1 In Fig. 238, if $\angle$AOB $= 128°$, calculate $\angle$APB and $\angle$AQB.

2 In Fig. 238, if $\angle$AQB $= 115°$, calculate the reflex $\angle$AOB and $\angle$APB.

3 In Fig. 238, if $\angle$APB $= 50°$, calculate $\angle$AOB and $\angle$OAB.

4 In Fig. 238, if $\angle$AQB $= 108°$, calculate $\angle$AOB and $\angle$OAB.

5 In Fig. 238, if $\angle$APB $= 60°$, prove that $\angle$AOB $= \angle$AQB.

O is the centre of the circle

FIG. 238

6 In Fig. 239, if $\angle$ABQ $= 95°$, $\angle$QBR $= 52°$, calculate $\angle$CQR, $\angle$CRQ, $\angle$QCR.

7 In Fig. 239, if $\angle$BQC $= 46°$ and $\angle$BCQ $= 37°$, calculate $\angle$CRQ, $\angle$QBC.

8 In Fig. 239, if ∠PQC=150° and ∠BCR=98°, calculate ∠CBR, ∠BRC.

9 In Fig. 239, if ∠CRS=102°, ∠BQC=61° and ∠CBR=28°, calculate ∠BCQ, ∠QCR, ∠PQB.

10 In Fig. 239, if ∠DCR=84° and ∠BCQ=37°, calculate ∠BRQ, ∠QBR and ∠PQB.

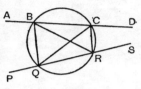

Fig. 239

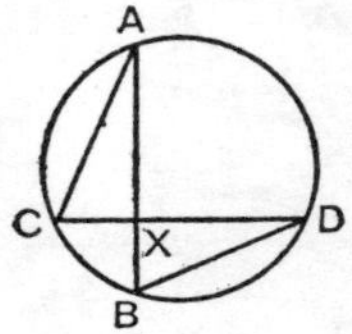

Fig. 240

11 In Fig. 240, if ∠BAC=33° and ∠AXC=90°, calculate ∠ABD.

12 In Fig. 240, if ∠AXC=90° and ∠BAC=x°, find ∠ABD.

13 In Fig. 241, if ∠ACD=137°, calculate ∠DAB and ∠DBA.

14 In Fig. 241, if ∠CDA=41°, calculate ∠CDB and ∠CAB.

15 In Fig. 241, if ∠CDA=x°, find ∠CDB and ∠CAB.

16 In Fig. 241, if ∠DAB=25°, calculate ∠ACD and ∠ABD.

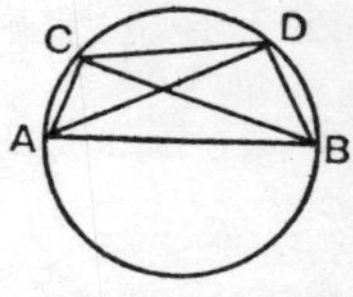

AB is a diameter

Fig. 241

17 ABCD is a cyclic quadrilateral. If ∠ABC=115° and ∠BCA=32°, calculate ∠BDC.

18 Two chords AB, CD of a circle intersect at the point X inside the circle. If ∠AXC=63° and ∠DAB=48°, calculate ∠ABC.

19 The diagonals AC, BD of a cyclic quadrilateral ABCD intersect at X. If ∠AXD=97°, ∠ACD=40° and ∠CBD=34°, calculate ∠BAD.

20 The centre O of the circumcircle of a triangle ABC lies inside the triangle. If ∠AOB=132° and ∠BOC=146°, calculate ∠ABC.

21 AB is a diameter of a circle, and P is a point on the circle. If the radius of the circle is 5 cm and AP = 8 cm, calculate the length of BP.

22 In Fig. 242, if ∠PAB = 48°, calculate ∠PBA and ∠PQB.

AB is a diameter

FIG. 242

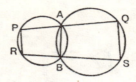

FIG. 243

23 In Fig. 242, if ∠PAB = x°, find ∠PBA and ∠PQB.

24 In Fig. 242, if ∠PQB = 72°, calculate ∠ABP.

25 ABCD is a cyclic quadrilateral; ∠ADC = 82°, ∠ABD = 31°. Calculate ∠DBC.

26 In Fig. 243, if ∠APR = 68°, calculate ∠ABS and ∠AQS.

27 In Fig. 243, if ∠QSB = 57°, calculate ∠PAB and ∠PRB.

28 In Fig. 243, if ∠APR = x°, state the numbers of degrees in ∠ABS and ∠AQS. Hence show that ∠APR and ∠AQS together make 180°. What conclusion can you draw from this fact?

29 In Fig. 244, if ∠CBQ = 41° and ∠BQC = 32°, calculate ∠BCD, ∠BAD, ∠APB.

30 In Fig. 244, if ∠ADC = 66° and ∠BQC = 29°, calculate ∠CBQ, ∠BCD, ∠APB.

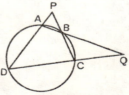

FIG. 244

31 In Fig. 244, if ∠PAB = x° and ∠PBA = y°, write down the numbers of degrees in ∠APB, ∠CBQ, ∠BCD, ∠BQC, ∠ADC.

32 Draw a circle, centre O, radius 3 cm. Mark a point T 5 cm from O, and construct the circle which has OT as a diameter. Let this circle cut the first circle at A and B, and join TA, TB. What do you notice about these lines?

39. DIRECTED NUMBERS

On a Celsius thermometer 0° (or zero) is the mark reached by the mercury column when the thermometer is placed in melting ice. The stem of the thermometer is graduated above and below this zero mark, and temperatures above the freezing point of water are denoted by $+1$, $+2$, $+3$, ... degrees, while temperatures below zero are denoted by -1, -2, -3, ... degrees.

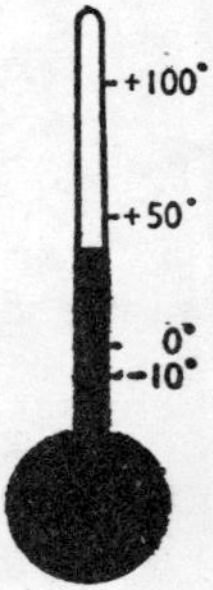

This use of $+$ and $-$ is quite different from the use of those signs which we have made previously. The expression $4+3$ meant that we were to carry out the instruction to add 3 to 4; the expression $4-3$ meant that we were to subtract 3 from 4. The signs $+$ and $-$ were *verbs*. In the new use of $+$ and $-$ given above, the signs are *adjectives*.

Fig. 245

For many purposes **signless numbers** are sufficient; e.g. the number of metres in a kilometre, or the number of days in a week. But when we want to represent such things as temperatures above and below zero, distances along a road to the north or south of a particular place, or times by the clock before or after midday, it is convenient to use numbers with the symbols $+$ or $-$ in front of them. Such numbers are called **directed numbers,** and they will be written

$$(+1), (+2), (+3), \ldots$$
and
$$(-1), (-2), (-3), \ldots$$

Thus a temperature of 20° above freezing point is denoted by $(+20)°$; one of 20° below freezing point is denoted by $(-20)°$.

EXERCISE 104 (Oral)

1 Referring to the Celsius thermometer (see Fig. 245):

(i) say what is meant by $(-5)°$, $(+42)°$;

(ii) use directed numbers to denote the following temperatures: 100° above freezing point, 15° below freezing point, 4° below freezing point.

2 A man has a balance of £100 in the bank. This can be denoted by (+100). How would you denote his balance after he has paid out a cheque for £70?

If he then pays out another cheque for £70, how would you then represent his bank balance?

3 If 3 p.m. is denoted by (+3), how would you denote 11 a.m., 7.30 p.m., 3 a.m., and 12 noon, all on the same day?

4 The speed of a train travelling north at 88 km per h is denoted by (+88). How would you denote the speed of a train travelling south at 48 km per h?

5 If the normal annual rainfall of a place is 104 cm, how much *above* normal is: (i) 134 cm, (ii) 66 cm?

6 A stone is thrown upwards from the top of a cliff, and it subsequently falls into the sea. The following table shows the height of the stone *above* the top of the cliff at one-second intervals:

Time in sec	0	1	2	3	4
Height in metres	2	9	6	−7	−29

Explain the meaning of the table, using signless numbers.

7 Re-state the following, using signless numbers:

(i) The lowest part of the Jordan Valley is (−396) m above sea-level.

(ii) In a competition to guess the weight of a parcel, one person over-estimates the weight by (+3) kg, while another over-estimates it by (−2) kg.

(iii) A man's watch is (−4) minutes fast.

(iv) The Battle of Hastings was fought in the year (+1066); Julius Cæsar landed in Britain in the year (−55).

(v) Moscow time is (+2) hours ahead of Greenwich; New York time is (−5) hours ahead of Greenwich.

Addition and subtraction We must learn how to add and subtract these directed numbers. Fig. 246 represents a *number-scale*, consisting of positive and negative numbers. By moving up and down this ladder, we can find out the 'rules of signs'.

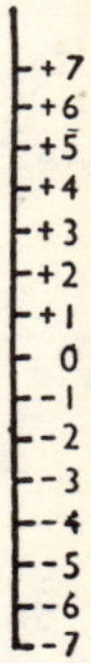

Let us consider *addition* first, e.g. $(+4)+(+3)$.

We start at $(+4)$ and move 3 steps up the ladder. This brings us to $(+7)$. Thus

$$(+4)+(+3)=(+7).$$

Now consider $(+4)+(-3)$. This should evidently be the same as $(-3)+(+4)$, which is obtained by starting at (-3) and moving 4 steps up the ladder. This brings us to $(+1)$, and so

$$(+4)+(-3)=(+1).$$

But if we started at $(+4)$, we should reach $(+1)$ by moving 3 steps *down* the ladder. This shows that $+(-3)$ is the same as moving 3 steps *down* the ladder.

We have now shown that

$+(+N)$ means: move N steps up the ladder, and is written $+N$.

$+(-N)$ means: move N steps down the ladder, and is written $-N$.

Now consider *subtraction*. We have found that

$$(+1)=(-3)+(+4).$$
$$\therefore (+1)-(+4)=(-3).$$

If we start at $(+1)$, how should we reach (-3)? The answer is, by moving 4 steps *down* the ladder.

Again, since

$$(+1)=(+4)+(-3).$$
$$\therefore (+1)-(-3)=(+4).$$

If we start at $(+1)$, we should reach $(+4)$ by moving 3 steps *up* the ladder.

Fig. 246

We have thus found that

- $-(+)$ means: move N steps down the ladder, and is written $-N$.
- $-(-N)$ means: move N steps up the ladder, and is written $+N$.

The **rule of signs** is thus:

$+(+N) = +N$; move up N steps.
$+(-N) = -N$; move down N steps.
$-(+N) = -N$; move down N steps.
$-(-N) = +N$; move up N steps.

Example *Carry out the following operations on the number-scale, and give the answers;*

(i) $(+2)-(+3)$, (ii) $(-2)-(-3)$, (iii) $(-3)+(-2)$.

(i) Start at $(+2)$ and move 3 steps down the number-scale, thus reaching (-1); $\therefore$ $(+2)-(+3)=(-1)$.

(ii) Start at (-2) and move 3 steps up the scale, thus reaching $(+1)$; $\therefore$ $(-2)-(-3)=(+1)$.

(iii) Start at (-3) and move 2 steps down the scale, thus reaching (-5); $\therefore$ $(-3)+(-2)=(-5)$.

EXERCISE 105 (Oral)

Say how the following operations can be performed on the number-scale, and give the answers:

1 $(-2)+(+5)$	**2** $(-2)-(+5)$	**3** $(+4)-(-2)$
4 $(-3)+(+3)$	**5** $(+2)-(-3)$	**6** $0+(-3)$
7 $(+2)+(-2)$	**8** $(-2)-(+3)$	**9** $(+2)-(+4)$
10 $(-3)+(-4)$	**11** $(+5)-(0)$	**12** $(-3)-(-3)$

Give the values of:

13 $(+6)-(+2)$	**14** $(-2)-(+5)$	**15** $(+3)+(-6)$
16 $(-2)-(-7)$	**17** $(+2)-(-3)$	**18** $(-6)+(-6)$
19 $(-3)+(+1)$	**20** $(-2)+(-4)$	**21** $(+5)-(+2)$
22 $(+1)-(+2)$	**23** $(-4)-(-7)$	**24** $(-4)+(-7)$

25 $(-9)+(-3)$ **26** $(-2)-(-2)$ **27** $(+2)+(-3)$
28 $(+4)-(+4)$ **29** $(+1)-(+5)+(+3)$
30 $(+3)+(-5)-(+4)$

Simplify:

31 $(+5a)-(+a)$ **32** $(-2x)-(-x)$ **33** $(+b)+(-3b)$
34 $(-y)+(-2y)$ **35** $(-x)-(+3x)$ **36** $(+2x)-(-3x)$
37 $(+5x)-(+5x)$ **38** $(-2b)-(-3b)$ **39** $(-y)+(-y)$
40 $(+a)-(+4a)+(+6a)$ **41** $0-(-3x)$
42 $(-2b)-(-8b)$ **43** $(+3t)+(-6t)-(-t)$
44 $(+3x)-(-7x)$ **45** $(+y)-(+4y)$ **46** $(+a)+(-a)$
47 $(-3x)+(-4x)$ **48** $(+2c)-(+4c)-(-c)$
49 $(+4b)+(+2b)+(-7b)$ **50** $(-x)-(-2x)+(-3x)$

Multiplication and division

Suppose a man is walking eastwards at v km per hour along a road, and that he passes a point O at noon, which we shall call zero hour. Then at t hours after 12 o'clock he is (vt) km east of O.

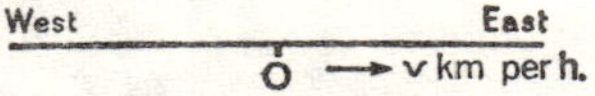

West   East
O → v km per h.

Fig. 247

The numbers v and t are to be thought of as directed numbers. Thus if $v=(+5)$, the man is walking *east* at 5 km/h; if $v=(-5)$, he is walking *west* at 5 km/h. Again, if $t=(+2)$, the time is 2 p.m.; if $t=(-2)$, the time is 10 a.m.

(i) Suppose that $v=(+5)$ and $t=(+2)$. The man's distance east of O at 2 p.m. is 10 km. Thus

$$(+5) \times (+2) = (+10).$$

(ii) Suppose that $v=(+5)$ and $t=(-2)$. The man's distance *west* of O at 10 a.m. is 10 km, and so his distance *east* of O is (-10) km. Thus

$$(+5) \times (-2) = (-10).$$

(iii) Suppose that $v = (-5)$ and $t = (+2)$. The man is walking westwards, and his distance *west* of O at 2 p.m. is 10 km. His distance *east* of O is therefore (-10) km. Thus

$$(-5) \times (+2) = (-10).$$

(iv) Suppose that $v = (-5)$ and $t = (-2)$. The man is again walking westwards, and his distance *east* of O at 10 a.m. is 10 km. Thus

$$(-5) \times (-2) = (+10).$$

This illustration shows the **rules of signs** for multiplication:

$(+x) \times (+y) = (+xy)$, usually written for shortness xy.
$(+x) \times (-y) = (-xy)$, usually written for shortness $-xy$.
$(-x) \times (+y) = (-xy)$, or $-xy$.
$(-x) \times (-y) = (+xy)$, or xy.

Notice carefully that the multiplication of two numbers with like signs (either two plus signs or two minus signs) gives a plus answer; and that two unlike signs give a minus answer.

The rules for division are deduced from those for multiplication. The illustration above shows that

$$(+5) \times (+2) = (+10),$$
$$(-5) \times (-2) = (+10),$$
$$(-5) \times (+2) = (-10),$$
$$(+5) \times (-2) = (-10).$$

From these four statements, it follows that

$$(+10) \div (+2) = (+5),$$
$$(+10) \div (-2) = (-5),$$
$$(-10) \div (+2) = (-5),$$
$$(-10) \div (-2) = (+5).$$

Notice that division of a plus number by a plus number, or of a minus number by a minus number, gives a plus answer; and that division of a minus number by a plus number, or of a plus number by a minus number, gives a minus answer.

The **rules of signs for multiplication and division** may thus be stated:

In multiplication and division of one directed number by another, like signs give a plus answer and unlike signs give a minus answer.

EXERCISE 106

Find the values of:

1 $(-2) \times (+3)$ **2** $(-10) \div (-2)$ **3** $(-5) \times (-4)$

4 $(+6) \times (-5)$ **5** $(-4) \times (-2)$ **6** $(-6) \div (+3)$

7 $(+24) \div (+6)$ **8** $0 \times (-3)$ **9** $(+3) \times (+4)$

10 $(-18) \div (-6)$ **11** $(-7) \div (+7)$ **12** $(-3) \times (-3)$

13 $(+2) \times (-6)$ **14** $(+2) \times (-8)$ **15** $\dfrac{(+24)}{(-3)}$

16 $\dfrac{(-9)}{(-1)}$ **17** $(+12) \div (-3)$ **18** $(-2) \times (-2) \times (-2)$

19 $\dfrac{(-3)}{(-3)}$ **20** $\dfrac{(-14)}{(+7)}$

Simplify:

21 $(-4x) \div (+x)$ **22** $(-6y) \div (-2)$

23 $(-3x) \times (-2x)$ **24** $(+ab) \div (-b)$

25 $(-xy) \div (-x)$ **26** $(-p) \times (+p)$

27 $(-4p) \div (+2p)$ **28** $(+18x) \div (-3x)$

29 $(-ab) \times (+bc)$ **30** $(-4a) \times (-2a)$

31 $(-2) \times (+3y)$ **32** $(-5) \times (-2d)$

33 $(+10x^2) \div (-2x)$ **34** $(-3x^2) \times 0$

35 $(-5f) \times (+2f)$ **36** $\dfrac{(-a) \times (-b)}{(-c)}$

If $a = (-1)$, $b = (+2)$, $c = (-3)$, $d = (+4)$ and $e = 0$, evaluate:

37 ab **38** bcd **39** a^2c **40** ac^2 **41** $\dfrac{c}{a}$

42 b^2ca **43** a^2de **44** $\dfrac{cd}{b}$ **45** $\dfrac{bd^2}{a}$ **46** $\dfrac{ad}{c}$

47 a^2bc **48** $\dfrac{ad}{b^2}$ **49** $\dfrac{e}{b}$ **50** $\dfrac{a}{b} \times \dfrac{d}{c}$

40. BRACKETS

We have already made use of brackets to show the order in which operations are intended to be done.   Thus

$$(4 \times 2) + 3 = 8 + 3 = 11,$$
but $$4 \times (2 + 3) = 4 \times 5 = 20.$$

When an expression in a bracket is multiplied by a number, we found that, in order to remove the bracket, every term inside must be multiplied by that number.   Thus

$$p(x + y) = px + py,$$
and $$p(x - y) = px - py.$$

To see what rules we must follow when removing brackets, let us consider these illustrations:

(i) $9 + (5 + 3)$.

This means: add 3 to 5, and add the result to 9.   The same answer would be obtained if we added 5 to 9 and then added 3 to the sum.

$$\therefore \ 9 + (5 + 3) = 9 + 5 + 3.$$

(ii) $9 - (5 + 3)$.

This means: add 3 to 5, and subtract the result from 9. The same answer would be obtained if we subtracted 5 from 9 and then subtracted 3 from the difference.

$$\therefore \ 9 - (5 + 3) = 9 - 5 - 3.$$

(iii) $9 + (5 - 3)$.

This means: subtract 3 from 5, and add the difference to 9.   The same answer would be obtained if we added 5 to 9 and then subtracted 3 from the sum.

$$\therefore \ 9 + (5 - 3) = 9 + 5 - 3.$$

(iv) $9 - (5 - 3)$.

This means: subtract 3 from 5, and subtract the difference from 9.   If 5 were subtracted from 9, we should be subtracting too much, and should require to add 3 to make up for it.

$$\therefore \ 9 - (5 - 3) = 9 - 5 + 3.$$

The rules for the **removal of brackets** are therefore:

If a bracket has a $+$ sign in front of it, the signs of the terms which were inside the bracket remain unchanged. If a bracket has a $-$ sign in front of it, a $+$ sign inside the bracket changes to $-$ and a $-$ sign changes to $+$.

Example 1

(i) $2 - 2x - (x + 1) = 2 - 2x - x - 1$
$$= 2 - 1 - 2x - x$$
$$= 1 - 3x.$$

(ii) $2(5x - 1) - 4(2x - 3) = (10x - 2) - (8x - 12)$
$$= 10x - 2 - 8x + 12$$
$$= 12 - 2 + 10x - 8x$$
$$= 10 + 2x.$$

(iii) $a - (b - c + d) = a - b + c - d.$

Insertion of brackets Sometimes it is useful to insert brackets. We must be careful when a bracket is inserted after a $-$ sign, as all the signs inside the bracket must be changed. It is best to check by removing the bracket mentally, after which the expression should be the same as it was before the bracket was inserted. Thus

$$a - x - 2y + z = a - (x + 2y - z),$$
$$2x - 4y - 3y = 2x - (4y + 3y)$$
$$= 2x - 7y.$$

Example 2 *Complete the following:*

(i) $x - 2y - 3z = x - (\ldots)$; (ii) $6a + 9b - 12c = 3(\ldots)$.

(i) $x - 2y - 3z = x - (2y + 3z).$
(ii) $6a + 9b - 12c = 3(2a + 3b - 4c).$

EXERCISE 107

Remove brackets, and simplify:

1 $x + (y - z)$ **2** $y - (x + z)$ **3** $(x - y) - z$
4 $(a - b) - (c + d)$ **5** $x + (x + 2y)$ **6** $3f + (2f - 2h)$
7 $1 - (x - 1)$ **8** $(x + 4) - (x - 1)$ **9** $3a - (a + b)$
10 $(1 + 2x) + (1 - 2x)$ **11** $8 - (3 + 2a)$ **12** $2p + (3 - p)$

13 $2(x^2 - 3x + 6)$ **14** $5(3x - 2)$ **15** $-(4 - 5y)$
16 $a + 5 + 2(a + 7)$ **17** $4(3 + b) - (2 - b)$
18 $3(x + 7) + 2(x - 3)$ **19** $3(a + 4) + (a - 1)$
20 $4x - (y - 3x)$ **21** $5(3c - 2) - (4 + 5c)$
22 $6(1 - 3t) + (t - 5)$ **23** $9 - (3 + 6x)$
24 $(x - 2y) + (2y - a)$ **25** $(1 + 3x) + (1 - 3x)$
26 $a - 7b + (5b - 2a)$ **27** $(2a - b) - (7a - 5b)$
28 $-3(x - 2y)$ **29** $5 - x^2 - (x^2 + 1)$
30 $(2a - 1) - (a + 1)$ **31** $1 - (2b - 4) - (b - 5)$
32 $3 - (2 - x) - (4 - x)$ **33** $4f + (3g - 5f)$
34 $(5a + 3b) + (2a - b)$ **35** $3y - (-2y)$

Complete the following:

36 $x + 2b - c = x + (\ldots)$ **37** $x - a - b = x - (\ldots)$
38 $a - b + c = a - (\ldots)$ **39** $p - q + r + s = p - (\ldots)$
40 $5x + 10 = 5(\ldots)$ **41** $1 + 14x - 7y = 1 + 7(\ldots)$
42 $x^2 + 3x = x(\ldots)$ **43** $ab^2 + a^2b = ab(\ldots)$
44 $3x^2 - 9x^3 = 3x^2(\ldots)$ **45** $2p^2 + 6pq = 2p(\ldots)$

Example 3   *Simplify* $2x(4x - 3) - 5(x + 1)$.

$$\begin{aligned}
2x(4x - 3) - 5(x + 1) &= (8x^2 - 6x) - (5x + 5) \\
&= 8x^2 - 6x - 5x - 5 \\
&= 8x^2 - 11x - 5.
\end{aligned}$$

You should multiply brackets by the number in front as the first step, and then remove brackets in a separate step. If you try to do both steps at once, you will make mistakes.

Example 4   *Solve the equation* $3(2x - 1) - 2(x + 1) = 4$.

$$\begin{aligned}
3(2x - 1) - 2(x + 1) &= (6x - 3) - (2x + 2) \\
&= 6x - 3 - 2x - 2 \\
&= 4x - 5.
\end{aligned}$$
$$\therefore \ 4x - 5 = 4.$$
$$\therefore \ 4x = 9.$$
$$\therefore \ x = \tfrac{9}{4} \text{ or } 2\tfrac{1}{4}.$$

EXERCISE 108

Remove brackets and simplify:

1 $2(4x+3y)-3(2x+y)$

2 $4(a-b)+3(b-a)$

3 $5(x-y)-4(x+y)$

4 $\frac{1}{x}(x^2+2xa)$

5 $\frac{1}{2}(2x-6)$

6 $3(p+q)-6(q-p)$

7 $\frac{3(x+1)-2(x-1)}{6}$

8 $\frac{a-(a-b)}{a}$

9 $x(x+2y)-y(x-y)$

10 $3(y-x)+4(x-y)$

11 $2x(3x-5)-5(x-4)$

12 $4(3a-2)-2(4-3a)$

13 $\frac{1}{2}x(a+8b)$

14 $\frac{1}{5}(10p-5q)$

15 $4(l+m)-3(l+2m)$

16 $4(p-2)-3(p+1)$

17 $3(x-2)+2(x-1)$

18 $2a(3a-b)$

19 $y(2y+x)-x(y-x)$

20 $3(x+1)+2(x-1)$

Solve the equations:

21 $x-(6-x)=12$

22 $3y=4-(1+y)$

23 $2x+3(x-2)=2x+3$

24 $2(t+2)+3(t+1)=t+31$

25 $3(y+2)+2(3y-2)=3y+4$

26 $3(z-2)+12(z+3)=5(z+20)$

27 $3t-(t+2)+7=t+30$

28 $5(3x+1)-2(2x+3)=3(x+1)$

29 $3(x+1)+2(x-1)=6$

30 $3(2y+1)-5(y-1)=15$

Brackets inside brackets Sometimes one or more sets of brackets are used inside another set of brackets. If so, different sorts of brackets, such as { } or [ ], should be used.

To simplify such an expression, **remove the inside bracket first**, as in the next example.

Example 5 *Simplify* $3x-\{x-(2y-x)\}$.

The expression $=3x-\{x-2y+x\}$
$=3x-\{2x-2y\}$
$=3x-2x+2y$
$=x+2y$.

Directed numbers have been written hitherto with brackets round them, e.g. $(+4)$, (-2). The purpose of this was to emphasize the distinction between the order 'add 4' and the positive number 'plus 4', or between the order 'subtract 2' and the negative number 'minus 2'. But this distinction is no longer necessary, and for shortness we shall write these numbers as 4, -2. The rules for the removal of brackets containing directed numbers, indeed all the laws for the algebra of these numbers, are the same as for the algebra of signless numbers, and therefore the pupil need never worry whether he is dealing with signless or directed numbers.

In future

$+(+2x)$ will be written as $+2x$, or merely $2x$,
$+(-2x)$,,   ,, $-2x$,
$-(+2x)$,,   ,, $-2x$,
$-(-2x)$,,   ,, $+2x$ or $2x$.

It is usual to write an expression so that it begins, if possible, with a positive term. Thus, $-x+2y$ is generally written as $2y-x$.

Example 6 *Simplify* $(+4x)-3[(-2x)-(+5x)]$.

The expression $= 4x-3[-2x-5x]$
$$= 4x-3[-7x]$$
$$= 4x+21x = 25x.$$

Example 7 *Simplify* $7a-8x+2x-9a+4$.

Collecting like terms together, we have

$$7a-9a-8x+2x+4$$
$$= -2a-6x+4 = 4-2a-6x.$$

EXERCISE 109

Simplify:

1 $2\{(3a+b)-(a-b)\}$ **2** $2x-3[4-(x-1)]$
3 $(+10y)-2\{y-3(3-y)\}$ **4** $a+b-\{a-[a-b]\}$
5 $x-3[x-4(x-1)+1]$ **6** $y-2\{x-4(y-x)\}$

7 $3x-[x-(1+x)+2]$ **8** $2p+q-[4p-3(q-p)]$

9 $x\{x(x+a)-a(x-a)\}$ **10** $3b+\{(a+2b)-(a-b)\}$

11 $4x-(x+2y)-[x-(2y-x)]$

12 $3a-4(b-c)-\{2c-3(a-c)\}$

13 $(+4)(-2x)$ **14** $-(+2)(-2x)$

15 $-2(a-3b)+a$ **16** $-(x-y)+z$

17 $(+3)(+5x)$ **18** $+(-2p)$

19 $3a+2\{(+2y)-(-a)\}$ **20** $2x-(x-y)-5y$

21 $0-2(a-b)$ **22** $3(1-a)-3a(1-a)$

23 $2p-q-(p+q)$ **24** $3(a+b)+7(a-b)$

25 $2[(+b)+(-c)]-3[(+b)-(-c)]$

26 $3x^2-2(1-x+x^2)$ **27** $a^2-(-a)^2$

28 $(2a)^2-2(+a)^2$ **29** $(-3x)(-3y)$ **30** $(-4a^2)(+3)$

31 $(-2x)(0)$ **32** $(+4a)(-5b)$ **33** $(-p)(+3q)$

34 $(+a)+(-2a)-(-3a)$ **35** $(-12x^2)\div(-3x)$

36 $(-27a^2b)\div(+9a)$ **37** $(+2x)-(-x)+3(+x+1)$

38 $(+x)+(-x)+(+x)$ **39** $\dfrac{(-2x)^3}{(+2x)}$

40 $2a-3\{(-5)-(-2a)\}$ **41** $0-2(x-y)-3(x+y)$

42 $\left(-\dfrac{a}{b}\right)\div(-a)$ **43** $(+x)\div(-x)$

44 $(-3x)^2$ **45** $(-2)(3a-2b-c)-(-1)(a-b)$

46 $(x-y)(-1)-2(y-x)(-1)$ **47** $\dfrac{(+x)(-y)}{(-a)(+b)}$

48 $-(-xy)^2$ **49** $(+6ab)\div(-bc)$ **50** $(-6x^6)\div(+3x^3)$

51 $2x-3y-4y$ **52** $2a-4b+6b$

53 $3a-6a-9a$ **54** $4p-6q+q$

55 $-8y+7x-9x$ **56** $3-7a+a-5$

57 $2-3x-2x-(1+x)$ **58** $4a+9x-3x-2x-11a$

59 $1+6a-10a$ **60** $(4+x-2y)-(-2+3x-y)$

41. SIMPLE INTEREST

You have to pay money (called 'rent') if you want to live in someone else's house or if you want to use a gas cooker hired from the gas company.   In the same way, if you borrow money from someone, you have to pay what is called **interest** for the use of that money, and the interest will depend on the sum borrowed and the time for which it is borrowed.   When you lend money to the Government through the Post Office Savings Bank, the Government pay you for the use of your money by giving you interest at the end of every year.

The sum of money which is borrowed is called the **principal.** The interest payable every year is generally expressed as a percentage of the principal.   This percentage is called the **rate of interest.**   If the rate of interest is 5% per annum (i.e. for each year), it means that the interest on £100 is £5 every year.   The interest on £200 would be £10 every year;   on £300 it would be £15 every year, and so on.   If £100 is borrowed for 2 years at 5% per annum, the interest would be £10;   for 3 years it would be £15, and so on.

Interest is usually paid annually to the lender.   If the interest for the whole period is added to the principal and the whole debt paid together, the sum so paid is called the **amount** of the loan, so that

$$\text{amount} = \text{principal} + \text{interest}.$$

Both these cases are called **simple interest.**

Sometimes, however, the interest is added to the amount owing, and the interest for the successive years continually increases, on account of the growth of the sum owed.   This method is called **compound interest.**   We are confining our work to simple interest in this section of the book.

The words 'per annum', meaning 'for each year', are usually abbreviated to 'p.a.'.

Example 1 *Find the simple interest on £200 for 3 years at 5% p.a.*

The interest on £100 for 1 year = £5.

∴   „   „   £200 „ 1 „   = £(5 × 2).

∴   „   „   £200 „ 3 „   = £(5 × 2 × 3)

= £30.

EXERCISE 110 (Oral)

Find the simple interest on:

1 £100 for 1 year at $3\frac{1}{2}\%$ p.a.

2 £100 for 3 years at 6% p.a.

3 £500 for 1 year at $2\frac{1}{2}\%$ p.a.

4 £150 for 1 year at 4% p.a.

5 £400 for 2 years at 3% p.a.

6 £200 for $1\frac{1}{2}$ years at 2% p.a.

7 £1000 for 2 years at 3% p.a.

8 £600 for 1 year at $3\frac{1}{2}\%$ p.a.

9 £300 for 2 years at 5% p.a.

10 £200 for 4 years at $2\frac{1}{2}\%$ p.a.

Find the amount at simple interest of:

11 £300 for 1 year at 4% p.a.

12 £500 for 2 years at $2\frac{1}{2}\%$ p.a.

13 £100 for 3 years at $3\frac{1}{2}\%$ p.a.

14 £800 for 2 years at $4\frac{1}{2}\%$ p.a.

15 £400 for 3 years at $1\frac{1}{2}\%$ p.a.

Example 2 *Find the simple interest on £384 for $2\frac{1}{2}$ years at 4% p.a.*

The interest on £100 for 1 year   = £4.

∴   „   „   £100 „ $2\frac{1}{2}$ years = £$(4 × 2\frac{1}{2})$.

∴   „   „   £384 „ $2\frac{1}{2}$ „   = £$\dfrac{384 \times 4 \times 2\frac{1}{2}}{100}$

= £$\dfrac{384 \times 4 \times 5}{100 \times 2}$

= £38·40.

Formula for simple interest   In the next example, a general formula for the simple interest is found, by taking £P as the principal, T years as the time, and R% as the rate. The steps in the argument are just the same as in the last example.

Example 3   *Find the simple interest on £P for T years at R% p.a.*

The interest on £100 for 1 year at R% = £R.

∴   „   „   £100 for T years at R% = £R × T.

∴   „   „   £P   „   „   = £$\dfrac{P \times R \times T}{100}$.

Hence we have a general formula:
If the simple interest on £P for T years at R% p.a. is £I, then

$$I = \frac{P \times R \times T}{100}.$$

In applying this formula, P is the number of £ in the principal.   T is the number of years, and any months or days must be expressed as a fraction of a year.   R is the rate per cent per annum.   I is the number of £ in the interest.

When finding T, take a year as 365 days, and be careful when reckoning the number of days between two given dates. For example, to find the number of days from March 7 to May 23:

March 7 to March 31 = 24 days.

March 31 to April 30 = 30 days.

April 30 to May 23 = 23 days.

Total period = 77 days.

Example 4   *Find to the nearest penny the simple interest on* £214·38 *for 4 years at* 3% *p.a.*

Here P = 214·38, R = 3, T = 4.

$$\therefore I = \frac{P \times R \times T}{100}$$

$$= \frac{214·38 \times 3 \times 4}{100} = \frac{214·38 \times 12}{100}$$

$$= 25·73 \text{ to two places of decimals.}$$

∴ the interest = £25·73, to the nearest penny.

Example 5   *Find to the nearest penny the simple interest on* £237·12 *from August 10 to October 14 of the same year at* $3\frac{1}{2}$% *p.a.*

First find the time in days.

$$\begin{array}{ll}
\text{August 10 to August 31} & = 21 \text{ days} \\
\text{August 31 to September 30} & = 30 \text{ days} \\
\text{September 30 to October 14} & = 14 \text{ days} \\
\text{Total period} & = 65 \text{ days}
\end{array}$$

$$\therefore P = 237·12, \ R = 3\tfrac{1}{2}, \ T = \frac{65}{365}.$$

$$\therefore I = \frac{237·12 \times 3\frac{1}{2} \times \frac{65}{365}}{100}$$

$$= \frac{237·12 \times 7 \times \overset{13}{\cancel{65}}}{2 \times \underset{73}{\cancel{365}} \times 100}$$

$$= \frac{237·12 \times 91}{14600}$$

$$\begin{array}{r}
237·12 \\
91 \\
\hline
237·12 \\
21340·8 \\
\hline
21577·92
\end{array}$$

$$\begin{array}{r}
146 \ ) \ 215·779 \ ) \ 1·477 \\
146 \\
\hline
69 \ 7 \\
58 \ 4 \\
\hline
11 \ 37 \\
10 \ 22 \\
\hline
1 \ 159
\end{array}$$

∴ the interest = £1·48, to the nearest penny.

EXERCISE 111

Find the simple interest on the following:

1 £460 for 2 years at $3\frac{1}{2}\%$ p.a.

2 £450 for 8 months at $4\frac{1}{4}\%$ p.a.

3 £630 for $3\frac{1}{2}$ years at 6% p.a.

4 £735 for $2\frac{1}{2}$ years at $3\frac{1}{3}\%$ p.a.

5 £62·50 for $4\frac{1}{2}$ years at 4% p.a.

6 £750 for 2 years 8 months at $3\frac{1}{2}\%$ p.a.

7 £560 for 4 years at $3\frac{1}{2}\%$ p.a.

8 £160 for 9 months at $3\frac{3}{4}\%$ p.a.

Find to the nearest penny the simple interest on:

9 £170·43 for $3\frac{1}{2}$ years at $2\frac{1}{2}\%$ p.a.

10 £208 for 2 years 8 months at $4\frac{1}{2}\%$ p.a.

11 £204·36 for 3 years at $2\frac{1}{2}\%$ p.a.

12 £2089 for 2 years at $3\frac{1}{2}\%$ p.a.

13 £610·47 for 1 year 3 months at 6% p.a.

14 £348·26 for 14 months at 5% p.a.

15 £456·76 for 2 years at $4\frac{1}{2}\%$ p.a.

16 £748 from October 17 to December 31 at 5% p.a.

17 £390 from August 6 to October 13 at $6\frac{1}{4}\%$ p.a.

18 £450 from May 3 to June 15 at 3% p.a.

19 Find the amount if £780 is lent for 2 years, simple interest being at $2\frac{1}{2}\%$ p.a.

20 Find the amount if £920 is borrowed for 1 year 3 months at $3\frac{1}{2}\%$ p.a.

21 A man invests £3060 at $4\frac{1}{2}\%$. Find the annual income he gets from his investment.

22 Find the simple interest on £560 for $4\frac{1}{2}$ years at $2\frac{1}{2}\%$ p.a.

23 A man borrows £327·75 from his bank for 6 months at 5%. Find how much interest the bank charges him.

24 Find, correct to the nearest centime, the amount at simple interest of 760 francs for 1 year 8 months at $3\frac{1}{2}\%$ p.a.

42. TANGENT PROPERTIES OF THE CIRCLE

Tangent and secant   If you draw a circle on your paper, and then draw any straight line at random, the line will do one of three things:

(i) It may cut the circle in two points, e.g. AB in Fig. 248. This is called a **secant.**

(ii) The line may meet the circle at one point only; e.g. in Fig. 248 CD meets the circle at T.   CD is called a **tangent,** T is called the **point of contact,** and the line is said to **touch** the circle at T.

(iii) The line may lie entirely outside the circle, and not meet the circle at all, e.g. XY in Fig. 248.

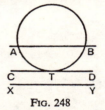

Fig. 248   Fig. 249

Notice that the line PQ in Fig. 249, although it meets the circle at only one point, is not a tangent, because, if produced, it would meet the circle at a second point.

Tangent as limit of a secant   Fig. 250 shows how the tangent can be regarded as the **limit of a secant.**   The secant

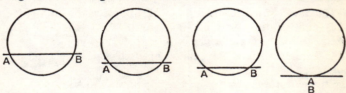

Fig. 250

AB gets shorter and shorter until, in the last figure, B and A become the same point.

We found on p. 231 that the perpendicular bisector of

any chord AB passes through the centre of the circle. What happens in the case when B and A are the same point?

Consider the secant PABQ in Fig. 251, cutting the circle at A and B. O is the centre of the circle.

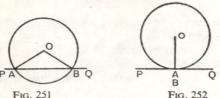

FIG. 251   FIG. 252

Since OA = OB (radii), then △ OAB is isosceles.

∴ ∠OAB = ∠OBA.

∴ ∠OAP = ∠OBQ.

Now move the chord until it reaches its limiting position, the tangent in Fig. 252.

A and B are now the same point, and the statement proved above, that ∠OAP = ∠OBQ, becomes

$$\angle OAP = \angle OAQ.$$

But these angles make 180°, since PAQ is a straight line.

$$\therefore \ \angle OAP = 90°.$$

Thus the tangent PAQ is perpendicular to the radius OA; in other words,

A tangent to a circle is perpendicular to the radius drawn through the point of contact.

This fact is used to draw the tangent at a point on a circle. If O is the centre, and A is a point on the circle, we join OA and make a right angle OAT, either with a set square or with compasses, as in Fig. 253. Then AT is the tangent at A.

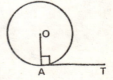

FIG. 253

Length of tangent If a line TA is drawn from a point T, outside a circle, to touch the circle at A, the length of TA is called the **length of the tangent** from T to the circle.

Tangents from an external point In Fig. 254 we have the two tangents TA, TB to a circle, centre O, from a point T outside the circle (or an *external* point, as it is called). A and B are the points of contact.

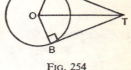

FIG. 254

Join OA, OB, OT.

Since the tangent to a circle is perpendicular to the radius drawn through the point of contact, the angles OAT, OBT are right angles.

The △s OAT, OBT are therefore two right-angled triangles with the same hypotenuse OT and the sides OA, OB equal (being radii).

We showed on p. 174 that two such triangles are congruent;

$$\therefore\ TA = TB.$$

In words,

The two tangents from an external point to a circle are equal.

It also follows from the congruent triangles that ∠OTA = ∠OTB; which means that

The centre of the circle lies on the bisector of the angle between the two tangents.

See Exercise 112, No. 20 for the method by which the tangents from an external point are constructed.

Inscribed circle The circle which touches the three sides of a triangle is called the **inscribed circle,** or sometimes the **incircle.** Its centre is called the **incentre.** (See Exercise 92, No. 12.)

To construct the inscribed circle, we make use of the fact that the centre of a circle lies on the bisector of the angle between the two tangents from an external point.

Since the sides of the triangle will be tangents to the required circle, we draw the bisectors of any two angles of the triangle, say ∠s ABC and ACB.

Let these bisectors meet at I, as in Fig. 255.

Draw IL perpendicular to BC, meeting it at L.

The circle with centre I and radius IL is the inscribed circle of the triangle ABC.

If L, M, N are the feet of the perpendiculars from I to the sides, these points are the points of contact of the inscribed circle with the sides of the triangle.

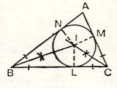

FIG. 255

EXERCISE 112

1 In Fig. 256, if ∠BAT = 34°, calculate ∠OAB and ∠AOB.

2 In Fig. 256, if ∠AOB = 78°, calculate ∠OAB and ∠BAT.

3 In Fig. 256, if ∠ABO = 70°, calculate ∠BAT.

4 In Fig. 256, if ∠AOB = 42°, calculate ∠BAT.

5 In Fig. 256, if ∠BAT = 29°, calculate ∠AOB.

6 In Fig. 256, if OA = 3 cm and AT = 4 cm, calculate OT.

7 In Fig. 256, if OB = 5 cm and OT = 13 cm, calculate AT.

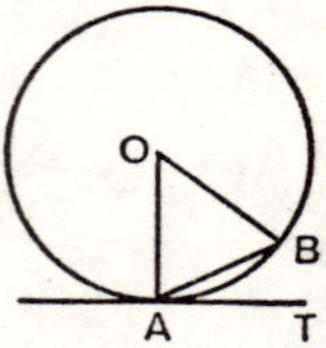

8 In Fig. 254, if OA = 8 cm and OT = 17 cm, calculate AT.

9 In Fig. 254, if ∠ATB = 72°, calculate ∠AOB.

10 In Fig. 254, if ∠AOT = 53°, calculate ∠ATB.

11 In Fig. 254, if ∠ATB = 48°, calculate ∠TAB.

12 In Fig. 255, if AM = 6 cm, BL = 5 cm and CL = 3 cm, calculate the lengths of AB, BC, CA.

13 In Fig. 255, if ∠ABC = 44° and ∠ACB = 62°, calculate ∠BIC.

O is the centre of the circle; AT is the tangent at A

FIG. 256

14 In Fig. 257, if ∠PAS = 30°, calculate ∠PAB and ∠ABP.

15 In Fig. 257, if ∠PAT = 140°, calculate ∠PAB, ∠PAS and ∠ABP.

16 In Fig. 257, if ∠PBA = 23°, calculate ∠PAB and ∠PAS.

17 In Fig. 257, if ∠PAS = $x°$, find ∠ABP.

If Q is any point on the major arc ABP, state the number of degrees in ∠AQP. Do you notice anything?

(∠PAS is called 'the angle between a tangent and a chord', and ∠AQP is called **the angle in the alternate segment**.)

AB is a diameter; TAS is the tangent at A

Fɪɢ. 257

18 In Fig. 258, if ∠PAS = $x°$ and R is any point on the minor arc AP, find ∠s PAB, PRB and BRA. Hence find ∠PRA. Compare your answer with ∠PAT. What do you notice?

19 Draw a circle with centre O and radius 3 cm. Mark two radii OA and OB, making ∠AOB equal to 125°. Construct the tangents at A and B to the circle. Measure the angle at which these tangents intersect, and verify your result by calculation.

AB is a diameter; TAS is the tangent at A

Fɪɢ. 258

20 Draw a circle with centre O and radius 4 cm, and mark a point P 7 cm from O. Construct the circle which has OP as a diameter, and let this circle cut the first circle at A and B. Explain why the angles OAP, OBP are right angles, and prove that PA and PB are the tangents from P to the circle.

21 Draw a triangle ABC in which AB = 6·6 cm, BC = 5·6 cm and CA = 7·2 cm, and construct the inscribed circle. Measure its radius.

22 Draw a triangle with sides 6 cm, 6 cm, 4½ cm, and construct its inscribed circle. Measure the radius of this circle.

43. EQUATIONS (II)

The rules for solving equations which were given on p. 108 can be summarized by saying that we can add equal numbers to, or subtract equal numbers from, both sides; and that we can multiply or divide both sides by the same number.

Suppose we have the equation $x+a=b$.

If we subtract a from both sides, we get

$$x+a-a=b-a, \quad \text{or} \quad x=b-a.$$

Now consider the equation $x-a=b$.

If we add a to both sides, we get

$$x-a+a=b+a, \quad \text{or} \quad x=b+a.$$

This shows that

A term can be moved from one side of the equation to the other, provided the sign in front of it is altered.

If the equation contains brackets, these should be removed by the rules given on p. 253. If the equation contains fractions, multiply every term (on both sides) by the L.C.M. of the denominators of the fractions, thus making the equation free from fractions.

Some of the equations which follow will be found to have negative answers.

Example 1 *Solve the equation*

$$6(x+4)-(2-x)=15.$$

Removing brackets,

$$6x+24-2+x=15.$$
$$\therefore 7x+22=15.$$
$$\therefore 7x=15-22.$$
$$\therefore 7x=-7.$$
$$\therefore x=-1.$$

Check.   If $x=-1$, then $6(x+4)-(2-x)$
$$=6\times 3-3$$
$$=18-3=15.$$

Example 2 *Solve the equation*

$$\frac{3x}{2} - \frac{2(x-3)}{3} + 4 = 0.$$

Multiply each term by 6 (the L.C.M. of 2 and 3);

$$\frac{6 \times 3x}{2} - \frac{6 \times 2(x-3)}{3} + 24 = 0.$$

$$\therefore 9x - 4(x-3) + 24 = 0.$$

$$\therefore 9x - 4x + 12 + 24 = 0.$$

$$\therefore 5x + 36 = 0.$$

$$\therefore 5x = -36.$$

$$\therefore x = -7\tfrac{1}{5}.$$

Check. If $x = -7\tfrac{1}{5}$, the left side of the equation

$$= -\frac{3 \times \overset{18}{\cancel{36}}}{\cancel{2} \times 5} - \frac{2 \times (-10\tfrac{1}{5})}{3} + 4$$

$$= -\frac{54}{5} + \frac{2 \times \overset{17}{\cancel{51}}}{\cancel{3} \times 5} + 4$$

$$= -10\tfrac{4}{5} + 6\tfrac{4}{5} + 4 = 0.$$

When checking the answer, it is essential to substitute in the *original* equation, not in the equation after it has been simplified. But it is often quicker, especially when there are awkward fractions, to go all through the working again.

EXERCISE 113

Solve the equations:

1 $2x + 1 = 2(2x-3) - 3(2x-1)$ **2** $2x + 1 \cdot 86 = 1 \cdot 5$

3 $2(3-2x) - (x+3) = 2(x+8) + 1$

4 $3(y+3) + 6(2y-1) = 6(2y+1)$ **5** $x + 1 \cdot 42 = -6 \cdot 78$

6 $(t+1) - 3(t+3) = 15$ **7** $2v - 3 \cdot 76 = v - 5 \cdot 61$

8 $5(x+1) = 3x - 2(x+1)$ **9** $1 \cdot 49 - x = 0 \cdot 63$

10 $12z - 3(2z-5) = 30 - 4z$ **11** $\dfrac{(x+2)}{2} + \dfrac{x}{3} = 1$

12 $3(x+1)-1=x-3$

13 $\dfrac{(y+1)}{2}+3=3(y+4)$

14 $3v-\dfrac{(1-2v)}{2}=5v$

15 $2(t-7)=6+\dfrac{t}{3}$

16 $2(y-5)=2-7y$

17 $x+1\frac{1}{2}=-5.38$

18 $x(x+4)-2(1+x)=1+x^2$

19 $\frac{1}{3}(2z+4)=\frac{1}{4}(z-8)$

20 $\frac{1}{2}(x-1)-\frac{1}{4}(3-x)=2$

21 $\dfrac{y}{2}-\dfrac{y}{3}=\dfrac{1}{5}$

22 $3x-5.4=1-(6.72-2x)$

23 $2x+\dfrac{x}{5}+22=0$

24 $2x+\dfrac{x}{3}=2\frac{1}{2}-5x$

25 $\dfrac{x}{4}-1=\dfrac{x}{2}-\dfrac{x}{3}$

26 $4x-2.7=-4.31$

27 $\dfrac{3p}{2}+9p=7$

28 $\dfrac{(5x-3)}{8}+1=\dfrac{(4x-3)}{5}$

29 $3(6-2x)-8(x+4)=0$

30 $0.7x+0.14=0$

31 $\dfrac{2x}{7}-x=10$

32 $\dfrac{(t+1)}{2}=\dfrac{(3t-1)}{11}$

33 $y+2.51=3.87-y$

44. ALGEBRAIC PROBLEMS

When solving a problem by algebra, begin by taking a letter to stand for some unknown number, and state what units you are using. Avoid making statements such as those on the left below; begin with clear statements like those in the right-hand column:

Wrong	*Right*
'Let the length be x';	'Let the length be x metres.'
'Let a cow $=x$';	'Let £x be the cost of a cow.'
'Let the weight be w.'	'Let w kg be the weight of the parcel.'
'Let his speed be x.'	'Let his speed be x km per hour.'

You should check the answer to a problem by using the facts given. It is useless to check in your equation, as the equation may be wrong.

Example 1 *A man bought some fourpenny stamps and some fivepenny stamps at a post office. The number of fivepenny stamps was 6 more than the number of fourpenny ones, and the total cost of all the stamps was £3. Find how many fourpenny stamps he bought.*

Suppose he bought x fourpenny stamps.
Then he bought $(x+6)$ fivepenny stamps.
The cost of the fourpenny stamps $= 4x$ pence.
The cost of the fivepenny stamps $= 5(x+6)$ pence.
The total cost $= 4x + 5(x+6)$ pence.
But the total cost $= £3 = 300$ pence.

$$\therefore 4x + 5(x+6) = 300.$$
$$\therefore 4x + 5x + 30 = 300.$$
$$\therefore 9x + 30 = 300.$$
$$\therefore 9x = 270.$$
$$\therefore x = 30.$$

$\therefore$ there were 30 fourpenny stamps.

Check. 30 fourpenny stamps cost 120p, 36 fivepenny stamps cost 180p. The total cost $= 300\text{p} = £3$.

Example 2 *A man walks from his home to a neighbouring town at 6 km per hour and then returns home by the same route at 5 km per hour. He finds that the total journey takes 2 min longer than if he went there and back at $5\frac{1}{2}$ km per hour. Find the distance of the town from his home.*

Let the distance of the town from his home be x km.

The time to walk x km at 6 km/h $= \dfrac{x}{6}$ hours.

The time to walk x km at 5 km/h $= \dfrac{x}{5}$ hours.

The total time $= \left(\dfrac{x}{6} + \dfrac{x}{5}\right)$ hours.

The time to walk $2x$ km at $5\frac{1}{2}$ km/h $= \dfrac{2x}{5\frac{1}{2}}$ h $= \dfrac{4x}{11}$ h.

$$\therefore \frac{x}{6} + \frac{x}{5} = \frac{4x}{11} + \frac{1}{30}.$$

(Notice that every term is a number of *hours*.)

Multiply every term by 330, the L.C.M. of 6, 5, 11, 30.

$$55x + 66x = 120x + 11.$$
$$\therefore 121x = 120x + 11.$$
$$\therefore x = 11.$$

$\therefore$ the distance of the town is 11 km.

Check.

The time to walk 11 km at 6 km/h $= \dfrac{11}{6}$ h $= 110$ min.

The time to walk 11 km at 5 km/h $= \dfrac{11}{5}$ h $= 132$ min.

The total time $= 242$ min $= 4$ h 2 min.

The time to walk 22 km at $5\frac{1}{2}$ km/h $= \dfrac{22}{5\frac{1}{2}}$ h $= 4$ h.

The problems in Exercise 61, Nos. 31–42, p. 111, could be revised before the following Exercise is commenced.

EXERCISE 114

The following problems should be solved by means of equations, even when the answer can be guessed or readily obtained by other means.

1 One number is 5 more than another. If the smaller number is trebled, the answer is 17 more than the larger number. Find the two numbers.

2 The length of a rectangle is 2 cm greater than the breadth, and the perimeter is 60 cm. Find the length and the breadth.

3 A man is twice as old as his son, and 4 years older than his wife. Their ages total 111 years. Find the man's age.

4 Find 3 consecutive even numbers whose sum is 114. (If the middle number is x, what are the other two numbers?)

5 A boy is allowed to score 3 marks for every sum he gets right, and (-1) mark for every sum he gets wrong. He does 20 sums altogether, and obtains 44 marks. How many did he get wrong?

6 A man bought some roses at 48p each and three times as many other plants at 8p each. He spent altogether £10·80. Find how many roses he bought.

7 A father is 35 years old and his son is 11. In how many years will the father be twice as old as the son?

8 Divide £3·30 among 3 boys A, B and C, so that B gets 40p more than C, and A gets $\frac{3}{8}$ as much as B and C together.

9 A has three times as many marbles as B. If he gives B 6 marbles, he will then have twice as many as B then has. How many marbles have they at first?

10 A boy cycles from P to Q at 20 km/h and returns at 16 km/h. The total journey takes $4\frac{1}{2}$ hours. Find the distance from P to Q.

11 A boy starts out from a town A to cycle towards a town B, 90 km away, at an average speed of 16 km/h. At the same moment a motorist leaves B and travels towards A at an average speed of 56 km/h. After how many hours do they meet?

12 A cyclist sets out along a certain road at an average speed of 16 km/h. Half an hour later a motorist starts from the same place to overtake him. If the motorist's average speed is 48 km/h, find how many kilometres he must go before he overtakes the cyclist.

13 A factory ordered some coal at £10 per tonne and some coke at £9 per tonne. The number of tonnes of coke was one more than twice the number of tonnes of coal, and the total bill was £107. Find the number of tonnes of coal.

14 If a man walks to the station at 5 km/h he misses his train by 1 min. If he runs at 10 km/h he has 2 min to spare. Find the distance to the station.

15 A grocer mixes 3 kg of cheap tea with 4 kg of dearer tea. If the dearer tea costs 28p per kg more than the cheap tea, and the mixture costs 82p per kg, find the cost of both sorts of tea.

16 How many kg of tea at 62p per kg must be mixed with 4 kg at 76p per kg to give a mixture worth 70p per kg?

17 What number must be added to the numerator and denominator of the fraction $\frac{8}{17}$ to make a new fraction which is equal to $\frac{3}{4}$?

18 The inscribed circle of a triangle touches the sides at L, M and N (see Fig. 255, p. 266). AB = 5 cm, BC = 6 cm, AC = 4 cm. If AM = AN = x cm, write down the lengths of BN and CM, and hence find x.

19 AB is a straight line 8 cm long, and P is a point in the line AB produced beyond B. If AP : BP = 7 : 5, find the length of BP.

20 The nth number in the set of numbers 17, 20, 23, 26, ... is $(3n+14)$. Test this by putting n equal to 1, 2, 3 and 4. How would you decide whether 215 is a number in this set, and, if so, how many terms of the set must be taken before it is reached?

Test in a similar manner where the number -70 comes in the set, and explain your answer.

21 A person bought some postcards at $2\frac{1}{2}$p each, and three times as many at $1\frac{1}{2}$p each. She spent 56p altogether. How many of each kind did she buy?

22 In a triangle ABC, AB is 1 cm less than BC, and 2 cm greater than AC. The perimeter of the triangle is 56 cm. Find the length of AC.

23 A number is doubled, and 3 is added to the result. The total is then multiplied by 7, and three times the original number is added. If the answer now comes to 344, find the original number.

24 The perimeter of a rectangle is 50 cm, and the length is 4 cm more than twice the breadth. Find the breadth of the rectangle.

25 In a triangle one angle is $x°$, a second angle is $2x°$ and the third is $3(x-2)°$. Find the angles of the triangle.

26 In 5 years time a boy will be twice as old as he was 4 years ago. How old is he now?

27 What is the sum of the angles of a quadrilateral? In a quadrilateral ABCD, $\angle A$ is twice $\angle D$, $\angle C = 80°$ and $\angle B = \angle C + \angle D$. Find all the angles of the quadrilateral.

28 What number must be added to both numerator and denominator of the fraction $\frac{33}{40}$ to give a new fraction which is equal to $\frac{4}{5}$. Explain your answer.

29 A man is at present aged 46 and he has a son aged 20. In x years time the man will be exactly three times as old as his son will be then. Find x, and explain your answer.

45. MENSURATION

Area of a rectangle The rule for the area of a rectangle was given on p. 44 as

Area of rectangle = length × breadth.

Volume of a cuboid The rule for the volume of a cuboid was given on p. 48 as

Volume of cuboid = length × breadth × height.

The **cross-section** of a solid means any cut through the solid perpendicular to its length or height. A solid is said to have a **uniform cross-section** if the cross-section is always the same wherever it is taken.

An argument similar to that used for finding the volume of a cuboid shows that

Volume of solid of uniform cross-section
$$= \textbf{area of cross-section} \times \textbf{length.}$$

Inverse problems If the area and the length of a rectangle are given, we can find the breadth by substituting in the formula

$$\mathbf{A} = \mathbf{\mathit{lb}},$$

and solving the equation for b.

Similarly, if the volume, length, and breadth of a rectangular block are known, we can substitute in the formula

$$\mathbf{V} = \mathbf{\mathit{lbh}}$$

in order to find h.

In the case of a solid of uniform cross-section A sq. units, and of length (or height) h units, the volume is given by the formula

$$\mathbf{V} = \mathbf{A}\mathbf{\mathit{h}}.$$

If V and A are known, we can find h by solving an equation.

Example *A rectangular sheet of metal, 2 m by $1\frac{1}{2}$ m, has a volume 4500 cm³. Find its thickness.*

The length = 200 cm and the breadth = 150 cm.

Let the thickness = h cm.

Then $200 \times 150 \times h = 4500$.

$$\therefore h = \frac{4500}{200 \times 150} = \frac{3}{20}.$$

$\therefore$ the thickness is $\frac{3}{20}$ cm = 1·5 mm.

EXERCISE 115

1 Find (i) the area of the floor, (ii) the total area of the walls, of a room 6·5 m long, 4·75 m wide and 3·5 m high.

2 A room is 8 m long, 7·6 m wide and 3·5 m high. The walls are to be distempered, allowing 25 m² for doors, windows, etc. Find the total area to be distempered.

3 A floor is 7·2 m long and 5·6 m wide. It has a carpet in the middle which reaches to 40 cm from each wall. Find the area of the whole floor and that of the carpet.

4 A room 7 m long and 6·5 m wide is to have the floor covered with carpet which is sold in a roll 50 cm wide. Find the total length of carpet required.

5 Find the volume of a tube of uniform cross-section 2·5 cm² and length 8·4 cm.

6 The length of a post is 3·75 m, and its cross-section is of area 42 cm². Find its volume in cubic centimetres.

7 The cross-section of a girder 3 m long is shown in Fig. 259, where the dimensions are given in centimetres. Find the volume of the girder in cubic centimetres.

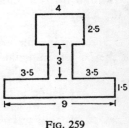

Fig. 259

8 A roll of copper wire, of cross-section 0·8 mm², is 750 m long. If copper weighs 8·8 g per cubic centimetre, find the weight of the roll of wire.

9 A tube of uniform cross-section 25 cm² contains water, and when a stone is dropped into the tube the water level rises 3·6 cm. Find the volume of the stone.

10 A box with a lid is made of wood 1 cm thick. The outside measurements are 36 cm by 32 cm by 20 cm. Find (i) the volume occupied by the box, (ii) the volume of space inside the box, (iii) the volume of wood used in making the box.

11 A lidless box measures externally 30 cm long, 24 cm wide and 16 cm deep. It is made of wood 1 cm thick, and the inside is lined with thin sheet metal. Find the area of metal needed, and the volume of wood used in making the box.

12 Find the weight of a kilometre of copper wire of cross-section 5·2 mm², if 1 cm³ of copper weighs 8·8 g.

13 Find an expression for the volume in cubic centimetres of a rectangular block which is x m long, y cm wide, z mm high.

14 Find an expression for the volume in litres of a pipe of uniform cross-section p m^2 and length q cm.

15 The volume of a rail of uniform cross-section 6·4 cm^2 is 1600 cm^3. Find the length of the rail.

16 The volume of a solid of uniform cross-section is 99·2 cm^3 and the height is 6·4 cm. Find the area of the cross-section.

17 Find the base area of a vessel of uniform cross-section, if the internal height is 25 cm and the capacity is $1\frac{3}{4}$ litres.

The remaining questions in this Exercise require a knowledge of the British Imperial units. The table for these was given on p. 53, and the following facts will also be found useful:

> 1 gallon is the volume of 10 lb of water.
> 1 ft^3 = $6\frac{1}{4}$ gallons (approximately).
> 1 ft^3 of water weighs about $62\frac{1}{2}$ lb.

18 A cistern without a lid is to be lined with zinc at £1·62 per yd^2. Find the cost, if the cistern measures internally 7 ft 9 in long, 5 ft wide and 2 ft 6 in deep.

19 Find the area of linoleum needed to cover a border 1 ft 9 in wide all round the edge of the floor of a room which is 22 ft long and 16 ft 6 in wide.

20 A floor 21 ft long and 18 ft wide is to be covered with carpet from a roll 27 in wide. Find the number of yards required.

21 A wooden block is 9 in long, $3\frac{1}{2}$ in wide and $6\frac{2}{3}$ in high. Find its volume in cubic inches.

22 Find in cubic inches the volume of a piece of wire 10 ft long and of cross-section 0·025 in^2.

23 A lawn 50 ft long and 25 ft wide is surrounded by a path 4 ft wide. Find the number of cubic feet of gravel needed to cover the path to a depth of 3 in.

24 An open box is made of wood 1 in thick. Its inside measurements are 14 in long, 12 in wide and 9 in deep. Find the volume of wood in the box.

25 A wooden post 5 yd long has a cross-section 45 in² in area. Find its volume in cubic feet, and its weight if 1 ft³ of the wood weighs 40 lb.

26 An iron bar is 14 ft long and has a cross-section 4 in². Find its weight, if a cubic foot of iron weighs 480 lb.

27 A rectangular field has an area 45 acres. If the width is 300 yd, find the length.

28 A tennis court is 120 ft by 50 ft. Find the area as a decimal of an acre, correct to two places of decimals.

29 Find in cubic feet the volume of rain which falls on an acre during a rainfall of 1 in. Find also the weight of this rainfall, correct to the nearest ton.

30 A railway company buys a strip of land 55 ft wide for a railway track. How many acres of land are needed for each mile of track?

31 A rectangular tank 8 ft long and 6 ft wide contains 15 in of water. How many gallons of water is this? What is the weight of the water?

32 A vessel of uniform cross-section contains 1 gallon of water. If the water is 9 in deep, find the area of the cross-section of the vessel, to the nearest square inch.

33 The bottom of a tank has an area of 40 ft² and 100 gallons of water are poured into it. Find the depth of the water.

34 A pipe, of uniform cross-section 60 in² and length 6 ft, is full of water. Find the number of gallons of water, and the weight of the water in pounds.

46. CIRCLES AND CYLINDERS

Circumference of a circle The ratio of the circumference of any circle to its diameter is a fixed number, whose value has been calculated to be about 3·14. This fixed number is denoted by the Greek letter π (pronounced 'pie').

Thus
$$\frac{\text{circumference}}{\text{diameter}} = \pi.$$

Let us take C cm to stand for the circumference, d cm for the diameter, and r cm for the radius, so that $d = 2r$.

From the definition above,
$$\frac{C}{d} = \pi.$$
$$\therefore C = \pi d = 2\pi r.$$

The value of π was in early times thought to be 3, as is shown in the Bible account of the building of King Solomon's temple (see I Kings vii, 23). Archimedes, a Greek mathematician of the third century B.C., showed that the value of π lay between $3\frac{1}{7}$ and $3\frac{10}{71}$. The correct value has now been proved to be 3·14159265 . . .

When working to four significant figures, take π as 3·142.

A convenient approximation to π is $3\frac{1}{7}$, which is 3·142857. . . . But it must be remembered that this is correct only to three significant figures, and is not so accurate as 3·142.

Do not be in too great a hurry to substitute a numerical value for π. It often cancels out of the working.

Take π to be 3·142 or 3·14, unless $3\frac{1}{7}$ seems more convenient. Give your answers to three significant figures.

Example 1 *Find the circumference of a circle of radius 4·5 cm.*

Circumference $= 2\pi r$
$$= 2\pi \times 4\cdot5 \text{ cm}$$
$$= 9\pi \text{ cm}$$
$$= (9 \times 3\cdot142) \text{ cm}$$
$$= 28\cdot278 \text{ cm}$$
$$= 28\cdot3 \text{ cm (to three significant figures).}$$

Example 2   *Find the radius of a circle whose circumference is* 8 *cm.*

Let the radius be r cm.
Then the circumference $= 2\pi r$ cm.
$$\therefore 2\pi r = 8.$$
Dividing both sides of this equation by 2π,

$$r = \frac{8}{2\pi}$$

$$= \frac{8}{2 \times 3\frac{1}{7}}$$

$$= \frac{\overset{2}{8} \times 7}{\underset{11}{2 \times 22}} = \frac{14}{11} = 1{\cdot}272 \ldots$$

$\therefore$ the radius $= 1{\cdot}27$ cm (to three significant figures).

EXERCISE 116

Give all answers to three significant figures.
In Nos. 1–8, take π as $3\frac{1}{7}$.

Find the circumference of a circle with:

1 Diameter 7 cm   **2** Radius 6·3 cm   **3** Radius 28 cm
4 Diameter 4·9 m   **5** Diameter 126 m   **6** Radius 5·6 cm
7 Radius 21 cm   **8** Radius 105 m

In Nos. 9–13, take π as 3·142.

Find the circumference of a circle with:

9 Radius 6 cm   **10** Diameter 15 m   **11** Diameter 1·6 m
12 Radius 4000 m   **13** Diameter 11 cm

In Nos. 14–16, take π as $3\frac{1}{7}$; in Nos. 17 and 18 take π as 3·14.

Find the radius of a circle whose circumference is:

14 440 m   **15** 8·8 km   **16** 33 cm
17 48 m   **18** 60 cm

In the rest of the Exercise, take whatever value of π seems appropriate.

19 The minute-hand of a clock is 10 cm long. Find how far the tip moves in an hour.

20 Find how many times a bicycle wheel, diameter 70 cm, revolves while the bicycle goes 8 km.

21 The radii of two circles are 11·7 cm and 15·6 cm. Find the ratio of their circumferences.

22 A circular running-track is 4 m wide. The inner radius is 100 m. Find how much farther it is to run round the outside edge than the inside edge.

Solve the same problem if the inner radius is: (i) 150 m, (ii) x metres.

23 The radii of two circles are x cm and $(x+1)$ cm. Find in terms of π how much the circumference of one exceeds that of the other.

24 A cyclist is travelling at 16 km per h. Find the number of revolutions per minute made by the wheels of his bicycle, if their diameter is 70 cm.

25 The minute-hand of Big Ben is 3·35 m long. Find how far the tip of this hand moves in a quarter of an hour.

Area of a circle   The formula for the area of a circle of radius r can be shown to be

$$A = \pi r^2.$$

The proof is too difficult for our present stage of mathematics; but Fig. 260 shows an interesting way of dividing

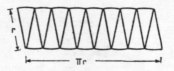

Fig. 260

the circle into 16 parts and fitting them together so as to form a figure which approximates roughly to a rectangle whose length is πr (half the circumference) and breadth r (the radius of the circle).

Example 3 *Find the area of a circle of radius $3\frac{1}{2}$ cm.*

$$\begin{aligned}
\text{Area} &= \pi r^2 \\
&= \tfrac{22}{7} \times (\tfrac{7}{2})^2 \text{ cm}^2 \\
&= \frac{\overset{11}{\cancel{22}}}{7} \times \frac{\overset{7}{\cancel{49}}}{\underset{2}{\cancel{4}}} \text{ cm}^2 \\
&= \tfrac{77}{2} \text{ cm}^2 \\
&= 38\tfrac{1}{2} \text{ cm}^2.
\end{aligned}$$

EXERCISE 117

Give all answers to three significant figures.

In Nos. 1–8, take π as $3\frac{1}{7}$.

Find the area of a circle with:

1 Radius 7 m   **2** Radius 21 cm
3 Diameter 28 cm   **4** Diameter 11·2 cm
5 Diameter 7 cm   **6** Radius 6·3 cm
7 Diameter 400 m   **8** Radius 10·5 cm

In Nos. 9–11, take π as 3·14.

Find the area of a circle with:

9 Radius 2·5 cm   **10** Diameter 1·6 m
11 Radius 40 km

12 Find the radius of a circle whose area is 154 cm². (Take π as $3\frac{1}{7}$.)

13 Find the ratio of the areas of two circles with radii 2 cm and 3 cm. (Do not substitute for π.)

14 The radii of two circles are 3 cm and 3·6 cm. Find the ratio (i) of their circumferences, (ii) of their areas. (Do not substitute for π.)

The circular cylinder A solid whose uniform cross-section is a circle is called a **circular cylinder**. Examples of such a solid are a round pencil, a cocoa tin, and a jam jar. The radius of the cross-section is called the *radius* of the cylinder, and the line which passes through the centres of all the cross-sections is called the *axis* of the cylinder. The length of the axis is sometimes called the *length* of the cylinder (as in the case of a round ruler), sometimes the *height* (as in the case of a jam jar), sometimes the *thickness* (as in the case of a penny).

Surface area of a cylinder   If you wrap a piece of paper round a cylinder so as to fit exactly, you can unroll the paper into a rectangle whose width is the same as the height of the cylinder and whose length is the circumference of the cylinder.

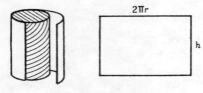

FIG. 261

If the radius is r units and the height h units, the circumference of the cylinder is $2\pi r$ units. The formula for the area of the curved surface, S sq. units, is therefore

$$S = 2\pi rh.$$

If the cylinder is solid, the *total* surface includes the two circular ends, which each have an area πr^2 sq. units.

∴ the *total* surface area $= (2\pi rh + 2\pi r^2)$ sq. units, which is the same as $2\pi r(h + r)$ sq. units.

Volume of a cylinder   By the rule

$$V = Ah$$

for the volume of a solid of uniform cross-section, the formula for the volume of a circular cylinder of radius r and height h is seen to be

$$V = \pi r^2 h.$$

Example 4 *Find the area of the curved surface and the volume of a circular cylinder of radius 3 cm and height 5 cm.*

Here $r = 3$, $h = 5$.

∴ the area of the curved surface

$$= 2\pi rh$$
$$= (2 \times \tfrac{22}{7} \times 3 \times 5) \text{ cm}^2$$
$$= \tfrac{660}{7} \text{ cm}^2$$
$$= 94 \cdot 3 \text{ cm}^2 \text{ (to three significant figures)}.$$

The volume of the cylinder

$$= \pi r^2 h$$
$$= (\tfrac{22}{7} \times 9 \times 5) \text{ cm}^3$$
$$= \tfrac{990}{7} \text{ cm}^3$$
$$= 141 \text{ cm}^3 \text{ (approx.)}.$$

EXERCISE 118

Give all answers to three significant figures.

In Nos. 1–8, take π as $3\tfrac{1}{7}$ or $3\cdot14$, whichever seems the more convenient.

Find the area of the curved surface and the volume of a circular cylinder with:

1 Radius 7 cm, height 12 cm.

2 Radius 1·4 cm, height 6 cm.

3 Radius 4 cm, length 10 cm.

4 Diameter 18 cm, height 5 cm.

5 Radius 3·5 cm, length 12 cm.

Find the *total* surface area of a solid circular cylinder with:

6 Radius 2 m, length 8 m.

7 Radius 10 cm, thickness 0·5 cm.

8 Radius 21 cm, length 12 cm.

Take π as $3\tfrac{1}{7}$ in Nos. 9–14.

9 A garden roller has a radius 28 cm and width 48 cm. Find in square metres the area rolled during 60 revolutions.

10 If $2\pi rh = 264$ and $r = 21$, find h.

11 If the area of the curved surface of a cylinder is 44 cm², and the height is 14 cm, find the radius.

12 Find the height of a cylinder whose radius is $3\frac{1}{2}$ cm and volume $423\frac{1}{2}$ cm³.

13 Find the radius of a cylinder whose volume is 198 cm³ and height 7 cm.

14 Find the length of a cylinder whose radius is 1 cm and *total* surface area 44 cm².

The rest of the Exercise involves a knowledge of British Imperial units.

Give all answers correct to three significant figures.

In Nos. 15–22, take π as $3\frac{1}{7}$.

Find the circumference and area of a circle with:

15 Radius 28 in.   **16** Diameter 7 yd.   **17** Diameter 42 yd.

18 Radius 1 ft 9 in.   **19** Radius 100 yd.

20 Find the radius of a circle whose circumference is 8 ft.

21 Find the radius of a circle whose circumference is 440 yd.

22 Find the radius of a circle whose area is 616 in².

In Nos. 23–25, take π as 3·142.

Find the circumference and area of a circle with:

23 Radius 6 in.   **24** Diameter 15 ft.   **25** Radius 40 miles.

In the rest of the Exercise, take π as $3\frac{1}{7}$ or 3·14, whichever seems the more convenient.

Find the area of the curved surface and the volume of a right circular cylinder with:

26 Radius 7 in, height 12 in.

27 Diameter 1 ft 6 in, height 5 in.

Find the *total* surface area of a solid circular cylinder with:

28 Radius 2 ft, length 8 ft.

29 Radius 1 ft 9 in, length 1 ft.

Take π as $3\frac{1}{7}$ in Nos. 30–34.

30 A garden roller has a radius of 14 in, and is 2 ft wide. Find in square yards the area rolled during 100 revolutions.

31 If the area of the curved surface of a cylinder is 29 ft² 48 in² and the height is 7 ft, find the radius.

32 Find the height of a cylinder whose radius is 3 ft 6 in and volume 1540 ft³.

33 Find the radius of a cylinder whose volume is 880 in³ and height 1 ft 5½ in.

34 Find the length of a solid cylinder whose radius is 4 in and *total* surface area 132 in².

47. PLAN AND ELEVATION (II)

Most of the examples in the first section on Plan and Elevation, p. 142, were cuboids. In this section we shall apply the same methods to the pyramid, the prism, the cylinder, and also to the sphere. A **sphere** is an object shaped like a billiard ball or tennis ball. You will come across formulae for the volume and surface area of a sphere later in your work. In the meantime you will need to have a general idea of what is meant by the word. Just as all points on the circumference of a circle are at a fixed distance from the centre of the circle, so all points on the surface of a sphere are at a fixed distance from the centre of the sphere. We call this fixed distance the *radius* of the sphere.

The prism We have already referred to solids with uniform cross-sections. If the solid has a uniform cross-section which is a triangle, a quadrilateral, or a polygon with any number of sides, it is often called a **prism**; if the uniform cross-section is a circle or an ellipse, the solid is called a **cylinder.**

The cuboid in oblique position In the earlier section the cuboid was always placed on the horizontal plane in such a position as to have four edges parallel to one or other of the two vertical planes. We shall now consider the problem of a cuboid placed in an oblique position.

Example *A rectangular block, 4 cm long, 3 cm wide and 2 cm high, is placed with the largest face on the horizontal plane and the longest edges making 30° with the XY line. Draw the plan, front elevation and end elevation.*

See p. 143 for the arrangement of the horizontal plane (which we shall in future call H.P.), the vertical plane A and the vertical plane B (which we shall call V.P. A and V.P. B).

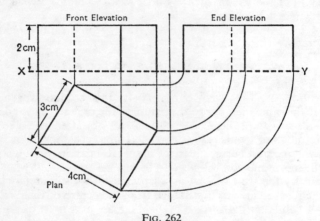

Fɪɢ. 262

We begin by drawing the XY line across the paper, and a line perpendicular to it to represent the trace of V.P. B.

Then we draw a rectangle 4 cm by 3 cm, which is the plan in the H.P. The 4 cm sides of this rectangle make 30° with XY.

Perpendiculars are drawn from the four corners of this rectangle to the XY line and to the trace of V.P. B, and thus the front elevation and the end elevation are obtained. Notice that one vertical edge in the front elevation and one in the end elevation are marked as dotted lines, to show that they are hidden detail.

EXERCISE 119

1 Describe the shape and position of the solids whose plan and elevation are shown in Fig. 263.

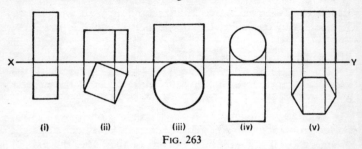

Fig. 263

Draw the plan, front elevation and end elevation of each of the solids described in Nos. 2–12.

2 A sphere, diameter 6 cm, resting on the H.P. and touching it at a point $3\frac{1}{2}$ cm from XY.

3 A hemisphere (or half-sphere) with its flat surface, of radius 2 cm, resting on the H.P., and the centre of the flat surface 3 cm from XY.

4 A circular cylinder, radius 2 cm and length 4 cm, standing with a circular end on the H.P. and the centre of that end $2\frac{1}{2}$ cm from XY.

5 The same cylinder as in No. 4, but lying with its curved surface touching the H.P., its axis at right angles to XY and one circular end touching V.P. A.

6 The same cylinder as in No. 4, but lying with its curved surface touching the H.P., its axis parallel to XY and $2\frac{1}{2}$ cm from XY.

7 A prism, cross-section a square of side 2 cm, length of prism 6 cm, one square face in contact with the V.P. A and one face in contact with the H.P.

8 The same prism as in No. 7; one square face on the H.P., the edges of this face making 45° with XY, and the nearest corner of this face $1\frac{1}{2}$ cm from XY.

9 The same prism as in No. 7; one square face on the H.P., the nearest corner of this face 1½ cm from XY, and two opposite edges of this face making 30° with XY.

10 A hexagonal prism, height 3 cm, the ends regular six-sided figures with each side 2 cm; standing with one end on the H.P., with one side of that end parallel to XY and 1 cm from XY.

11 A triangular prism, length 4 cm and the ends equilateral triangles of side 3 cm; a side face in contact with the H.P., the 4 cm edges making 40° with XY, and the nearest corner of that face 1 cm from XY.

12 A cube with edges 3 cm long, standing on the H.P. with one face touching the V.P. A, and a circular cylinder of height 3½ cm, radius 1 cm, standing on top of the cube, the axis of the cylinder passing through the centre of the top face of the cube.

Describe the shape and position of the solids whose plan, front elevation and end elevation are shown in Figs. 264, 265.

13   **14**

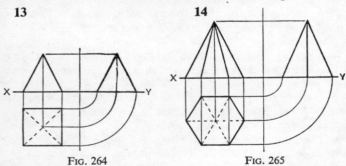

Fig. 264   Fig. 265

15 A square pyramid 3 cm high has a base which is a square of side 4 cm. It stands on the horizontal plane with two edges of the base parallel to XY. Draw its plan, front elevation and end elevation.

16 The same square pyramid as in No. 15 stands on the H.P. with two opposite sides of the base inclined at an angle of 30° with XY. Draw its plan, front elevation and end elevation. (Remember that the vertex of the pyramid is vertically above the centre of the base.)

48. AVERAGES

There are several different meanings to the word average, all with different uses. The most common of these, and the one you have probably met already, is the **arithmetic mean,** often called simply the **mean.** It is frequently referred to as the *average*. Suppose that a cricketer scores 16, 3, 29, 0, 48 and 12 in six completed innings. We say that his average is obtained by adding together all his scores and dividing by the number of innings:

$$\frac{16+3+29+0+48+12}{6}, \text{ which equals } \frac{108}{6} \text{ or } 18.$$

Example 1 *The readings of the barometer on seven days of a certain week are 764, 763, 755, 764, 766, 767 and 762. Find the mean of these readings.*

The sum of the readings = 5341.

∴ the mean $= \frac{5341}{7} = 763.$

If the numbers are large and there are a lot of them to be added together, quick methods of calculating the mean can be employed. Thus, all the readings in Example 1 are approximately 760, and we need only calculate the mean reading *above* 760 (regarding a reading below 760 as a negative reading *above* 760).

The sum of the readings above 760

$$= 4+3-5+4+6+7+2$$
$$= 21.$$

The mean $= \frac{21}{7} = 3.$

∴ the mean of the readings = 760 + 3 = 763.

Example 2 *The marks of 20 boys in a test were:*

$$\begin{array}{ccccc} 2 & 18 & 21 & 8 & 36 \\ 64 & 17 & 23 & 58 & 63 \\ 33 & 29 & 41 & 32 & 19 \\ 20 & 41 & 40 & 49 & 10 \end{array}$$

Find the mean of these marks.

Since the marks are spread out from 2 to 64, let us take 30 as an **assumed mean**. We write down the deviations from 30, i.e. the amounts by which the marks exceed or fall short of that number, an excess being positive and a deficiency negative.

Deviation from 30

+					-				
6	34	28	33	3	28	12	9	22	13
11	2	11	10	19	7	1	11	10	20
Total = 157					Total = 133				

Mean mark $= 30 + \dfrac{157 - 133}{20} = 30 + \dfrac{24}{20} = 31$ approximately.

Example 3 *The average age of 6 men is 45, and 5 of the men are 47, 40, 38, 46 and 43 years old. Find the age of the sixth man.*

The sum of the ages of all 6 men $= 45 \times 6 = 270$.
The sum of the ages of 5 men $= 214$.
∴ the age of the sixth man $= 270 - 214 = 56$.

Example 4 *A grocer mixes 7 kg of tea at 59p per kg with 5 kg of tea at 47p per kg. Find the average cost per kilogramme of the mixture.*

7 kg of tea at 59p per kg cost 413p.
5 kg of tea at 47p per kg cost 235p.
∴ 12 kg of the mixture cost 648p.
∴ 1 kg costs 54p.
∴ the average cost of the mixture is 54p per kg.

Notice that this answer is not the mean of 59p and 47p, for this would be $\frac{1}{2}(59 + 47)\text{p} = \frac{1}{2} \times 106\text{p} = 53\text{p}$. The reason is that there are more kilogrammes of the dearer tea than of the cheaper tea.

The next example also illustrates the danger of taking an arithmetic mean as the answer to a problem without considering the matter.

Example 5 *A motorist travels 60 km at 48 km per hour, and $7\frac{1}{2}$ km at 30 km per hour. Find his average speed for the whole journey.*

The time to travel 60 km at 48 km/h $=\dfrac{60}{48}$ h $= 1\frac{1}{4}$ h.

The time to travel $7\frac{1}{2}$ km at 30 km/h $=\dfrac{7\frac{1}{2}}{30}$ h

$$=\dfrac{15}{60} \text{ h} = \tfrac{1}{4} \text{ h.}$$

∴ the time to travel $67\frac{1}{2}$ km $= 1\frac{1}{2}$ h.

Average speed for the journey $=\dfrac{67\frac{1}{2}}{1\frac{1}{2}}$ km/h

$$=\dfrac{135}{3} = 45 \text{ km/h.}$$

Note. The mean of 48 km/h and 30 km/h is 39 km/h.

Example 6 *A boy can swim at 10 km per hour in still water. In a stream flowing at 4 km per hour, he swims down-stream for a certain distance and then swims back to his starting-point. Find his average speed for the whole distance.*

His speed down-stream is 14 km/h, and his speed up-stream is 6 km/h.

Suppose he swims a distance a km down-stream.

The time to swim a km down-stream $=\dfrac{a}{14}$ h.

The time to swim a km up-stream $\quad=\dfrac{a}{6}$ h.

Total time $\quad=\left(\dfrac{a}{14}+\dfrac{a}{6}\right)$ h $=\left(\dfrac{3a}{42}+\dfrac{7a}{42}\right)$ h

$$=\dfrac{10a}{42} \text{ h} = \dfrac{5a}{21} \text{ h.}$$

Average speed $=\dfrac{\text{total distance}}{\text{total time}} = 2a \div \dfrac{5a}{21}$ km/h

$$= 2a \times \dfrac{21}{5a} = \dfrac{42}{5} = 8\tfrac{2}{5} \text{ km/h.}$$

EXERCISE 120

Find the average of:

1 2, 4, 6, 8, 10, 12, 14   **2** 0·7, 2·7, 1·2, 0·4, 3·5

3 843, 851, 861, 848, 857   **4** 42p, 51p, 37p, 26p

5 13 years 4 months, 13 years 7 months, 13 years 9 months, 14 years 1 month, 12 years 11 months, 12 years 10 months.

Use an assumed mean, as in the worked example on p. 292, to find the mean of the following sets of numbers:

6	95	103	113	109	78
	127	83	100	94	90
	104	119	101	88	86

7	58·4	62·7	61·6	55·0	47·2
	59·0	51·3	45·5	60·2	49·1
	42·8	53·1	52·6	58·7	61·8

8	1817	2122	2946	1941	1968
	2223	2004	1861	1919	2310
	2011	1897	2411	2018	1822

9 If 5 kg of tea at 60p per kg, 8 kg at 42p per kg and 3 kg at 44p per kg are mixed together, find the average cost per kg of the mixture.

10 Find the average cost per kg of a mixture which consists of 12 kg at 7½p per kg, 8 kg at 7p per kg and 4 kg at 11½p per kg.

11 A factory buys 15 tons of coal at £8·40 per ton, 10 tons at £10·50 per ton and 10 tons at £12·60 per ton in the course of a year. Find the average cost per ton for the year.

12 A boy cycles 30 km at 15 km/h and returns by the same route at 12 km/h. Find his total time and his average speed for the whole journey.

13 A motorist travels to a town 54 km away at an average speed of 60 km/h and returns at an average speed of 48 km/h. Find his average speed for the whole journey.

14 The average age of 6 men is 37, and one of them is 42. Find the average age of the other five men.

15 A man travels for 1 h at 45 km/h, then for 3 h at 63 km/h, then for 2 hr at 36 km/h. Find his average speed for the whole journey.

16 A batsman has scored 21, 13, 42, 20 and 8 in 5 completed innings. How many runs must he score in the next innings to make his average 25 for the 6 innings?

17 During the cricket season a batsman scores r runs in x innings. He was n times not out. Find his batting average for the season.

REVISION PAPERS

PAPERS 31–35 (§26–33)

Paper 31

1 Draw a triangle ABC in which BC = 5·1 cm, AC = 6·9 cm and $\angle$ B = 70°. Measure AB.

2 Draw a straight line 9 cm long, and by a geometrical construction divide it into 7 equal parts.

3 ABC is an isosceles triangle in which AB = AC = 10 cm, BC = 16 cm and D is the mid-point of BC. Calculate AD.

4 Simplify: (i) $\dfrac{7xy}{4ab} \times \dfrac{16a^2}{14x^2}$, (ii) $\dfrac{1}{x} + \dfrac{1}{2x} + \dfrac{1}{3x} + \dfrac{1}{4x}$.

5 A marble, rolled down a smooth groove cut in a sloping board, moves through the following distances in 1, 2, 3, ... sec:

Time in sec	0	1	2	3	4	5	6
Distance in cm	0	3	12	27	48	75	108

Draw a graph in which the distance rolled is plotted against the number of seconds which have elapsed, and find the distance through which the marble rolls in $4\frac{1}{2}$ sec.

6 If 24 men earn £252 in 7 days, how many men will earn £342 in 6 days?

Paper 32

1 Simplify: (i) $2x^2 \times 4xy \times 3y^2$, (ii) $2ab \times 2bc \times 2ca$, (iii) $\dfrac{x^6 y^3}{x^2 y^5}$.

2 If 8 fires burn 5·4 tonnes of coal in $13\frac{1}{2}$ days, in how many days at the same rate will 5 fires burn 7 tonnes?

3 Express the ratio 4 mm : 7·91 m in the form $1 : n$.

4 The distance in kilometres of a point on the horizon at sea when seen from a place above sea-level is given in the following table:

Height in metres	0	10	25	50	75	100
Distance in kilometres	0	11·3	17·9	25·3	30·9	35·7
Height in metres	150	200	250	300		
Distance in kilometres	43·7	50·5	56·5	61·9		

Draw a graph of these values, and estimate from your graph how high above sea-level you would have to be to see a distance of 48 kilometres.

5 Draw a quadrilateral ABCD in which $\angle A = 120°$, AB = 2·8 cm, AD = 2·4 cm, DC = 5·2 cm and $\angle D = 60°$. Measure BC.

6 In Fig. 266, if AX = XB = 2 cm, BC = 2·8 cm and AC = 3·8 cm, calculate AY and XY.

Fig. 266

Paper 33

1 Calculate the side of a rhombus whose diagonals are 10 cm and 24 cm long.

2 Verify the statements of the Egyptian priest Ahmes (about 1800 B.C.) that:

 (i) $\frac{5}{21}$ is the sum of the fractions $\frac{1}{7}$, $\frac{1}{14}$, $\frac{1}{42}$;

 (ii) $\frac{2}{29}$ is the sum of $\frac{1}{24}$, $\frac{1}{58}$, $\frac{1}{174}$, $\frac{1}{232}$.

3 Simplify: (i) $\dfrac{ab}{a^3b^3}$,   (ii) $\dfrac{x^3y^2}{3xy^6}$,   (iii) $\dfrac{1}{t}+\dfrac{1}{2t}$.

4 ABC is an isosceles triangle in which AB = AC; L, M are the feet of the perpendiculars from B, C to AC, AB respectively. Prove that the triangles BLC, CMB are congruent, and deduce that BL = CM.

5 If $a:b=4:9$ and $b:c=12:19$, find three whole numbers proportional to a, b, c.

6 The price of tobacco goes up in the ratio $6:5$ and a man decreases the quantity he smokes in the ratio $2:3$. In what ratio does the money he spends on tobacco alter?

Paper 34

1 Values of the age of a male and the number of years he is expected to live are given in the following table:

Age in years	0	10	20	30	40	50	60
Number of years expected to live	44·1	49·6	41	33·1	25·6	18·9	12·9

Taking scales of 1 cm to 5 years, draw a graph, and estimate how many more years a man aged 36 may expect to live.

2 E is the mid-point of the side AC of $\triangle$ABC. Construct the triangle, if AB = 6 cm, AC = 5 cm and BE = 4·2 cm. Measure BC.

3 Draw a straight line AB 5 cm long, and without further measurement construct a point P on it such that $AP=\frac{1}{2}PB$.

4 A rectangle is 15 m long and 8 m wide. Calculate the length of its diagonal.

5 Find the values of:

(i) $\dfrac{2\frac{1}{2}+1\frac{2}{3}}{2\frac{1}{2}-1\frac{2}{3}}$,   (ii) $(13\frac{1}{2}-11\frac{1}{4})(13\frac{1}{2}+11\frac{1}{4})$.

6 Simplify:

(i) $3x^5\times 5x^3$.   (ii) $6a^6\div 3a^3$,   (iii) $\sqrt{36y^8}$.

Paper 35

1 If 19 men working $7\frac{1}{2}$ h per day can do a certain piece of work in 24 days, how many hours a day must 45 men work to do it in 8 days?

2 Divide £315 in the ratios $3:7:11$.

3 In Fig. 267, if AB = BC = 2 cm, AP = 1·5 cm and CR = 3·5 cm, calculate BQ. (Find BL and LQ.)

4 In Fig. 268, if AB = 26 cm, CD = 19 cm and BD = 24 cm, calculate AC.

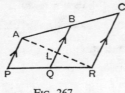

FIG. 267   FIG. 268

5 Simplify:

    (i) $\dfrac{(4x)^2}{20x^4}$,   (ii) $\dfrac{1}{3y}+\dfrac{1}{6y}$,   (iii) $\sqrt{9x^6}$.

6 The following table shows the distances travelled by a car accelerating from rest:

Time in sec	0	1	2	4	5	6	7	8	10	11	12
Distance in metres	0	3	10	33	50	70	87	109	160	188	216

Draw a graph to show these values, and estimate the distance travelled (i) in 3 seconds, (ii) in 9 seconds.

PAPERS 36–40 (§34–41)

Paper 36

1 Find to the nearest penny the simple interest on £525 for $2\frac{1}{2}$ years at $3\frac{1}{2}$ per cent p.a.

2 The base ABCD of a cube (see Fig. 269) rests on a table. The cube is rolled over, without slipping, so that the face BCGF rests on the table. It is then rolled over again so that FGHE rests on the table, and then again so that ADHE rests on the table. Sketch the locus of the point A.

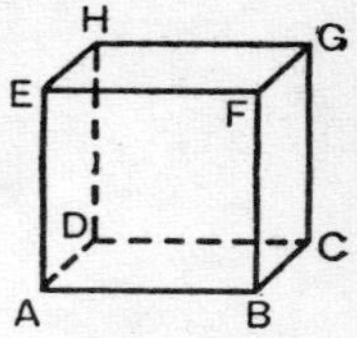

Fig. 269

3 Express as percentages the fractions $\frac{1}{10}$, $\frac{1}{100}$, $\frac{1}{8}$, $\frac{1}{12}$, $\frac{2}{3}$, $\frac{7}{2}$.

4 Simplify: (i) $3(x+7)-2(x-3)+4(2x-1)$,

(ii) $-(-3a)+(-4a)-(+2a)$,

(iii) a^2bc when $a=-1$, $b=+2$, $c=-3$.

5 Calculate the length of a chord of a circle which is at a distance 5 cm from the centre, if the radius of the circle is 13 cm.

6 Name three capital letters of the alphabet which have symmetry about a line, and three which have symmetry about a point.

Paper 37

1 In Fig. 270, $\angle ACD = 52°$ and O is the centre of the circle. Calculate $\angle AOB$.

2 Draw a straight line AB and mark a point S 1 cm from AB. P is any point in the line AB. SP is produced 1 cm to Q. Plot the locus of Q.

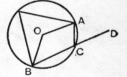

3 Draw a circle of radius 4 cm and mark a point P $2\frac{1}{2}$ cm from the centre. Construct a chord APB which is such that AP = PB.

Fig. 270

4 Find the simple interest on £492·75 for 100 days at 3 per cent p.a.

5 If 12% of a sum of money is £30, find the sum.

6 Draw a triangle ABC in which AB=4 cm, AC=8 cm and ∠A=60°. Find by construction a point P which is such that BP=3 cm and PA=PC. Measure PA, and state its length.

Paper 38

1 Goods are bought at £250 per tonne and sold at 29p per kg. Find the gain per cent.

2 Simplify: (i) $-(-8x)-(-7x)+(-3x)$,

(ii) $(15y^3) \div (-5y)$, (iii) $(3a)(-3b)(-3c)$.

3 Draw two straight lines AOB, COD, intersecting at 60°. Construct the locus of points (i) 2 cm from AB, (ii) 1 cm from CD. Mark clearly the points which lie on both loci, and measure their distances from O.

4 Without using a protractor or set square, construct a triangle ABC in which AB=5·5 cm, BC=6·5 cm and the angle ABC=120°. Construct the circumcircle of the triangle, and measure its radius.

5 Calculate to the nearest penny the simple interest on £500 from April 4 to June 9 at 4 per cent p.a.

6 In Fig. 271, AB=AC=AD. If ∠BAC=40° and ∠CAD=36°, calculate the angles of △BCD. (Consider A as the centre of a circle through B, C, D.)

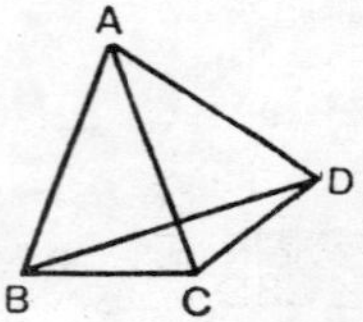

FIG. 271

Paper 39

1 Remove brackets, and simplify:

(i) $3x+(3x-2y)-2(x+4y)$,
(ii) $3\{a-(t-a)\}-2\{t-(a-t)\}$.

2 Draw a triangle ABC in which BC = 4·2 cm, ∠B = 38°, ∠C = 112°. Produce the sides in both directions, and construct the locus of points: (i) 1 cm from AB, (ii) equidistant from AB and AC. Mark clearly the points which lie on both loci, and measure their distances from B.

3 (i) Evaluate 3½% of £4·86, to the nearest penny. (ii) Express 37·2 m as a percentage of a kilometre.

4 An article was sold for £31·20 at a loss of 2½%. Find the cost price.

5 Construct two circles of radii 4 cm and 5 cm such that the length of their common chord (i.e. the distance apart of their two points of intersection) is 6 cm. (Begin by drawing the common chord.)

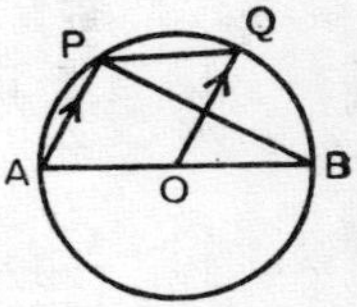

6 In Fig. 272, if O is the centre of the circle and AB is a diameter, and if ∠PAB = 62°, calculate ∠s QOB, QPB and APQ.

Fig. 272

Paper 40

1 The diagonals AC, BD of a cyclic quadrilateral ABCD intersect at X. If ∠AXD = 94°, ∠ACD = 41° and ∠CBD = 36°, calculate ∠BAD.

2 Draw a triangle ABC in which AB = 4·5 cm, BC = 4·1 cm and CA = 4·9 cm. Construct the locus of points (i) equidistant from AB and BC, (ii) 3·2 cm from C. Mark clearly all the points which lie on both loci, and measure their distances from B.

3 A length of 5·5 m was incorrectly measured as 5·1 m. Find the error as a percentage of the true value.

4 An article was sold at a profit of $7\frac{1}{2}$ per cent of the cost price. If the profit was £12, find the selling price.

5 A circle has a radius of 13 cm. Two parallel chords (on the same side of the centre) are 10 cm and 24 cm long. Calculate their distance apart. (Draw the perpendicular from the centre of the circle to the chords.)

6 Draw a triangle ABC in which AB = 6·8 cm, the angle A = 62° and the angle B = 48°. Construct the circumcircle of the triangle, and measure its radius.

PAPERS 41–45 (§42–48)

Paper 41

1 A cricketer has an average of 35 runs per innings after 8 completed innings. In his ninth innings he scores 62. Find his new average.

2 A number of coins, some of them 5p pieces and the rest 10p pieces, make up £2·35. The number of 10p pieces is one more than twice the number of 5p pieces. Find the number of each.

3 Draw a triangle ABC with sides 5·4 cm, 6·6 cm and 4·8 cm. Construct the inscribed circle of the triangle, and measure its radius.

4 Solve the equations:

(i) $4(x-7)-2(x-5)=9$,

(ii) $\dfrac{y+2}{3}-\dfrac{2y+5}{4}=\dfrac{5(y+2)}{6}$.

5 A hexagonal prism, whose height is 7 cm and whose ends are regular six-sided figures with each side 2 cm, stands with one end on the horizontal plane and with one side of that end parallel to the XY line and 1 cm from it. Draw the plan, front elevation and end elevation.

6 Find the area of a circle whose radius is 1·5 cm. (Take π as 3·142.)

Paper 42

1 A bicycle wheel is 70 cm in diameter. Find how many revolutions it makes in a kilometre. (Take π as $\frac{22}{7}$.)

2 Draw the plan and front elevation of a pyramid standing on the horizontal plane, the base of the pyramid being a square of side 3 cm with two edges parallel to the XY line, the height of the pyramid being 5 cm.

3 Solve the equation

$$\tfrac{1}{3}(x-1)+\tfrac{1}{2}x=\tfrac{1}{4}(x+1).$$

4 Draw a circle with centre O and radius 3 cm. Mark two radii OA, OB making the angle AOB equal to 73°, and construct the tangents at A and B to the circle. Measure the angle between these two tangents, and verify your answer by calculation.

5 If 5 is added to a certain number, the result is the same as if 45 is subtracted from three times the number. Find the number.

6 A tank is 2 m long and $1\frac{1}{2}$ m wide, and 90 litres of water are poured into it. Find through how many centimetres the water-level rises.

Paper 43

1 In Fig. 273, AP$=a$ cm, BQ$=b$ cm, CR$=c$ cm and DS$=d$ cm; P, Q, R and S are the points of contact of AB, BC, CD and DA with the circle. By expressing both sides of the equation in terms of a, b, c, d, prove that

AB$+$CD$=$BC$+$DA.

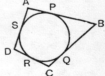

FIG. 273

2 Solve the equation

$$\frac{4x-7}{3}-\frac{2x+3}{2}=\frac{8-x}{6}.$$

3 The average age of a class of 30 boys is 14 years 4 months. Five boys whose average age is 15 years 2 months leave the class. Find the average age of the 25 remaining boys.

4 Calculate the volume of a circular cylinder whose radius is 9 cm and height 3·5 cm. (Take π as $\frac{22}{7}$.)

5 An empty rectangular tank is 3 m long, 2 m wide and 1 m deep. All the rainfall over an area of 120 m² drains into the tank. Find in centimetres the depth of the rainfall necessary to fill the tank.

6 Draw the plan, front elevation and end elevation of a cuboid 5 cm long, 3 cm wide and 2 cm high, standing on its end on the horizontal plane with the 2 cm edges inclined to XY at 30°.

Paper 44

1 The radii of two circles are 22 cm and 26·4 cm. Find the ratio (i) of their circumferences, (ii) of their areas.

2 Solve the equation

$$2x + 1 + \tfrac{2}{3}(1 - x) = \tfrac{4}{3}(3 - 2x).$$

3 In Fig. 274, X, Y, Z are the points of contact of the inscribed circle with the sides of the triangle ABC. If AY = 4 cm, BZ = 5 cm and CX = 2 cm, calculate the lengths of BC, CA and AB.

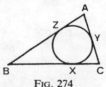

Fig. 274

4 In Fig. 274, if $\angle$ABC = 48° and $\angle$ACB = 62°, calculate the numbers of degrees in the angles BXZ and CXY. Find also the angles of the triangle XYZ.

5 Find what number must be added to the numerator and denominator of the fraction $\frac{5}{13}$ to make a new fraction which is equal to $\frac{3}{5}$.

6 Draw the plan, front elevation and end elevation of a cube, with edges 4 cm long, standing on the horizontal plane with two opposite faces inclined at 60° to the XY line.

Paper 45

1 The centre of a circle of radius 8 cm is O. A point P is such that OP = 17 cm. Calculate the length of the tangent from P to the circle.

2 In a circle, whose centre is O, three radii OA, OB, OC are drawn. $\angle AOB = 110°$, $\angle BOC = 134°$ and $\angle AOC = 116°$. Tangents are drawn to the circle at A, B, C to form a triangle. Calculate the angles of this triangle.

3 An open box is made of wood $\frac{1}{2}$ cm thick. Its inside measurements are 14 cm long, 12 cm wide and 8 cm deep. Find the volume of wood in the box.

4 AB is a line 14 cm long, and P is a point in AB produced such that $\frac{AP}{BP} = \frac{5}{3}$. Denoting the length BP by x cm, form an equation in x and hence find the length of BP.

5 Find the total surface area, including the two ends, of a cylinder whose height is 4 cm and whose base-radius is 3 cm. (Take π as $\frac{22}{7}$.)

6 Solve the equations:
  (i) $2(3t + 5) + 3(t - 2) = 2(2t + 7)$,
  (ii) $0·6(2x - 0·5) + 0·5x = x - 0·4$.

PAPERS 46–50 (§26–48)

Paper 46

1 The temperature of a hot body that is cooling is shown by the following table:

Number of minutes elapsed	0	1	2	3	4
Temperature (°C.)	93	83·8	75·6	67·8	61·1

Number of minutes elapsed	5	7	8	9	10
Temperature (°C.)	55	44·6	40·1	36·1	32·9

Draw the graph, and estimate the temperature of the body after it has been cooling for 6 min.

2 In Fig. 275, ABC is the base and V the vertex of a tetrahedron. D, E, F, G are the mid-points of VB, VC, AB, AC respectively. Apply the mid-point theorem to the triangles VBC, ABC, and hence prove that ED is parallel and equal to GF. What kind of figure is EDFG?

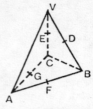

FIG. 275

3 Construct a cyclic quadrilateral ABCD in which AB = 4·6 cm, BC = 3·8 cm, the angle ABC is a right angle and AD = DC. (Start with the triangle ABC and draw its circumcircle. On what line does D lie if AD = DC?) Measure AD.

4 Simplify:

(i) $(-3) \times (+8)$, (ii) $(-5x) \times (-4y)$, (iii) $\dfrac{a}{-b} \times (-b)^3$.

5 After falling in price by 10%, a car was worth £720. What was it worth originally?

6 Solve the equation $3x - 2·7 = -4·41$.

Paper 47

1 Find the error per cent in taking π as $3\frac{1}{7}$, assuming the correct value to be 3·1416. (Answer to 2 decimal places.)

2 Find the H.C.F. and L.C.M. of $16a^3b^2$, $24a^3bc$, $56a^2bc$.

3 Four rods form a parallelogram ABCD. AB is held fixed, while AD and BC turn about A and B. (See Fig. 276.) P is the mid-point of the rod CD. Plot the locus of P.

(Hint: let O be the mid-point of AB. Consider the quadrilateral ADPO. What can you say about the length of OP?)

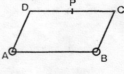

FIG. 276

4 If a men earn £b in d days, how much will x men earn in f days at the same rate?

5 In Fig. 277, if OA : AP = 3 : 2 and OC = 6·9 cm, calculate OR.

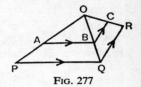

Fig. 277

6 After 5% had been deducted from a bill, the amount to be paid was £60·42. Find the original amount of the bill.

Paper 48

1 Give the locus (i) of the mid-point of a variable chord of a circle, if the chord is of a fixed length, (ii) of the mid-point of a straight rod whose ends slide on the inside of a hollow sphere.

2 Solve the equation $(4x-3)-(2-5x)=1+x$.

3 An article is sold for £47·70 at a loss of $16\frac{2}{3}\%$ of the cost price. Find the cost price.

4 Find the angles of an isosceles triangle, if each of the angles at the base is four times the vertical angle.

5 Draw the plan, front elevation and end elevation of a circular cylinder of length 6 cm, base-radius 2 cm, lying on the horizontal plane with its length parallel to XY.

6 A cylindrical tank $1\frac{1}{2}$ m in diameter holds 990 litres of water. Calculate the depth of the water. (Take π as $3\frac{1}{7}$.)

Paper 49

1 Find (i) the total area of the walls, (ii) the volume, of a room $5\frac{1}{2}$ m long, $4\frac{1}{4}$ m wide and 4 m high.

2 Solve the equation $10(x-1)=28(x-3)-35(x-6)$.

3 A regular pentagon ABCDE is inscribed in a circle. P is any point on the minor arc AB. Calculate $\angle$APB.

4 A and B are fixed points. What is the locus of a point P if $\angle$APB$=90°$, (i) in the plane of the paper, (ii) in space?

5 The volume of a circular cylinder is 186 cm³ and the radius is 7 cm. Find its height, to the nearest millimetre.

6 Find the simple interest on £136 for 3 years at 6% p.a.

Paper 50

1 Evaluate: (i) 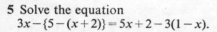, (ii)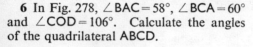

2 Draw a series of parallel chords of a circle, plot the locus of their mid-points, and state what the locus is.

3 The length of a rectangular field is three times the breadth. If the perimeter is 336 m, find the breadth.

4 At an election in which there were two candidates, one received 54 per cent of the votes, and he had 344 votes more than his opponent. Find the number of votes cast.

5 Solve the equation
$$3x - \{5 - (x + 2)\} = 5x + 2 - 3(1 - x).$$

6 In Fig. 278, $\angle BAC = 58°$, $\angle BCA = 60°$ and $\angle COD = 106°$. Calculate the angles of the quadrilateral ABCD.

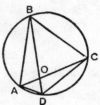

Fig. 278

PAPERS 51–65 (§1–48)

Paper 51

1 Perform the calculations (i) $2012_3 + 1202_3$, (ii) $220_3 \times 121_3$.

2 Find the simple interest on £450 for 1 year 4 months at $4\frac{1}{2}\%$ p.a.

3 Find by drawing the radius of the circle inscribed in a triangle ABC, where AB = 6·5 cm, BC = 6 cm and CA = 2·5 cm.

4 From the formula $s = \dfrac{v^2 - u^2}{2a}$, find s if $v = 30$, $u = 18$ and $a = 32$.

5 Solve the equation $10(2x - 3) = 12x - 5(2x - 3)$.

6 In Fig. 279, find the angles ABC, ADC in terms of x. Hence form an equation for x, and solve it. (Hint: $\angle$ABC is an exterior angle of $\triangle$BPC.)

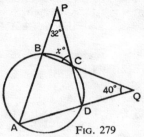

Fig. 279

Paper 52

1 (i) Express $52\frac{1}{2}$p as a percentage of 60p. (ii) A man bought an article for £296 and sold it at a profit of 15%. Find the selling price.

2 Draw an isosceles triangle ABC in which AB = AC, BC = 5 cm and $\angle$BAC = 34°.

Find by geometrical construction the point P in the side AC which is equidistant from A and B. Measure PC.

3 AB is a chord of a circle whose centre is O and radius 25 cm; D is the foot of the perpendicular from O to AB, and OD = 24 cm. Calculate the length of AB.

4 Simplify:

(i) $(3x^2 - 2x + 1) - 2(x^2 + 5x - 3)$,

(ii) $\dfrac{(ab) \div (-b)}{-(-a)^2}$,

(iii) $3x + 4\{(2x + 3y) - (y - x)\} + 2(x - 3y)$.

5 Simplify:

(i) $(\frac{3}{4} \times 4\frac{2}{3}) + 13\frac{1}{8}$,

(ii) $\dfrac{\frac{1}{2} + \frac{1}{3} - \frac{1}{4}}{(\frac{1}{2} + \frac{1}{3}) \times \frac{1}{4}}$.

6 Solve the equation

$$\frac{x}{20} + \frac{1}{4} = \frac{x-2}{36}.$$

Paper 53

1 Draw a parallelogram PQRS in which PQ = 4 cm, QR = 6 cm and $\angle$PQR = 70°. Measure QS.

2 O is the centre of the circumcircle of the triangle ABC. The angle OCA = 28° and the angle OBA = 32°. Calculate the angle OCB.

3 Perform the calculations: (i) $1011_2 + 1100_2$, (ii) $1011_2 \times 1011_2$, (iii) $1001_2 \div 11_2$.

4 The height of a pyramid is 6 cm and the sides of its square base are each 4 cm long. The pyramid is placed with its base on a horizontal plane, with two sides of the base parallel to the XY line. Draw the plan and elevation of the pyramid.

5 (i) Simplify $(3a - 7b - c) - (3c - a - 2b)$. (ii) Find the values of $\frac{1}{2}x^2 - 4x$ when $x = 4, 0, -2$.

6 Find (i) in cubic metres, (ii) in litres, the volume of a cuboid 5·4 m long, 4·5 m wide and 75 cm high.

Paper 54

1 Evaluate $\dfrac{8 \cdot 62 \times 0 \cdot 63}{200 \times 0 \cdot 09}$.

2 Simplify:

(i) $3(x^2 - 4x + 2) - 2(x - 2x^2)$,

(ii) $\dfrac{1}{2x} - \dfrac{2}{3x}$,

(iii) $\dfrac{6a^2b^2}{36(ab^2)^3}$.

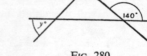

Fig. 280

3 In Fig. 280, find the value of y.

4 Find the simple interest and the amount when £320 is lent for $2\frac{1}{2}$ years at $3\frac{1}{2}\%$ p.a.

5 In the triangle ABC the angle B is four times the angle A, and the angle C is 40° more than twice the angle A. Find the angle A, and state which sides of the triangle are equal.

6 Draw a triangle ABC in which AB = 5·2 cm, $\angle$BAC = 59° and $\angle$ABC = 48°. Construct its circumcircle and measure the radius.

Paper 55

1 (i) Simplify $(\frac{5}{6} - \frac{2}{9}) \div (2\frac{1}{3} + 2\frac{5}{9})$. (ii) Express as denary numbers 10001_2, 1234_6, 321_5.

2 (i) Divide 5·0616 by 0·342.
(ii) Multiply 46 700 by 0·0023.

3 Evaluate $9\frac{1}{2}\%$ of £72 + $7\frac{1}{2}\%$ of £34.

4 Construct a quadrilateral ABCD in which AB = 5 cm, $\angle$A = 78°, $\angle$B = 68°, BC = 4·2 cm and $\angle$C = 101°. Measure CD.

5 Draw a square ABCD with its sides 4·2 cm long. On AB as base, and using ruler and compasses only, construct an equilateral triangle APB so that P lies inside the square. Calculate the number of degrees in $\angle$APD.

6 An open tank is $(x + 3)$ m long, x m wide and 4 m deep. Find an expression for the inside area of the tank.

Paper 56

1 Solve the equation $6x - (x + 1) = 14 + 2(x - 4)$.

2 Write down the time to walk x km at 6 km per hour. A man walks x km to a neighbouring village at 6 km per hour, and returns home at 5 km per hour. The total time for the journey is 3 h 18 min. Find the value of x.

3 If the selling price of an article is £2·65 and the gain is 25%, find the cost price of the article.

4 Find the L.C.M. and the H.C.F. of 169, 585 and 975.

5 Find the interior angle of a regular polygon which has 20 sides.

6 Draw a line AB 8·4 cm long. Without any calculation, divide AB into 5 equal parts. Mark the point P which divides AB in the ratio 3 : 2.

Paper 57

1 In Fig. 281, O is the centre of the circle and $\angle COA = 54°$. Calculate the number of degrees in $\angle OAB$.

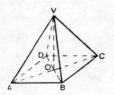

Fig. 281   Fig. 282

2 Fig. 282 shows a pyramid VABCD on a rectangular base ABCD. V is vertically above O, the intersection of AC and BD. AB = 6 cm, BC = 8 cm, VO = 10 cm. Draw the plan, front elevation and side elevation of the pyramid standing on the horizontal plane with AB and DC parallel to the XY line.

3 (i) An article increases in price from £1·05 to £1·68. Find the increase as a percentage of the original price.
(ii) Express 38_{10} as a number with base 2, and 615_{10} as a number with base 8.

4 A man pays £5 for keeping 10 horses in a field for 8 weeks. How much should he pay for keeping 22 horses for 6 weeks?

5 (i) Express $\frac{7}{3}$, $\frac{15}{3}$, $\frac{151}{9}$ as mixed or whole numbers, and $\frac{1}{4}$, $\frac{3}{8}$, $\frac{4}{25}$ as decimals.
(ii) Add together 6·25 m, 47 cm, 236 mm, giving the answer in metres.

6 A boy bought $4n$ stamps for 63p and sold them at 2p each. If his profit was 15p, find the value of n.

Paper 58

1 By what multiplying factor must a number be multiplied (a) to increase it in the ratio 3 : 2, (b) to increase it by 7%, (c) to decrease it by 11%?

2 The distances travelled by a train during the first 10 minutes of its run are given in the following table:

Time in minutes	0	2	4	5	6	8	10
Distance in kilometres	0	0·5	1·3	2·2	3·7	5·1	5·4

Draw the travel graph, and estimate from your graph (i) the distance travelled in the first 7 minutes, (ii) the time taken to go 3·2 km, (iii) when the train was travelling fastest.

3 A, B, C, D represent four towns. B is 60 km from A on a bearing of 055° from A. C is 70 km from A on a bearing of 018° from A. D is equidistant from A and C, and C is equidistant from AB and AD. Make an accurate scale drawing, using a scale of 1 cm to 10 km, and find the distance of D from B.

4 AB is a diameter of a circle and X, Y are two points on the circle on the same side of AB. If $\angle AXY = 118°$, calculate $\angle$s BXY, BAY, ABY.

5 Simplify: (i) $\dfrac{a}{3ab} - \dfrac{c}{6bc}$, (ii) $\dfrac{4rs}{15t^2} \times \dfrac{5st}{6r^2}$.

6 (i) Solve the equation $5(2x+1) = 7(x-2)$.
(ii) Express $r\%$ of £6 in pence.

Paper 59

1 Find to the nearest penny the simple interest on £604·68 for 1 year 3 months at 3% per annum.

2 (i) What number, when increased by 7%, becomes 321?
(ii) A greengrocer sells potatoes at 3p per kg, thereby gaining 20% on his cost price. Find how much per tonne the potatoes cost him.

3 Simplify: (i) $\dfrac{6a^2b^2}{15ab^5}$, (ii) the square root of $36x^4t^{10}$, (iii) $3m(3m-2p) - 2p(3m-2p)$.

4 Draw a convex quadrilateral ABCD in which AB = 6 cm, $\angle ABC = 62°$, BC = 5·5 cm, DC = 3 cm, AD = 4 cm. Measure BD.

5 The solid shown in Fig. 283 has a hole of square cross-section of side 1 cm passing through the middle of it. ABCD and EFGH are two parallel squares of sides 6 cm, 3 cm respectively. The height of the solid is 4 cm, and the sides all slope at the same angle. Draw the plan, front elevation and end elevation of the solid standing on the H.P. with AB parallel to the XY line.

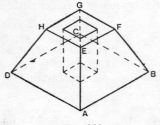

FIG. 283

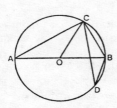

FIG. 284

6 In Fig. 284, AB is a diameter of a circle whose centre is O. If $\angle$ ABC = 63°, calculate $\angle$s CAB, CDB and COB.

Paper 60

1 A man is 25 years older than his son. In 13 years' time he will be twice as old as his son's age then. Find their present ages.

2 Draw accurately the net of a pyramid on a square base, if the side of the base is 2 cm and the slant edges are all of length 3 cm.

3 The diameter of a locomotive wheel is $1\frac{1}{2}$ m. How many revolutions does it make while the locomotive goes 3 km? (Take π as $\frac{22}{7}$.)

4 A swimming bath with a horizontal bottom is 25 m long and 16 m wide. What is the rise in level when 6000 litres of water are pumped in?

5 (i) Solve the equation $\frac{2x}{3} - \frac{x}{2} = 1$.

(ii) Simplify: (a) $6x^4 \div 2x$,   (b) $3x^2 \times 2x^3$,
(c) $2[b - a - 3(b + 2a)] - 4[2(a - b) - 3(a + 2b)]$.

6 The inscribed circle of a triangle ABC touches BC at X, CA at Y and AB at Z; $\angle A = 50°$, $\angle B = 60°$. Calculate the angles of $\triangle XYZ$.

Paper 61

1 Calculate the area of the curved surface of a cylinder of radius 21 cm, length 20 cm. (Take π as $3\frac{1}{7}$.)

2 The floor of a room is a rectangle 7 m by 5 m. A border 60 cm wide all round has to be stained. Find the cost at 6p per square metre, correct to the nearest penny.

3 Solve the equations:

(i) $\dfrac{2(x+7)}{3} - 12 = 4x$, \qquad (ii) $\dfrac{2y}{7} = 21 - \dfrac{3(y+1)}{7}$.

4 A hill slopes upwards directly towards a church tower, and the angle it makes with the horizontal is 19°. A man finds that at a certain point on the hill the angle of elevation of the top of the tower is 22°. After walking 100 m up the hill, he finds the angle of elevation to be 35°. By means of an accurate scale-drawing, find the height of the top of the tower above his first position.

5 Draw a triangle ABC in which AB = 5·4 cm, BC = 7·2 cm, AC = 6·4 cm. Construct through A a straight line AX parallel to BC, and also the bisector of $\angle ABC$ to meet AX at D. Explain why the triangle ABD is isosceles, and measure BD.

6 Two places, A and B, are 80 kilometres apart. A train leaves A at noon and travels towards B at a steady speed of 56 km per hour. At the same moment another train leaves B and travels towards A at a steady speed of 48 km per hour. Draw graphs showing the distances of the two trains from A at various times up to 1 p.m., and hence find when and where the trains meet.

Paper 62

1 Apples were bought at £125 per tonne and sold at 16p per kg. Find the gain per cent on the cost price.

2 (i) Add together 0·61 km, 143 m and 320 cm, and give the answer in metres.

(ii) If 1 cm^3 of petrol weighs 0·78 g, find the weight of 1½ litres.

3 If 4 is added to a number, the answer is the same as if twice the number is subtracted from 20. Find the number.

4 A man walks up a hill for x kilometres at 3 km per hour, rests for 45 min, then returns down the hill for x km at **6 km** per hour. Write down an expression in terms of x for the total time taken in hours.

If the whole journey takes 2½ h, find x.

5 A stone is thrown upwards into the air, and its height in metres above the ground is given in the following table:

Time in sec	0	1	2	2½	3	4	5
Height in metres	0	20	30	32	31	22	3

Draw a graph showing these values, and estimate from it (i) the greatest height the stone reaches, (ii) the height of the stone after 4½ seconds.

6 In △ABC, ∠A = 40° and ∠C = 110°. Calculate the acute angle between the bisectors of ∠A and ∠C.

If BA and BC are both produced, calculate the angle between the bisectors of the exterior angles so formed at A and C.

Paper 63

1 (i) Divide 278·4 by 0·32. (ii) Perform the calculations $2012_3 + 1202_3$ and $220_3 \times 121_3$.

2 (i) Find the L.C.M. of x^2yz^3 and $3y^3zt$, and the H.C.F. of $10ab^2cd^3$ and $5a^2b^2d$.

(ii) Simplify: (a) $\dfrac{12a^3b^4c}{(-2ab)^2}$, (b) $\dfrac{-18p^3q^3}{(-3pq) \times (-3p^2)}$.

3 A square piece, of side $\frac{x}{2}$ cm, is cut out of a square sheet of metal of side x cm, as in Fig. 285. Find (i) the total length of the edges, (ii) the area of the portion remaining.

4 Draw $\triangle ABC$ in which AB = 6 cm, AC = 4·5 cm and $\angle B = 34°$. Measure the two possible values of $\angle ACB$.

Without drawing another accurate figure, say whether there would still be two triangles which satisfy the data if AC were 7·5 cm and the other data were unchanged.

FIG. 285

5 V is the vertex and ABCD is the rectangular base of a pyramid. P, Q, R, S are the mid-points of VA, VB, VC, VD. Prove that PQRS has its opposite sides equal.

6 Draw a straight line POQ across the middle of a sheet of squared paper, with O near the centre of the paper and PO, OQ each equal to 4 cm. With centre P, draw circles of radii 2, 3, 4, ... 10 cm, and do the same with centre Q. Hence plot the locus of points X which are such that XP + XQ = 12 cm.

Paper 64

1 (i) Find by calculation the length of the side of a rhombus whose diagonals are 10 cm and 24 cm.

(ii) A is a point distant 25 cm from the centre of a circle of radius 7 cm, and T is the point of contact of the tangent from A. Calculate the length of AT.

2 Draw a triangle ABC in which AB = 4 cm, AC = 6 cm and $\angle A = 60°$. Construct the circumcircle of the triangle, and measure its radius.

3 (i) Simplify $2x - \{4x - y - (2x - 5y)\}$.

(ii) If $a = 1$, $b = 2$, $c = -3$, $d = -4$, find the values of $\frac{a+b}{c-d}$, $\frac{b+d}{c-a}$ and $\frac{ad}{c}$.

4 The radius of a circle is 3 cm. Find its circumference and area, each to three significant figures. (Take π as 3·142.)

5 A box without a lid is $3x$ m long, $2x$ m wide and x m deep. Find expressions, in their simplest form, for the volume of the box and the area of the four sides and bottom.

6 In Fig. 286, PQ touches the circles at P and Q; A and B are the centres of the circles; $AP = 2$ cm, $BQ = 7$ cm, $AB = 13$ cm. Calculate the length of PQ. (Hint: draw AX perpendicular to BQ.)

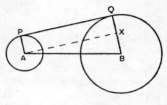

FIG. 286

Paper 65

1 In Fig. 287, AB is a diameter of the circle, CD is a chord; AB and CD are produced to meet at P. If $\angle CAD = 36°$ and $\angle DAB = x°$, write down the numbers of degrees in $\angle PDB$ and $\angle PBD$.

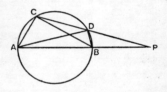

If, also, $\angle DPB = 30°$, find the value of x.

2 Solve the equation $2(7x - 6) - 3(x + 3) = 16x - 11$.

FIG. 287

3 Given the formula $A = \dfrac{a+b}{2} \times h$, find b when $A = 234$, $h = 18$ and $a = 10$.

4 Find to the nearest penny the simple interest on £361 for 6 months at $4\frac{1}{2}\%$ p.a.

5 The radius of a solid circular cylinder is r cm, and the height is equal to the diameter. Find, in terms of π and r, an expression for the *total* surface area of the cylinder.

6 After 14 completed innings a cricketer finds that his average is $47\frac{1}{2}$ runs per innings. How many runs must he get in the next innings (assuming he completes the innings) in order to bring his average per innings to 50?

INDEX

See also Table of Contents

319